Hans Zell Resource Guides

The African Studies Companion:
A Resource Guide & Directory

Hans Zell Resource Guides

No. 1: The African Studies Companion:
   A Resource Guide & Directory

No. 2: Displaced Peoples and Refugee Studies:
   A Resource Guide

The African Studies Companion: A Resource Guide & Directory

HANS M. ZELL

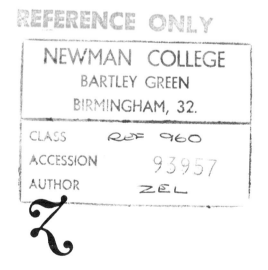
HANS ZELL PUBLISHERS
London · Munich · New York · 1989

© Copyright Hans M. Zell 1989
Hans Zell Publishers
An imprint of the K.G. Saur division of Butterworths
Shropshire House, 2–10 Capper Street, London WC1E 6JA. England

British Library Cataloguing in Publication Data
Zell, Hans M. (Hans Martin), *1940–*
    The African studies companion: a resource guide and
    directory. – (Hans Zell resource guides; no. 1).
    1. African studies. Information sources
    I. Title
    960'.07

ISBN 0–905450–80–9

Library of Congress Cataloging-in-Publication Data
Zell, Hans M.
    The African studies companion: a resource guide & directory/
    Hans M. Zell.
        176 p./23.5 cm — (Hans Zell resource guides: no. 1)
        ISBN 0–905450–80–9
        1. Africa—Study and teaching—Handbooks, manuals, etc.
    I. Title. II. Series
    DT19.8.Z45 1989
    960'.07—dc20   89–16722
                                                                      CIP

Typeset by DMD, St. Clements, Oxford
Printed and bound in Great Britain
by Unwin Brothers Limited, The Gresham Press
Old Woking, Surrey.

Contents

V. PUBLISHERS WITH AFRICAN STUDIES LISTS 85

VI. DEALERS AND DISTRIBUTORS OF AFRICAN STUDIES MATERIALS 101

Preface

The African Studies Companion aims to identify, within the covers of a single, compact volume, a wide variety of sources of information in African studies. It includes annotated listings of the major reference tools; bibliographies and continuing sources; journals and magazines; major libraries and documentation centres; publishers with African studies lists; dealers and distributors of African studies materials; organizations; African studies associations; foundations and donor agencies supporting African studies research or which are active *in* Africa; and awards and prizes in African studies.

For the librarian, the *African Studies Companion* will provide them with a quick guide to reference sources, as well as supporting collection development. For the individual Africanist scholar, it aims to serve as a convenient desk-top compendium; and I hope it will also prove useful for teachers who seek to develop courses on the subject, or for students starting off in African studies.

For the most part this book includes general and current reference sources only. For more specialist sources readers will need to consult other tools, for example Yvette Scheven's highly acclaimed *Bibliographies for African Studies 1970–1986*, or Laurence Porges's equally valuable (especially for francophone material) *Sources d'Information sur l'Afrique Noire Francophone et Madagascar*. Also useful is *Africa: A Directory of Resources*, compiled by Thomas Fenton and Mary Heffron, although this covers primarily North American resources. For the 'names and numbers' type of listings (i.e. sections VI and VII), readers are throughout referred to either fuller annotated directories, or to a variety of alternative and/or supplementary sources of information of data, readily available elsewhere.

It has not been easy to pack so much information into a two hundred page book. I had originally planned to include details of the world's top research centres and institutions in the African studies field, providing at least a brief outline of their activities and research. In the end, however, this was not possible within the constraints of the space available, and in any event this information is at least partially covered by the annotated listings of the major libraries and documentation centres in Europe and North America with substantial African studies collections.

Acknowledgements

Information for some sections in the *African Studies Companion* was gathered by means of a series of questionnaire mailings. I realize that completing questionnaires can be a tedious and time-consuming business, and I am indebted to all those librarians, journal editors, publishers, and donor agency representatives who completed and returned our questionnaires, thus ensuring accurate and up-to-date information. It is my hope that, for subsequent editions of this resource guide, those who failed to respond on this occasion can be persuaded to do so in future. Whereas I have done all I can to ensure accuracy and completeness in the directory type listings, the Publishers cannot of course accept responsibility for accidental omissions or errors.

Finally, I wish to acknowledge editiorial help provided by my colleague Mary Jay in the preparation of certain sections of this book.

Oxford,
June 1989   Hans M. Zell

Introduction

This directory and resource guide seeks to bring together a wide variety of sources of information in the African studies field. It also identifies significant organizations, and donor agencies active or supporting research in the field. Information is provided in ten chapters, and there is also a list of acronyms and abbreviations in African studies.

Scope and definitions

The majority of listings identify *general* sources of information; chapter I covers the major general reference tools on African studies, but does *not* include monographs or any other material not of a reference book nature (unlike some of the other titles in the 'Hans Zell Resource Guides' series, on more specialist subjects, which will include annotated listings and critical evaluations of the core literature on the subject covered). However, whereas the emphasis is on general African studies resources, broad reference works on the Third World are not included, except for one or two.

More specific comments on scope and definitions are given in the introductory sections to each chapter.

Entries and annotations

Most of the entries are extensively annotated, providing, for many sections, a whole array of specifics. Annotations are descriptive not critical, intending to place not judge the books or journals, etc. listed.

Entries are consecutively numbered throughout. Fairly extensive cross-referencing forms an integral part of the book, thus enabling users to move from one entry to others of relevance.

The fullest possible bibliographic data is furnished for each book or journal entry, including prices/subscription rates and other essential acquisitions data.

Data gathering

Information for chapters III, IV, V, VIII, and IX was collected by means of a series of questionnaire mailings. Whereas, overall, the response rate was quite satisfactory (about 75%), a small number of journal editors or publishers, librarians, associations, or donor agencies, could not unfortunately be persuaded to complete and return our questionnaire, despite persistence on our part and several follow-up mailings. All these entries are flagged with a † dagger symbol, and information provided is either incomplete and/or we supplemented details from secondary sources. It must follow, however, that all information contained in entries with dagger symbols must be used with caution.

Index

We have thought long and hard how a resource guide of this nature could be most usefully indexed; indexing that should not duplicate the arrangement of entries *per se*, but that should provide various additional means of access. In the end we decided on a simplified, single combined index, based on an anticipation of the most likely needs of users.

Abbreviations

In order to save space this book contains a great many abbreviations. Keys to abbreviations used are provided at the beginning of each chapter. The following *general* abbreviations are also used throughout:

BP   – Boite Postal (PO Box)
Co   – Company
CP   – Caixa Postal/Case Postale (PO Box)
EM   – Electronic mail address
Fax – Facsimile address
Inc – Incorporated
Ltd – Limited Company
n/a – not available (not disclosed)
POB – Post Office Box
PMB – Private Mail Bag
Tel – Telephone (however, the abbreviation 'Tel' is generally omitted, and numbers only, with area/STD codes etc. given in parentheses, immediately follow address details)
Tx   – Telex number (with details of Answerback where provided, but without Telex country codes)
†   – indicates no reply received to questionnaire mailing

Currencies

Details of currencies/prices are given in the conventionally abbreviated forms. $ indicates US Dollars throughout, unless otherwise specified.

I. MAJOR GENERAL REFERENCE RESOURCES

This section provides a select listing of some of the key references resources in the African studies field, primarily those written in English. It is confined to listings of *general* reference works and bibliographies only. For subject bibliographies, specialist resources, directories, etc. – for example on African art, African literature, African history, etc. – consult Yvette Scheven's *Bibliographies for African Studies, 1970–1986* (*see* **27**), or, for francophone Africa, Laurence Porges's *Sources d'Information sur l'Afrique Noire Francophone et Madagascar* (*see* **24**).

1. Major general reference works on African studies

1 The African Book World & Press: A Directory/Répertoire du Livre et de la Presse en Afrique. Ed. by Hans M. Zell 4th rev. ed. Oxford: Hans Zell Publishers (New York: K.G. Saur), 1989. 336pp. £75.00/ $135.00

> A reference tool on the African book world and print media providing comprehensive information on libraries, publishers and the retail booktrade, research institutions with publishing programmes, magazines and periodicals, major newspapers, as well as the printing industries. Most entries are extensively annotated. Arranged in 52 country-by-country sections, the fourth edition includes 4,435 entries, each entry providing a whole array of specifics on the scale of activities of the institutions and organizations listed. Also includes annotated listings of African book trade events, literary prizes and awards, African news agencies, and a directory of dealers in African books in Europe and North America.

2 African Books in Print. An Index by Author, Title and Subject/ Livres Africaines Disponibles: Ed. by Hans M. Zell 3rd ed. London: Mansell Publishing, 1984. 2 vols. 1,402pp. £85.00 set

> Lists 18,724 titles in print as at the end of 1982, from 604 African publishers and research institutions with publishing programmes. Lists books, together with full bibliographic data, by author, title, and under some 1,300 subject headings. Covers material in English and French, plus some 4,000 titles in 102 African languages. Cumulates the quarterly *African Book Publishing Record* (*see* **99**). New 4th ed. forthcoming in 1991.

3 'African Historial Dictionaries' series. Series Editor: Jon Woronoff. Metuchen, N.J.: Scarecrow Press, 1975– var.pp.

> This series currently comprises 40 volumes on individual African countries. They provide, in dictionary form, basic information about each country's geography, history, economic and social aspects, events, institutions, and major persons and leaders. The biographical entries cover past and present political leaders, statesmen, diplomats, military leaders, educators, labour leaders, religious leaders, prominent traders and business leaders, and entrepreneurs.

4 **African International Organization Directory, 1984/85**. Ed. by the Union of International Associations. Munich: K.G. Saur, 1984. 603pp. £52.00/$82.00

A condensed version, covering African countries, of the *Yearbook of International Organizations*. Three parts: (1) African Organization Descriptions; (2) African Secretariat Countries; (3) International Organizations with African Membership, plus several indexes. 1984/85 ed. is only ed. published to date.

5 Asamani, J.O. **Index Africanus**. Stanford: Hoover Institution Press, 1975. 659pp. (Hoover Institution on War, Revolution and Peace, Bibliographical series, 53)

Lists almost 26,000 articles from over 200 periodicals, published between 1885 and 1965. Arranged geographically and by topic with an author index.

6 Besterman, Theodore. **A World Bibliography of African Bibliographies**. Revised and brought up to date by J.D. Pearson. Oxford: Blackwell (Totowa, NJ: Rowman and Littlefield), 1975. 241 columns

An extract of 1,136 titles from Besterman's *A World Bibliography of Bibliographies* (4th ed. 1963), together with a further 498 items added by J.D. Pearson, and published between 1963 and 1973. Entries are arranged under geographical divisions and thereafter in regional or subject divisions; plus an author and title index.

7 Boston University. Libraries. **List of French Doctoral Dissertations on Africa, 1884–1961**. Boston: G.K. Hall, 1966. 334pp. $69.00

2,981 titles arranged by country and/or area.

8 Cason, Maidel K. **African Newspapers Currently Received by American Libraries**. Rev. ed. Evanston: Melville J. Herskovits Library of African Studies, Northwestern University Library, 1988. 17pp. gratis

A union list that aims to help researchers to locate African newspapers in US libraries. The list surveys the holdings of 15 libraries. Arrangement is by country of publication, with library location symbols indicated with each newspaper.

9 Cooperative Africana Microform Project. **CAMP Catalog**. Cumulative edition. Chicago: Cooperative Africana Microform Project and Center for Research Libraries, 1985. 642pp.

7,590 entries arranged in alphabetical order; with subject index.

10 Duignan, Peter, and Helen F. Conover. **Guide to Research and Reference Works on Sub-Saharan Africa**. Stanford: Hoover Institution Press, 1971. 1,102pp. (Hoover Institution on War, Revolution and Peace, Bibliographical series, 46)

A major and pioneering reference source for material published to 1969/70. 3,127 fully annotated entries arranged in topical and geographical sections, each with extensive details about bibliographies and other reference works, as well as serials. The book's interpretation of 'reference works' is very liberal, and includes many specialized monographs, as well as periodical articles. Indexes by author, names, titles, subject, and geographical.

11 Duignan, Peter. **Handbook of American Resources for African Studies**. Stanford: Hoover Institution Press, 1966. 234pp. (Hoover Institution on War, Revolution and Peace, Bibliographical series, 29)

Describes the holdings of 95 library and manuscript collections, 108 church and missionary libraries and archives, 95 art and ethnographic collections, and 4 business archives. Partially updated by Jean Gosebrink's *African Studies Information Resources Directory* (*see* **16**), published twenty years later.

12 Easterbrook, David L. **Africana Book Reviews, 1885-1945: an Index to Books Reviewed in Selected English-language Publications**. Boston: G.K. Hall, 1979. 247pp.

Brings together 1,725 reviews from 44 journals.

13 Fenton, Thomas P., and Mary J. Heffron. **Africa: A Directory of Resources**. Maryknoll, NY: Orbis Books, and Oakland: Third World Resources [464 19th St., Oakland CA 94612], 1987. 144pp. $9.95

One in a series of twelve volumes on Third World regions and issues, providing annotated listings – with full acquisitions data and prices – of books, articles, pamphlets, AV materials, catalogues and curriculum guides, together with listings of organizations and alternative sources of information for the study of Africa. Focusses on resources that are in favour of a 'radical analysis' of African/Third World affairs. Covers primarily US-published material, and omits material on Africa North of the Sahara.

14 Fredland, Richard. **A Guide to African International Organizations**. Oxford: Hans Zell Publishers (New York: K.G. Saur), forthcoming 1989/90. c.240pp.

Records some 500 international organizations which have appeared on the African continent in this century, and provides extensive critical analysis and commentary on these organizations, together with historical background, etc. For organizations active today it also includes such details as addresses and names of executive personnel; with numerous tables and maps.

15 Gibbs, James. **A Handbook for African Writers**. Oxford: Hans Zell Publishers (New York: K.G. Saur), 1986. 226pp. £25.00/$36.00

Provides a companion for African writers – how to present a manuscript, finding a publisher, dealing with literary agents, advice about contracts, remuneration, copyright, writing for the media, and more. A series of address listings give details about publishers in Africa, Europe and North America, and there are also annotated listings of magazines and literary periodicals. And the experience of several generations of African writers is distilled in a section entitled 'Patterns of Publication' in which eleven authors are quoted on the major issues confronting aspiring writers.

16 Gosebrink, Jean E. Meeh. **African Studies Information Resources Directory**. Oxford: Hans Zell Publishers (New York: K.G. Saur), 1986. 585pp. £50.00/$80.00

Provides a comprehensive reference and research tool for identifying sources of information and documentation on sub-Saharan Africa located in the United States. Conceived as a partial revision of Peter Duignan's *Handbook of American Resources for African Studies* (*see* **11**) it includes 437 entries (many with extensive sub-divisions) and is arranged alphabetically in four major sections:

(1) Information Resources for African Studies: describes collections and information services in libraries and other repositories, public and private institutions and organizations, government agencies, museums, and professional and academic associations. Full details on library holdings, including microforms, map collections, collections of visual and aural documentation, archival and manuscript materials, collections of computerized data, and information and documentation services. Information about conditions of access, and publications issued by each institution or organization, is also provided, as are telephone numbers, contact persons, etc.

(2) Resources in Church and Mission Organizations: Gives similar information as (1), arranged alphabetically by religious denomination or tradition, for church and mission organizations which have done work in Africa.

(3) Bookstores, Book Dealers and Distributors of Africa-related Materials.

(4) Publishers. With an index to subjects, persons, places and institutions, and organizations mentioned in the text.

17 Henige, David. **A Union List of African Archival Materials in Microform**. 2nd ed. Madison: University of Wisconsin, Madison Memorial Library, 1984. 45pp.

Provides an inventory of the holdings in 17 libraries, and lists 299 titles; with country index and P.R.O. numerical list.

18 **International African Bibliography 1973–1978; Books, Articles and Papers in African Studies**. Ed. by J.D. Pearson. London: Mansell, 1982. 374pp. £50.00

Cumulates 24 consecutive issues (vols. 3–8) of *International African Bibliography* (*see* **106**), and adds some 3,000 further entries. Arrangement is by subject and regions, and thereafter sub-divided by country/subject.

19 Mary, Geo T. **Afrika-Schrifttum: Bibliographie deutschsprachiger wissenschaftlicher Veröffentlichungen über Afrika südlich der Sahara/ Etudes sur l'Afrique: Bibliographie des Travaux Scientifiques sur l'Afrique au sud du Sahara parus en langue Allemande**. Wiesbaden: Franz Steiner Verlag, 1966, 1977. 2 vols. 688pp., 295pp.

A bibliography of German scholarly publications on Africa South of the Sahara for the period 1871 through 1963. Volume I is arranged by broad subject categories, and volume II is a subject index in German, French and English.

20 Northwestern University. **Catalog of the Melville J. Herskovits Library of African Studies, Northwestern University Library, and Africana in Selected Libraries**. Boston: G.K. Hall, 1972. 5,671pp. 8 vols. $750.00 First Supplement. 1978. 4,380pp. 6 vols. $500.00

> Facsimile reproductions of the catalog cards of this major library on African studies (see **345**). Altogether reproduces over 200,000 cards.

21 Northwestern University. Melville J. Herskovits Library of African Studies. **Joint Acquisitions List of Africana: 1978**. Boston: G.K. Hall, 1980. 764pp. $95.00 **Joint Acquisitions List of Africana: 1979**. Boston: G.K Hall, 1981. 662pp. $100.00 **Joint Acquisitions List of Africana: 1980**. Boston: G.K. Hall, 1982. 856pp. $130.00

> A record – as computer-produced entries, totalling some 39,000 entries for the three volumes – of materials catalogued by the leading African studies libraries in the USA. Unfortunately not continued beyond 1980. (*see* also **107**).

22 Panofsky, Hans E. **A Bibliography of Africana**. Westport, Conn: Greenwood Press, 1975. 350pp. (Contributions in Librarianship and Information science, 11)

> A guide to and inventory of the principal bibliographies and bibliographic sources of Africana, arranged by discipline and geographic area. Six parts: (1) The Study of Africa, (2) Bibliographies and Serials, (3) Guide to Resources by Subject and Discipline, (4) Guide to Resources in Non-African Areas, (5) Guide to Resources in African Nations, and (6) On Collecting and Disseminating Africana.

23 Pluge, John jr. **African Newspapers in the Library of Congress**. Washington, D.C.: Library of Congress, Serial and Government Publications Division, 1984. 144pp.

> Lists over 900 newspapers, arranged by country, city, title, plus a title index.

24 Porges, Laurence. **Sources d'Information sur l'Afrique Noire Francophone et Madagascar. Institutions, répertoires, bibliographies**. Paris: La Documentation Française/Ministère de la Cooperation, 1988. 389pp. Fl50.00

> A comprehensive guide to sources of information about francophone Black Africa and Madagascar, containing 1,498 mostly annotated entries, and several indexes. Part one lists sources about research institutions, associations and societies, libraries and documentation centres, official publications, magazines and periodicals, theses, and general and specialist bibliographies. Part two provides an inventory of bibliographies, directories and other sources of information on a country-by-country basis, with each country section also including information about institutes, research centres and universities, as well as museums, archival collections, and more.

25 **Répertoire de Périodiques Paraissant en Afrique au Sud du Sahara (Sciences Sociales et Humaines)**. Comp. by M. Aghassian. Paris: Centre National de la Recherche Scientifique, Centre de Documentation Sciences Humaines, 1982. 83pp.

> Lists 344 periodicals on Africa South of the Sahara in the social sciences and the humanities, giving library locations and including a directory of libraries in Paris and their addresses.

26 **Resources for African Studies in Canada**. Comp. by the Canadian Assoc. of African Studies. Ottawa: Canadian Association for African Studies, 1976. 264pp.

> A compendium of information on African Studies in Canada, including details about African studies programmes at Canadian universities, and names of scholars and teachers. In English and French. Now inevitably very dated.

27 Scheven, Yvette. **Bibliographies for African Studies, 1970–1986**. Oxford: Hans Zell Publishers (New York: K.G. Saur), 1988. 637pp. £58.00/$100.00

> This volume presents at a glance the bibliographical record of 40 specific disciplines and 57 geographical areas and nations, while at the same time providing a panoramic view of African Studies for the last 17 years. It cumulates Yvette Scheven's earlier volumes for 1970–1975, 1976–1979, and 1980–1983, and adds bibliographies from 1984, 1985, and 1986. Almost 100 subject and geographical sections provide access to bibliographies in the social sciences and humanities, for all sub-Saharan countries. This access is further enhanced by a detailed index of subjects, authors, and some titles.
> International in scope, the volume includes 3,245 entries. A special feature is the listing of bibliographies which appear regularly in periodicals or series. Almost all titles were examined by the compiler, who records the number of items for each bibliography; whether it is annotated; how it is arranged; its scope; special features; and whether it is indexed. Library locations are indicated for the more esoteric items.

28 Travis, Carole, and Miriam Alman. **Periodicals from Africa: a Bibliography and Union List of Periodicals Published in Africa**. Boston: G.K. Hall, 1977. 619pp.

> Lists 17,000 titles with locations in 60 British libraries, covering all countries except Egypt. *First Supplement* by D.S. Blake and C. Travis (Boston: G.K. Hall, 1984, 217pp.) gives a further 7,000 titles published through August 1979. A *Second Supplement*, by D.S. Blake is in preparation. Published for SCOLMA.

29 U.S. Library of Congress. African Section. **African Newspapers Available on Positive Microfilm**. Washington, D.C.: Library of Congress, Photoduplication Service, 1984. 27pp.

> Details of some 400 newspapers (current and ceased), arranged by country, city and title.

30 U.S. Library of Congress. African Section. **Sub-Saharan Africa: A Guide to Serials**. Washington, D.C.: Library of Congress, African Section, 1970. 411pp.

> Lists monographic series, annual reports of institutions, yearbooks, directories, and journals and periodicals, arranged alphabetically by title, and indexed by subjects and organizations.

31 Wallenius, Anna Britta. **Africana Scandinavica, 1960–1968: Books on Africa Published in Denmark, Finland, Norway and Sweden: a Selected Bibliography**: Uppsala: Scandinavian Institute of African Studies, 1971. 104pp.

> Presents some 1,200 titles (with an English translation of the titles), arranged by broad subject categories and geographical sub-divisions.

32 Wallenius, Anna Britta. **Africana Suecana, 1945–1965: An Analytical Approach to Swedish Printed Material on Africa**. Uppsala: Institutionen för Allmän och Jämförande Etnografi, Uppsala Universitet, 1975. 490pp. (Occasional Papers, 4)

> Lists almost 3,000 items, with an emphasis on the humanities and the social sciences, arranged by topics, with several indexes. Includes English translations of titles.

33 Witherell, Julian. **The United States and Sub-Saharan Africa: Guide to US Official Documents and Government-Sponsored Publications, 1785–1975**. Washington, D.C.: Library of Congress, 1978. 949pp.

> Over 8,800 annotated entries, in five chronological sections which are sub-divided by region or country (and 1952–75 further sub-divided by subjects). Covers largely holdings at the Library of Congress, plus some at 45 other libraries; very extensively indexed. Continued by Witherell's *The United States and Sub-Saharan Africa: Guide to Official Documents and Government-Sponsored Publications, 1976–1980*, listing a further 5,074 entries. (1984, 721pp.)

2. Some reference sources on microfiche/film

34 **African Official Statistical Serials, 1867–1982**. Cambridge: Chadwyck-Healey (Alexandria, Chadwyck Healey), 2,330 microfiche £5,500 for complete collection. For orders for single volumes or selections of volumes unit prices are: 1–49 microfiche £6.00, 50–99 microfiche £5.00, 100+ microfiche £4.00

> Consists of general statistical compendia – economic, financial, social, demographic statistics – issued by the governments of nearly every African nation. Available as a complete collection or by individual countries.

35 Boston University. Libraries. **Catalog of African Government Documents**, 3rd ed. Boston: G.K. Hall, 1976. Microfilm. 14,100 cards 1 reel $82.00
> Author catalog of monographs and serials covering all of Africa. 13,500 entries.

36 International African Institute. **Cumulative Bibliography of African Studies**. Boston: G.K. Hall, 1973. Microfilm. Author Catalog, 4 reels $200.00 Classified Catalog, 6 reels $300.00
> Contains all the titles of the books and articles listed in the quarterly bibliography published in the journal *Africa* (*see* **148**), from 1929 to 1970, and in the *International African Bibliography* (*see* **106**) during 1971 and 1972.

37 The New York Public Library. Schomburg Center for Research in Black Culture. **Schomburg Clipping File-Africa**. Cambridge: Chadwyck-Healey (Alexandria: Chadwyck Healey), 1986. 1,362 microfiche [with Index to the Schomburg Clipping File] £1,850/$2,950
> A collection of newspapers and magazine clippings, pamphlets and ephemera on all aspects of the Black experience held by the Schomburg Center. This is a selection from the complete file, covering material devoted to the various countries of Africa.

38 Northwestern University. Melville Herskovits Library of African Studies. **Africana File Listing as of April 1988**. Evanston: Melville J. Herskovits Library of African Studies, Northwestern University Library, 1988.
Microfiche (61 fiche) $50.00
> An index of all major publications in Northwestern University Library's (see **345**) extensive Africana vertical files, containing African government publications, political party and trade union materials, and company reports. 16,000 records are accessible by 37,000 index entries. Volume holdings of serials are included. There is a combined index by author, title, and added entry, in a single alphabetical sequence.

39 U.S. Library of Congress. African Section. **Africa South of the Sahara: Index to Periodical Literature, 1900-1970**. Boston: G.K. Hall, 1971. Microfilm 8 reels $365.00 First Supplement. 1973. 1 reel $135.00 Second Supplement. 1981. 3 reels $265.00
Third Supplement: Washington, Library of Congress, 1985. 306pp.
> Records serial articles relating to Africa South of the Sahara from 1900 onwards. The main work cites 80,000 references from 1,530 journals; arranged geographically with broad subject divisions. First Supplement 14,100 entries; Second Supplement, 41,000 entries covering 1972–1976, and Third Supplement, a further 4,199 citations to articles published in 1977.

3. Encyclopaedias

40 **The Arts and Civilization of Black and African Peoples**. Edited by Joseph Okpaku, Alfred Opubor, and Benjamin Oloruntimehin. New Rochelle, N.Y.: The Victoria Corporation, 1987. 10 vols. $425.00 per set (institutions) $395.00 per set (individuals)

    A ten volume encyclopaedia – the outcome of a Colloquium on Black Civilization held during the 2nd World Black and African Festival of Arts and Culture in Lagos, Nigeria, in 1977 – covering practically every aspect of the evolution and cultures of Black people in all parts of the world. Contents of individual volumes range from the arts and literature, to philosophy, religion, education, and science and technology.

41 **The Cambridge Encyclopedia of Africa**. General Editors: Roland Oliver and Michael Crowder. Cambridge: Cambridge University Press, 1981. 492pp. illus. pl. col. pl. maps £18.50

    A one-volume encyclopaedic guide to the past and present of Africa, covering its physical environment, archaeology and history, natural resources, political economy, society, religion, art, tourism, and more. With contributions by almost a hundred African studies scholars, and a substantial amount of illustrative material in both black and white and in full colour.

42 **Encyclopaedia of the Third World**. Ed. by George T. Kurian. 3rd ed. New York: Facts on File, 1987. 3 vols. 2,384pp. $195.00

    A comprehensive survey of 124 'Third World' countries, providing an overview of each nation's political, economic and social systems. Each national chapter follows the same format of 36 subject headings, with some 400 subtopics. Includes maps of each country, and an extensive index.

4. Annuals & Yearbooks

43 **Africa Contemporary Record. Annual Survey and Documents** New York: Holmes & Meier, London: Rex Collings [1970–76] vol. I, 1968–69, published annually, latest volume ca. 1,300pp. each vol. £185.00 Edited by Colin Legum & John Drysdale [to 1988]; edited by Marion Duro [from 1989]

    An annual work of analysis of political, economic, social and international developments covering all the countries in the African continent. Detailed articles and reviews on each African country. Also records the year's key documents from organizations such as the OAU, the UN, and the US House Committee on Foreign Affairs, and provides summaries and statistics regarding population growth, per capita GNP, oil and gas production, foreign aid, etc.

44 **The Africa Review**. [1988 edition] Saffron Walden: World of Information, 1988. 12th ed. 256pp. £28.00/$64.00 (in the US order from World of Information, PO Box C-430, Birmingham, AL 35283–0430)

> Annual economic and business survey. Includes individual articles on economic and political developments and a general overview, together with chapters on each African country, each with analysis of the year's events, a country profile, key indicators, key facts, a business directory and business guide with listings of useful addresses, etc.

45 **Africa South of the Sahara**. [1989 edition] London: Europa Publications, 1989. 18th ed. 1,179pp. £75.00

> Annual survey and directory, covering political, social and economic developments during the preceding year in 51 African countries. Each country section includes background essays, economic, demographic and statistical survey/data, plus a wide-ranging directory of essential names and addresses. Part one of the book, 'Background to the Continent' provides a history of the continent and includes a series of essays by acknowledged experts on African affairs, covering topics such as recent political events, economic trends, evaluations of industrial and agricultural development prospects for sub-Saharan Africa, and of production, marketing and price movements in the principal African commodities. Part two, preceding the individual country surveys, provides details about the activities of African regional organizations.

46 **New African Yearbook**. [1988 edition] London: IC Magazines Ltd., 1988. 7th ed. (in the US order from Franklin Watts Inc.) 412pp. £29.95/$49.95

> Annual publication covering all 48 African countries and offshore islands in alphabetical order, emphasizing basic factual material. Each country has sections on political history, the economy, current events, plus basic facts and the most up-to-date statistical data available. Also lists basic information on the main Pan-African organizations. Outline maps for each country.

5. Directories of research and teaching

47 **Directory of African and Afro-American Studies in the United States**. Comp. by Hanif M. Rana and John A. Distefano. 7th ed. Los Angeles: African Studies Association/Crossroads Press, 1987. 281pp. $40.00

> Published by the African Studies Association (*see* **585**), this is a guide to 388 programmes of African and Afro-American studies in the United States, with entries listed state by state. Information given includes full name and address, telephone number, contact person, faculty and course listings, degree offerings, regional emphasis, special features, library holdings of Africana, and financial aid available at each instittuion. With index of faculty and staff,

alphabetical index of institutions, index of programme titles and degree offerings, and index of African language courses offered.

48 **A Directory of British Africanists**. Ed. by Richard Hodder Williams. Bristol: University of Bristol, on behalf of the Royal African Society [order from Richard Hodder-Williams, Reader in Politics, University of Bristol, Bristol BS8 1TH], 1986. 85pp. £4.50

> A who's who of British Africanists, giving full names and institutional addresses/affiliations. Lists 443 UK African studies scholars, with details of subject/regional interests, primary research areas, publications, and more. Indexes by discipline and by country of research. (New 2nd edition scheduled for publication late in 1989.)

49 **Directory of Women in African Studies**. Comp. by the Women's Caucus of the African Studies Association. Los Angeles: African Studies Association/Crossroads Press, 1984. 45pp. $8.00

> Entries include current position and address of each scholar, and details about her discipline, geographic area studied/areas of specialization, and recent publications.

50 **Etudes Africaines en Europe. Bilan et Inventaire**. Comp. by the Agence de Coopération Culturelle et Technique. Paris: ACCT & Editions Karthala, 1981. 2 vols. 655pp., 714pp.

> Massive two-volume inventory of current (as at 1980) African studies research and African studies documentation in Europe. In addition to articles on various areas of African studies research, there are extensive 'Répertoire' sections, giving details about academic institutions throughout Europe offering courses and undertaking research in African studies, with information on staff, areas of specialization, etc. With indexes to names of institutions, individual scholars, disciplines, geographic areas studied, and African languages studied.

51 **International Guide to African Studies Research/Etudes Africaines. Guide International de Recherches**. Ed. by the International African Institute and comp. by Philip Baker. 2nd ed. Oxford: Hans Zell Publishers (New York: K.G. Saur), 1987. 276pp. £45.00/$72.00

> Provides information on nearly 1,500 research bodies, academic institutions and international organizations throughout the world. Each entry includes the following information: Full name and address; telephone and telex numbers; name of Head/Director, and details of staff (including their area of specialization); principal areas of current African studies research; courses offered and degrees awarded; number of students engaged in African studies; library holdings; publications. Additional information – e.g. financial support; links with (other) African institutions and organizations; and more. A series of indexes provide access to users' requirements by names of institutions, names of individual scholars, by subject or topics of research, by regional or country specialization, and by persons undertaking research into specific African ethnic groups.

52 Inventaire: Instituts de Recherche et de Formation en Matière de Développement: Afrique/Directory: Development Research and Training Institutes: Africa. Paris: OCDE, 1986. 156pp.

Country-by-country listing of research institutions in Africa, giving details of activities, courses offered, principal areas of research, publications issued, etc.

53 Répertoire: Projects de Recherche en Matière de Développement: Afrique/Register: Development Research Projects: Africa. Paris OCDE, 1986. 523pp.

An inventory of over 1,100 research projects in alphabetical order by country. Provides full name and address, institutional affiliation, nature of research, finance, etc.

54 Répertoire des Institutions d'Enseignement Supérieur Membres de l'AUPELF 1986. vol. 1: Algérie à Zaire (sauf France) 2nd ed. Montréal: Association des Universités Partiellement ou Entièrement de Langue Française (AUPELF), 1986. 420pp.

Provides full details of 32 teaching institutions in 21 francophone countries, with information on courses offered and diplomas awarded, services to students, library facilities, university presses, etc.

6. Teaching aids and children's material

55 Beyer, Barry K. **Africa South of the Sahara. A Resource and Curriculum Guide**. New York: Thomas Y. Crowell, 1969. 138pp.

A practical source (now rather dated of course) of information for teaching about Africa, and for teachers who seek to develop units on Africa. Part one contains data and ideas that aim to serve as guidelines for teaching on Africa; part two is a guide to resources, and lists some 500 items.

56 Crane, Luise. **Curriculum Material for Teachers**. 2nd ed. Urbana, Ill.: Center for African Studies [Room 101, 1208 West California Street, Urbana, IL. 61801], 1985. 353pp. $15.00

Lists some 80 items: basic bibliographies/filmographies, audio-visual material, biographical material, information resources, children's books for teaching about Africa and its languages and cultures. Indexed. Entries are coded for age or grade levels. A second edition is in preparation for publication in 1990.

57 Hartwig, G.W., and W.M. O'Barr. **The Student Africanist Handbook** Cambridge, Mass.: Schenkman Publishing, 1975. 160pp.

Offers references for information on both traditional and contemporary Africa, covering the literature in a variety of disciplines. Also presents topically organized references and on a country-by-country and regional basis, and offers assistance in working with publications of government and international organizations, and national archives.

58 Maxwell, Margaret. **African Studies Handbook for Elementary and Secondary School Teachers**. 3rd ed. Amherst, Mass: Center for International Education, School of Education, University of Massachusetts, 1983. 221pp.

> 450 entries in five sections, providing introductory lessons, and covering teacher and student resources and audio-visual materials.

59 Schmidt, Nancy J. **Children's Books on Africa and their Authors: An Annotated Bibliography**. New York: Africana Publishing Co., 1975. 290pp. $30.00

> Over 800 fully annotated entries, with biographical information on authors, and several indexes. Updated by Schmidt's *Supplement to Children's Books on Africa and their Authors: An Annotated Bibliography* (New York: Africana, 1979), listing a further 700 items published through 1977.

7. Theses and Dissertations

60 Lauer, Joseph J.; Kagan, Alfred; Larkin, Gregory. **American and Canadian Doctoral Dissertations and Master's Theses on Africa, 1974–1987**. Atlanta: African Studies Association/Crossroads Press, forthcoming 1989. $75.00

> Comprehensive listing of complete references for more than 8,500 American and Canadian dissertations and theses on Africa. Arranged by country and region, and indexed by subject and author. Update of entry **62**.

61 McIlwaine, J.H. St. J. **Theses on Africa, 1963–1975. Accepted by Universities in the United Kingdom and Ireland**. London: Mansell Publishing, 1978. 140pp. £20.00

> Originally published as an annual publication 1966–1970 (published by Frank Cass. London on behalf of SCOLMA; six volumes published to the volume covering 1967–68), this volume covers theses presented at British academic institutions between 1963 and 1975. Contains 2,335 entries, arranged geographically and by broad subject headings, with an author index.

62 Sims, Michael and Alfred Kagan. **American and Canadian Doctoral Dissertations and Master's Theses on Africa, 1886-1974**. Waltham: African Studies Association, Brandeis University, 1976. 365pp.

> Lists 6,070 theses classified by geographical area and thereafter by discipline; indexed by subject and author. Continued by entry **60**.

8. Guides to film and video resources

63 **Africa on Film and Videotape: A Compendium of Reviews** East Lansing: African Studies Centre, Michigan State University [100 Center for International Programs, Michigan State University, East Lansing, MI 48824–1035], 1982.

> Lists over 750 reviews of films and videotapes on Africa, and that are available in the USA; includes critical annotations, and full details of length, date released, director/producer, distributor, etc. Indexed by topic, country, and by language.

64 Ballantyne, James and Andrew Roberts. **Africa: A Handbook of Film and Video Resources**. London: British Universities Film & Video Council [55 Greek Street, London W1V 51R], 1986. 120pp. £11.00 (with Supplementary List, May 1987, 23pp. £2.50)

> Describes major archival collections of non-fiction films on Africa in Great Britain, together with a separate section with details of films on Africa which can be hired or borrowed, and covering mostly history, politics and ethnography. The latter part arranged by subject with country subdivisions, and country, title and distributor indexes. The subject sections give details of distributor, year released, production company, length and other technical details, together with a brief annotation. Also includes a list of distributors' addresses and a bibliography.

65 Cyr, Helen W. **A Filmography of the Third World, 1976-1983. An Annotated List of 16mm Films**. Metuchen, N.J.: Scarecrow Press, 1985. 285pp. £24.00

> Continues *Filmography of the Third World* (Scarecrow, 1976) and lists 1,300 new titles. Chiefly documentary but also short and feature-length fictional films, experimental cinema and cinema as art. Also lists distributors.

66 **Films & Video for Black Studies**. Comp. by Rebecca A. Hodges. 2nd ed. University Park: Black Studies Program and Audio-Visual Services, Penn State University, 1987. 24pp. gratis (with 8pp. Supplement, 1989)

> An updated version of a Penn State Black Studies film catalogue published in 1973, providing an annotated listing of films and tapes that are available for rental and purchase from the Penn State Audio-Visual Services (in US only); gives year of issue, running time, rental fee/purchase price, etc., with subject index. Mostly about the Black Experience in the US, but also includes about 40 films/tapes on African topics.

67 **Films and Video Resources about Africa**. Urbana-Champaign: University of Illinois Film Center, University of Illinois [1325 S.Oak Street, Urbana, IL 61801], 1985. 34pp. gratis

> Describes over 200 films and videos on African topics available for rental from the University of Illinois Film Center. The guide was

produced in association with the University of Illinois's Center for African Studies.

9. Guides to library and archival collections

68 **Afrika-bezogene Literatursammlungen in der Bundesrepublik und Berlin (West)**. Ed. by Heidrun Henze. Hamburg: Deutsches Institut für Afrika-Forschung, Dokumentationsleitstelle im ADAF, 1972. 214pp. (Dokumentationsdienst Afrika, 2)

> A guide to libraries and institutes with African studies collections in West Germany. Gives full name and address, telephone number, contacts, access, hours, size of book and serials collections, subject areas covered, strength of collections, etc. With indexes by names of institutions, subject, and geographic areas.

69 Bleken, Sidsel. **Nordisk Samkatalog over Tidsskrifter utgitt i Utviklingsland. Nordic Union Catalogue of Periodicals Issued in Developing Countries**. 2nd ed. Fantoft: Chr. Michelsen Institute [Fantoftvegen 38, 5036 Fantoft, Norway], 1986. 139pp.

> Records the holdings of periodicals issued in developing countries in 17 libraries in Scandinavia. Gives title, place of publication, publisher, ISSN, library code and holdings; plus an index by country of publication.

70 Conseil International des Archives. **Sources de l'Histoire de l'Afrique du Sud du Sahara dans les Archives et Bibliothèques Francaises. v. 1: Archives, v. 2: Bibliothèques, v. 3: Index**. Zug, Switzerland: Inter Documentation Co., 1976. 3 vols. 959pp., 932pp., 178pp. (Guides des Sources de l'Histoire des Nations, 3 & 4)

> Descriptions of archival holdings relating to Africa in libraries (public, government, private) in France. Extensively indexed. (For other volumes in the series *see* entries **71–78**).

"Guides to the Sources for the History of the Nations/Guides des Sources de l'Histoire des Nations/Quellenführer zur Geschichte der Nationen" Ed. by the International Council on Archives/Conseil International des Archives.

> The aim of this vast project is to provide easy access to the rich source materials preserved in European libraries and archives relating to the history of countries formerly under colonial rule. In addition to the preceding entry **70** the following titles also cover archival holdings on Africa (listed chronologically by year of publication):

71 *2nd series*
vol. 9:
Sources of the History of Africa South of the Sahara in the Netherlands. Comp. by M.P. Roessingh & W. Visser. Munich: K.G. Saur Verlag [for International Council on Archives], 1978. 241pp. DM88.00

72 *3rd series*
vol. 3, pt. 1:
Sources of the History of North Africa, Asia and Oceania in Denmark.
Comp. by C. Rise Hansen. Munich: K.G. Saur Verlag, 1980. 842pp.
DM298.00

73 vol. 3, pt. 2:
**Sources of the History of North Africa, Asia and Oceania in Finland,
Norway, Sweden.** Comp. by Berndt Federley *et al.* Munich: K.G. Saur
Verlag, 1981. 233pp. DM168.00

74 vol. 5:
**Sources de l'Histoire du Proche Orient et de l'Afrique du Nord dans les
Archives et Bibliothèques Françaises.** Ed. by the Commission Française
du Guide des Sources des Nations. pt. 1: Archives, pt. 2: Bibliothèque
Nationale. Munich: K.G. Saur Verlag, 1984 [pt.2]. 2 vols. 480pp.
DM228.00 (pt. 1 in preparation)

75 vol. 6:
**Quellen zur Geschichte Nordafrikas, Asiens und Ozeaniens in der
Bundesrepublik Deutschland bis 1945.** Ed. by Ernst Ritter. Munich:
K.G. Saur Verlag, 1984. 386pp. DM168.00

76 vol. 8:
**Quellen zur Geschichte Afrikas, Asiens und Ozeaniens im Oester-
reichischen Staatsarchiv bis 1986.** Ed. by the Generaldirektion des
Oestereichischen Staatsarchiv. Munich: K.G. Saur Verlag, 1986. 272pp.
DM198.00

77 vol. 9:
**Sources of the History of Latin America, Africa, Asia, Australia and
Oceania in Hungary.** Munich: K.G. Saur Verlag, forthcoming 1989. c.
520pp. c.DM198.00

78 vol. 10:
Sources of the History of Africa, Asia, Oceania in Yugoslavia. Ed. by
the Union of Societies of Archivists in Yugoslavia. Munich: K.G. Saur
Verlag, forthcoming 1989. c.250pp. c.DM168.00

79 Henige, David. **A Union List of African Archival Materials in
Microform.** 2nd ed. Madison: Univ. of Wisconsin, 1984. 45pp.
    Provides details of African archival materials in microform available
    in 18 US libraries. Lists almost 300 titles.

80 Matthews, Noel, and M. Doreen Wainright. **A Guide to Manuscripts and Documents in the British Isles Relating to Africa.** Ed. by
J.D. Pearson. London: Oxford University Press, 1971. 321pp.
    Substantial guide to archival collections, and relating to explorers,
    missionaries, traders, administrators, politicians, etc. Indexed by
    author, subject, and geographically.

81 Nyquist, Corinne and Leo P. Spencer. **The Lonely Africanist: A Guide to Selected U.S. Africana Libraries for Researchers**. Los Angeles: African Studies Association, 1984. 16pp.

> A basic guide, giving information about access to 18 major Africana libraries, collection strengths, etc.

82 Schomburg Center for Research in Black Culture. **Index to the Schomburg Clipping File**. Cambridge: Chadwyck-Healey, 1986. 176pp. £35.00

> An index to the microfiche edition of the Schomburg collection of periodical and newspaper clippings. Lists almost 7000 subjects, of which 650 are on Africa and which are listed separately. (*See also* **37**).

83 **The SCOLMA Directory of Libraries and Special Collections on Africa in the United Kingdom and Western Europe**. Ed. by Harry Hannam 4th ed. Oxford: Hans Zell Publishers (New York: K.G. Saur), 1983. 183pp. £19.50/$35.00

> Details of Africana collections in the United Kingdom and the Republic of Ireland, and significant holdings of African materials in the libraries of Western Europe. Contains 275 entries, each entry providing full name and address, telephone number, name of chief librarian and/or person in charge of the African collection, hours of opening, conditions of access, loan and reference facilities, size and description of the collection, and details of any relevant publications issued. (*See also* entry on SCOLMA **599**).

84 South, Aloha. **Guide to Federal Archives Relating to Africa**. Waltham, Mass.: Crossroads Press, 1977. 556pp. $75.00

> Guide to federal archival holdings in the USA; lists over 800 record groups. Information for each entry includes details of footage of Africa-related material, geographic areas covered, etc. Extensively indexed.

85 South, Aloha. **Guide to Non-Federal Archives and Manuscripts in the United States Relating to Africa**. Oxford: Hans Zell Publishers (New York: K.G. Saur, Inc.), 1989. 2 vols. 1,266pp. £140.00/$250.00 set 2 vols.

> This massive two-volume guide, published for the National Archives, Washington DC, describes textual and non-textual materials, relating to the African continent and offshore islands located in public and private manuscript and archival depositories in the United States. Entries in the *Guide* indicate the scope and content of each collection, as well as the subject of documents contained in a collection or series. The types of documents include correspondence, letterbooks, journals, logbooks, photographs and slides, sound recordings and films. (Includes an extensive 127pp. index.)

86 Stenderup, Vibeke. **Nordisk Biblioteksguide för U-Landsdoku-mentation. Nordic Library Guide to Documentation on Developing Countries**. Aarhus: Nordiska Vetenskapliga Bibliotekarieförbundet [distr. by Bibliothekscentralen, Telegrafvej 5, DK-2750 Ballerup, Denmark], 1981. 100pp.

> A guide to Nordic research libraries with holdings of books, periodicals, reports and other material on developing countries. Covering 156 libraries. In addition to full name and address and telephone/telex numbers, each entry gives a brief description about the nature of each collection, information and documentation services provided by each library, publications issued, etc. Descriptions are in Swedish, but there is an English subject/geographical index.

10. Africanist documentation and bibliography

87 **La Documentation Africaniste en Europe. Africanist Documentation in Europe. Actes du Colloque, Paris, 22–23 mars, 1986**. Strasbourg: Conseil Européen des Etudes Africaines [3 rue de l'Argonne, F-67083 Strasbourg Cedex], 1987. 174pp. F60.00

> The proceedings of a conference held in Paris in 1986 and coinciding with the first General Assembly of the European Council on African Studies (*see* **594**). Contains 17 papers on the state of Africanist documentation in Europe, including surveys of Africana library collections in several European countries. Two papers in English, the rest in French.

88 Larby, Patricia M. **New Directions in African Bibliography**. London: SCOLMA, 1987. 159pp. £6.50

> The proceedings of SCOLMA's Silver Jubilee Conference, this collection of papers looks at future trends in African studies and their implications for libraries. Includes contributions and overviews on African studies research and documentation in Europe, North America, and Africa.

89 Pearson, J.D., and Ruth Jones, eds. **The Bibliography of Africa. Proceedings and Papers of the International Conference on African Bibliography, Nairobi 4–8 December, 1967**. London: Frank Cass; New York: Africana Publ. Corp., 1970. 374pp.

> Papers from an international conference on African bibliography and bibliographic services, aspects of bibliographic control, etc. in Africa. Now inevitably very dated.

90 Standing Conference on Library Materials in Africa. **Progress in African Bibliography. SCOLMA Conference, Commonwealth Institute, London 17–18 March, 1977. Proceedings**. London: SCOLMA, 1977. var.pp. £6.75

> Fourteen papers presented at the 1977 SCOLMA conference, together with reports on the discussions that took place, on

developments in African bibliography since the Nairobi conference (*see* **89**), bibliographical control for African studies, and the acquisition of African materials.

91 Sternberg, Ilse, and Patricia M. Larby. **African Studies. Papers Presented at a Colloquium at the British Library, 7–9 January 1985**. London: The British Library in association with SCOLMA, 1986. 351pp. £17.95 (British Library Occasional papers, 6)

Although not strictly a reference work, this volume is useful as a current overview of the state of African studies in the UK and (to some extent) in Africa. The papers describe the resources available to researchers, the currency of guides and indexes to those resources, publishing and distribution problems for African studies in the UK, and international library and archival collaboration in the African studies field.

11. Some biographical sources

92 **Africa Who's Who**. London: Africa Journal Ltd., 1981. 1,169pp.

Supercedes earlier *African Yearbook & Who's Who* published in 1977. It covers over 7,000 Africans (alive in 1980) from all walks of life, providing fairly extensive biographical data on each. This is the only edition published to date.

'African Historical Dictionaries' series *see* **3**

93 **Dictionary of African Biography/Encyclopaedia Africana** Accra: Encyclopaedia Africana Project; Algonac, Mich.: Reference Publications Inc., 1977– 20 vols.
Vol. 1: Ethiopia-Ghana 370pp. $59.95 1977
Vol. 2: Sierra Leone-Zaire 1979 374pp. $59.95
Vol. 3: South Africa-Botswana-Lesotho-Swaziland 1988 $59.95

An ambitious project that had its roots in an idea for a comprehensive 'Encyclopaedia Africana' first proposed as far back as 1909 by W.E.B. du Bois, and revived by Kwame Nkrumah in the early 1960s. Unfortunately the project has been plagued by numerous problems, political upheavals, and funding difficulties. To date only three volumes have appeared. Written by Africanist scholars each volume contains a series of full biographies (preceded by a historical introduction). Volume 1 contains 152 biographies on Ethiopia and 138 on Ghana; volume 2 135 biographies on Sierra Leone, and 103 on Zaire. And the latest volume, on Southern Africa and published late in 1988, contains 268 entries, together with photographs, maps, bibliographies, extensive cross-references and an index.

94 Lipschutz, Mark R., and R. Kent Rasmussen. **Dictionary of African Historical Biography** 2nd ed. Berkeley: University of California Press, 1986. 328pp.

Arranged in dictionary form and contains some 850 biographical sketches of African historical figures. The second edition has a supplement that also covers 57 post-1960 political leaders.

95 **Makers of Modern Africa. Profiles in History**. London: Africa Journal Ltd., 1981. 592pp.

Includes 500 life histories – many with portraits or photographs – of eminent Africans now dead.

II. CURRENT BIBLIOGRAPHIES AND CONTINUING SOURCES

Only the major *general* current bibliographies and continuing sources are listed here; for more specialist continuing sources readers are again referred to the Scheven and Porges bibliographies (*see* **24** and **27**).

96 Accessions List Eastern Africa

Nairobi: Library of Congress Field Office [PO Box 30598], 1968– Six times yearly ISSN 0090–371X free (also available on microfiche) Edited by James C. Armstrong

> A record of the publications acquired by the Library of Congress Office, Eastern Africa, covering monographs and serials, and arranged by country. An *Annual Publishers Directory*, which appears at the end of each year, lists publishers whose monographs and serials have been included in the bimonthly *Accessions Lists* and in the *Annual Serials Supplement*.

97 Africa Bibliography

Manchester: Manchester University Press (in association with the International African Institute), 1985– [in North America order from St. Martin's Press] Annual ISSN 0266–6731 £22.50
Edited by Hector Blackhurst

> Records books, articles, pamphlets, and essays in edited volumes, principally in the social sciences, environmental sciences, humanities and the arts. Covers the whole of Africa (and not confined to works in English); classified into a general section, subject, and geographically, and subdivided by broad subject groups. With author and subject indexes. The latest annual volume – covering works published on Africa during 1987 – included over 4,000 entries.

98 Africa Index to Continental Periodical Literature.

Oxford: Hans Zell Publishers (New York: K.G. Saur), 1976–Annually price varies

> Provides access to articles from journals published in all African countries except South Africa, in all subjects except medicine. Organized by broad subject divisions, with author, geographical and subject indexes, plus a cumulative list of periodicals indexed since publication of the first volume. [Note: no further volumes have been published since *Africa Index no. 6 (1981)*, and which appeared in 1985. However, the project is about to be revived, using the bibliographic resources at Northwestern University's Africana collections. It is planned to reactivate *Africa Index* with the most current material, with an attempt to be made later to catch up with the backlog of indexing for the retrospective periods 1982–1986.]

99 The African Book Publishing Record
Oxford: Hans Zell Publishers, 1975–Quarterly ISSN 0306–0322 £75.00/
$130.00 annually
Edited by Hans M. Zell

> Provides systematic and comprehensive coverage of new and
> forthcoming African publications, giving full bibliographic and
> ordering information on new African-published material in English
> and French, as well as including significant titles in the African
> languages. Access is by subject, by author, and by country of
> publication. Cumulated every 4–5 years in *African Books in Print* (*see*
> **2**). In addition to its bibliographic coverage, ABPR also includes an
> extensive book review section, reviews of new African serials, and
> articles on publishing and book development in Africa (*see also* **157**).

100 'Africana Reference Works: An Annotated List of 1984–85 Titles'
Edited by Joe Lauer, et al, *The African Book Publishing Record* XII, 2, 1986,
pp.81–92 (*see also* **99**)

> Records, classifies and annotates new reference works covering
> Africa, building on a series first published in *ASA News* (*see* **206**),
> since July/September 1982 and beginning with 1980 books. Coverage
> is generally limited to titles in Western European languages.
> Continued with:
> 'Africana Reference Works: An Annotated List of 1986 Titles',
> *The African Book Publishing Record*, XIII, 2, 1987, pp.93–98;
> 'Africana Reference Works: An Annotated List of 1987 Titles',
> *The African Book Publishing Record*, XIV, 2, 1988, pp.87–93;
> 'Africana Reference Works: An Annotated List of 1988 Titles', [from
> 1989– edited by Yvette Scheven et al]
> *The African Book Publishing Record*, XV, 2, 1989, pp.79–87.

**101 Ausgewählte neuere Literatur . . ./A Selected Bibliography of
Recent Literature on Economic and Social Topics Concerning Africa/
Bibliographie Sélectionnée de littérature récente . . .**
Hamburg: Institut für Afrika Forschung, Dokumentations-Leitstelle
Africa, 1977–Quarterly

> Arranged geographically with subject sub-divisions; with indexes
> (through 1982 only) by subject, author, and geographical.

**102 Bibliographie de l'Afrique Sud-Saharienne, Sciences Humaines et
Sociales: Périodiques.**
Comp. by Marcel d'Hertefelt and Anne-Marie Mouttiaux. Tervuren,
Belgium: Musée Royal de l'Afrique Centrale. 1925–1930, 1932–Annually

> Arranged by author, with detailed subject index and list of
> periodicals indexed. Beginning with 1986 (covering 1981–1983
> publications) it indexes only journal articles. First known as
> **Bibliographie Ethnographique du Congo Belge et des Régions
> Avoisinantes**; from 1962–1981 (covering 1960–1977) it was entitled
> **Bibliographie Ethnographique de l'Afrique Sud-Saharienne**, and
> from 1978–1980 the title was **Bibliographie de l'Afrique Sud-
> Saharienne, Sciences Humaines et Sociales.**

103 **Bibliographie des Travaux en Langue Française sur l'Afrique au Sud du Sahara (Sciences Sociales et Humaines)**.
Comp. by Zofia Yaranga. Paris: Centre d'Etudes Africaines. 1977–
Annually
> Lists monographs, articles, contributions to collected works, arranged by subject and geographically, with author and subject indexes.

104 **A Current Bibliography on African Affairs**
Farmingdale, NY: Baywood Publishing Co., 1963– [New series 1968–]
Quarterly ISSN 0011–3255 $75.00 annually
Edited by Paula Boesch
> Each issue features articles and commentary, review articles and bibliographic essays, plus a topical and geographical list of books, documents, and periodical articles. An author index is included in each issue.

105 **Current Contents Africa**
Frankfurt am Main: Abt. Afrika, Stadt- und Universitaetsbibliothek (distr. by K.G. Saur Verlag, Munich), 1978– [New series, v.6, no.2, 1981–]
Quarterly ISSN 0721–5207 DM138.00 annually
Edited by I.D. Wolcke-Renk
> Reproduces the contents pages of over 200 Africanist periodicals and major non-Africanist journals when they publish relevant articles.

106 **International African Bibliography**
London: Mansell Publishing, 1971–Quarterly ISSN 0020–5877 £44.00/ $80.00 annually
Edited by David Hall
> Lists books, articles and papers in all fields of African studies, although principally in the social sciences and the humanities. Arranged by general topics and geographically with a subject index. Compiled at the Library of the School of Oriental and African Studies, University of London, each issue normally contains about 800–900 entries, and includes material in English, French, Italian, Spanish, Portuguese and some other languages. The annual index (in no. 4 of each volume) contains an Author/Personality Index, Ethnic Groups Index, Language Index, and Selective Index of Other Names and Special Terms.

107 **Joint Acquisitions List of Africana**
Evanston, IL.: Melville J. Herskovits Library of African Studies, Northwestern University Library, 1962–Six times yearly ISSN 0021–731 X $30.00
Edited by Daniel Britz
> A joint list of monographs and serials acquired (in the current year and preceding five years), by 21 US libraries, and arranged by main entry. Annual cumulations for 1979, 1980 and 1981 were published by G.K. Hall (*see* **21**) but not thereafter.

108 US Imprints on Sub-Saharan Africa: A Guide to Publications Catalogued at the Library of Congress, vol. 1, 1985–Washington, D.C.: Library of Congress, African section, 1986–

> Annual listing of titles catalogued during the previous year, arranged alphabetically by main entry and with title and subject indexes.

109 United States and Canadian Publications and Theses on Africa [1962–1970]
Stanford: Hoover Institution Press

> Annual (to 1970) listings of books, pamphlets, articles and doctoral theses, arranged by topics and geographically. Originally published by the African Section of the Library of Congress, the seventh and final volume covered 1966, and was published in 1970.

III. JOURNALS AND MAGAZINES

This is a *selective* listing of the major African studies periodicals and magazines, arranged alphabetically by country. It includes a number of journals not specifically on Africa – e.g. Black studies, Third World studies, Commonwealth literatures, etc. – but which have strong Africa interests.

Information for this section was gathered by means of a questionnaire mailing. Unfortunately not all journals approached responded, despite at least one follow-up chaser mailing, and listings of journals which failed to complete and return our questionnaire are restricted to a basic entry giving name and address, ISSN, frequency, subscription rates, and name of editor where known. All such entries are flagged with a † dagger symbol.

When questionnaires were duly completed and returned, the following details are provided: full name and address; telephone, telex, fax numbers (and electronic mail address for some); year first published, ISSN, frequency, circulation, and subscription rates (surface postage, unless otherwise indicated); name of editor/s and name/s of book review editor/s (and address if different from main address); a brief outline of contents and scope given in *italics*, and as provided by journal editors or publishers themselves; details whether the journal welcomes contributions and articles, and in what particular areas; average length suggested for contributions; payment offered (if any) and/or number of free copies of issue, or offprints, provided to contributors; type of illustrations used; and special editorial requirements.

Abbreviations used:

Ann	– annually
Biwk	– bi-weekly/fortnightly
b/w	– black and white illustrations
Book rev	– journal carries book reviews
Book rev ed	– Book Review Editor
Circ	– circulation
col	– colour illustrations
Contrib	– Contributions [welcomed in . . .]
d-s	– double-spaced
Ed/Eds	– Editor/Editors
Edit req	– Editorial requirements
fn	– footnotes
h-t	– half-tones
Ill	– illustrations [type used]
inst	– institutional subscription rate
indiv	– individual subscription rate
L	– Length [average length suggested for contributions]
line	– line illustrations

26   *Journals and Magazines*

Mon	– monthly
2Mon	– Twice monthly
No contrib	– No contributions [does not publish unsolicited articles]
NP	– No payment offered
P	– Payment offered
photog	– photographs
Qtly	– quarterly
refs	– references
Stud	– student subscription rate
Subs	– Subscription rates [annually]
w	– words [number of, for contributions]
Wk	– weekly
2Yr	– twice yearly
3Yr	– three times yearly
6Yr	– six times yearly/bi-monthly

EUROPE AND THE AMERICAS

Austria

110 Africa Press Clips
Postfach 88, A-1000 Vienna,
Tx: 111010 TZST
1987– 0259–5796 Qtly Circ: 15,000
Subs: $20 Stud: $17
Ed: Eric Silver Book rev
Book rev eds: Abayomi Williams,
Marie-Annette Koch
'Development-oriented, general interest magazine covering politics, business and economics, science and technology, banking, industry, trade, health and entertainment. Also carries paid supplement on countries, institutions and various topics'
Contrib: all areas, except current affairs; nothing negative about, or unduly critical of, Africa; articles previously published elsewhere preferred
L: 5pp NP + 2 copies Ill: line, h-t, photog, maps
Edit req: d-s, A4

111 Zeitschrift für Afrikastudien
Haydng 14/8, A-1060 Vienna
(02235) 89902 (Christian Neugebauer)
1987– 2Yr Circ: 500
Subs: Europe AS360 inst AS180 indiv
elsewhere AS400 inst AS200 indiv
Ed: Michael Neugebauer
Book rev
Book rev ed: Michael Neugebauer,
Herbstrasse 72/78, A-1160 Vienna
'Promotes four political objects: anti-racism, anti-imperialism, anti-colonialism and anti-neocolonialism. Interdisciplinary approach. Learned journal for African studies'.
Contrib: philosophy, labour-unions, history, politics, economy, culture, literature, documents, international relations
L: 25pp NP 2 copies Ill: line
Edit req: single-side pp, disk provision (5¼" disk, 360 kbyte), software must be indicated, author's full name, address & affiliation, abstract of less than 150w in French or German language, refs, bibliography at end

Brazil

112 Africa
CP 8105, C. Universitária,
00508 São Paulo
(210) 9416 Tx: 21519
1978– 0100–8153 Ann Circ: 1,500
Subs: $10
Ed: Fernando August Albuquerque
Mourão

'Concentrates on human sciences in general; dissemination of research on Africa from Brazil and elsewhere; establishment of interchange with academic institutions; a cultural link between Brazil and Africa. Articles are published in Portuguese, French, English, Spanish and Creole of Cabo Verde'
Contrib: human sciences in general
L: 30pp NP 30 offprints + 4 copies Ill: photog, b/w
Edit req: two copies, d-s, 14, résumé of up to 10 lines, refs at end of articles; style sheet available from ed

Canada

113 African Literature Association Bulletin
Department of Comparative Literature, University of Alberta, Edmonton, Alberta, Canada T6G 2J9
(403) 492 5535 Fax: (403) 492 7219
EM: SARNOLD @ UALTAVM
1975– 0146–4965 Qtly Circ: 1,000
Subs: $40 inst $30 indiv Stud $10
Ed: Stephen H. Arnold Book rev
'News, reviews, articles pertaining to African literature and scholarship (plus cinema and adjacent arts) in all languages'
Contrib: conference reports, memorial tributes and historical occasions
L: 5pp NP 5 copies Ill: h-t, photog
Edit req: hard copy plus raw text in Ascii on floppy disk, if possible

114 Canadian Journal of African Studies
Innis College, University of Toronto, 2 Sussex Avenue, Toronto, Ont. M5S 1J5
(416) 978 3424 Fax: (416) 978 5503
1967– 0008–3968 3 Yr Circ: 1,000
Subs: Can$55 Stud: Can$20
Ed: Roger Riendeau Book rev
Book rev ed: Jacques Bernier, Dept. de Geographie, Université Laval, Ste-Foy, PQ G1K 7P4

115 Journal of Asian and African Studies
Department of Sociology, York University, 4700 Keele Street, Downsview, Ontario M3J 1P3
(416) 736 5507
1966– 2 Yr Circ: n/a Subs: n/a
Ed: K. Ishuaran Book rev
'Publishes scholarly studies on Asia and Africa. The focus of the journal is interdisciplinary'
Contrib: social sciences
L: 20pp NP 10 offprints
Ill: line, h-t, photog, b/w Edit req: d-s

116 Journal of Developing Societies
Department of Sociology, York University, 4700 Keele Street, Downsview, Ontario M3J 1P3
(416) 736 5507
1966– 2Yr Circ: n/a
Subs: n/a
Ed: Yogendra Malik, Department of Political Science University of Akron, Ohio 44325, USA
'Deals with development issues – emphasis is on interdisciplinary approach'
Contrib: social sciences
L: 20pp NP 10 offprints Ill: line, h-t, photog, b/w
Edit req: d-s

Denmark

117 Kunapipi
Anna Rutherford, Department of English, University of Aarhus, 8000 Aarhus C
6136711
1970– 0106–5734 3Yr Circ: n/a
Subs: Kr150 inst Kr100 indiv
Ed: Anna Rutherford Book rev
'An arts magazine with special but not exclusive emphasis on the literatures written in English. It publishes creative material as well as articles, and it tries to cover a wide area of history, sociology, film and art as well as literature'

Contrib: in areas above
L: 12pp P: for creative material only Ill:
photog,   drawings,   lithographs,
paintings
Edit req: d-s, fn at end, MHRA Style
Sheet, self-addressed envelope

France

118 Afrique Contemporaine†
Centre d'Etude et de
Documentation sur l'Afrique
et l'Outre-Mer
29–31 quai Voltaire, 75340
Paris Cedex 07
(1) 40 15 70 00 Tx: 204826 DOCFRAN
1962– 0002–0478 Qtly Subs: FF150
Ed: Laurence Porges

119 Afrique Expansion†
Publications du Moniteur,
17 rue d'Uzes, 75002 Paris
(1) 42 96 15 50
1984– 0762–3399 Wk Subs: Fl,500
Ed: Jerome Savin

120 APELA. Bulletin de Liaison Association pour l'Etude des Littératures Africaines
5 Square Henri Delormel,
75014 Paris
1984– 0769–4563 2Yr Circ: 150
Subs: FF100/$16.50 free to members of
the Association Ed: Virginia Coulon
'*Reports/news of past, present or future
events relating to African literatures; list of
recent publication of interest to our
members*'
Contrib: information about events
relating to African literatures; no
articles or studies on African literatures

121 Bulletin de l'Afrique Noire†
Ediafric, 10 rue Vineuse,
75116 Paris
Cedex 16
1956– 0045–3501 Wk Subs: FF3,500

122 Cahier d'Etudes Africaines†
Institut National des
Languages et Civilisations
Orientales, 2 rue de Lille,
75007 Paris
1960– 0008–0055 Qtly Subs: F446 inst
F238 indiv
Ed: Pierre Alexandre

123 Jeune Afrique
51 Avenue des Ternes,
75017 Paris
47665242 Tx: 280674 GRUPJIA
Fax: 46226638
1960– 0021–6089 Wk Circ: n/a
Subs: France FF620 Africa FF1,800
elsewhere FF2,200
Ed: Hugo Sada Book rev
Book rev ed: Marcel Peju
'*Popular weekly news, current affairs and
cultural magazine*'
Contrib: all areas
L: 1pp P: various Ill: photog, drawings

124 Journal des Africanistes†
Société des Africanistes,
Musée de l'Homme, Place du
Trocadero, 75116 Paris
1931– 0399–0346 2Yr Subs: FF250
Ed: G. Calame-Griaule

125 Marches Tropicaux et Mediterranéens†
René Moreux & Cie, 190 Blvd
Haussmann, 75008 Paris
1945– 0025–2859 Wk Subs: F2,850
Ed: Serge Marpaud

126 Notre Librarie
Club des Lecteurs d'Expression
Française, 57 Boulevard des
Invalides, 75007 Paris, France
47831438
1969– 0755–3854 Qtly Circ: n/a
Subs: France FF100 elsewhere FF200
Ed: Club des Lecteurs d'Expression
Française Book rev
Book rev ed: Marie Clotilde Jacquey
'*Articles on literature from Africa, Indian
Ocean Islands, Caribbean Islands, biblio-*

graphic issues, special issues on the literature of one African country, thematic
issues. Mostly French language'
Contrib: in areas above
P: FF250 per printed page Ill: photog

127 Peuples Noirs, Peuples Africains
82 Avenue de la Porte des
Champs, 76000 Rouen
35893197
1978– 0181–4087 6Yr Circ: n/a
Subs: FF240 Stud: FF40
Ed: Editions des Peuples Noirs
Book rev
*'All cultural and political subjects concern-
ing Black peoples'*
Contrib: in areas above
L: 1,000–5,000w NP 5 copies Ill: none

128 Politique Africaine
Centre d'Etudes d'Afrique
Noire, BP 101, 33405 Talence
56 80 60 57
1980– Qtly Circ: 3,000
Subs: FF320
Ed: René Otayek Book rev
*'Current affairs, political life of (mostly)
Black Africa. Social and cultural topics'*
Contrib: field studies of political life in
contemporary Africa
L: 3,000–6,000w NP 3 copies Ill:
photog

129 Présence Africaine. Revue Culturelle du Monde Noire†
Société Nouvelle Présence
Africaine, 25 bis rue des
Ecoles, 75005 Paris
(1) 43 54 13 74, 43 26 66 43
1947– 0032–7638 Qtly Subs: F300/$75
Ed: Yande Christiane Diop

130 Revue Française d'Histoire d'Outre-Mer†
Société d'Histoire d'Outre
Mer, 1–2 rue Robert de Flers,
75015 Paris
1913– 0300–9513 Qtly Subs: FF280
Ed: Jean Devisse

Germany (Federal Republic)

131 Africana Marburgensia
Seminar für Religionsge-
schichte, Am Plan 3,
D-3550 Marburg/Lahn
(06421) 283930
1968– 0174–5603 2Yr Circ: 500
Subs: exchange basis only
Eds: Hans-Jürgen Greschat & Hans-H.
Münkner Book rev Book rev ed: Hans-
Jürgen Greschat
*'African studies – African religions;
African traditions and change (social,
economic and legal aspects)'*
Contrib: in areas above, preferably
from Africa/African authors
L: 10–20pp NP 10 copies Ill: none

132 Afrika. Review of German-African Relations†
Afrika Verlag,
Türltorstrasse 14,
Postfach 1144,
D-8068 Pfaffenhofen an der
Ilm
(98441) 5051 53
1960– 0340–5796 Mon Subs: DM17
Ed: Inga Krugmann

133 Afrika Spectrum
Institut für Afrika-Kunde,
Neuer Jungfernstieg 21,
D-2000 Hamburg 36
(040) 3562523/524
1966– 0002–0397 3Yr Circ: 500
Subs: DM80
Ed: Harald Voss Book rev
*'Africanist journal covering the social
sciences in general (Africa except Egypt
covered by 'Orient', published by the
Deutsches Orient-Institut, Hamburg).
Articles published in German, English,
French. Each issue contains sections
'Current African Legislation', indexed
from African government gazettes, book
reviews, and reports on conferences and
research activities'*
Contrib: social, economic and political
conditions and developments in
Africa, except Egypt, and reports on

conferences and research activities
L: articles 20–25pp reports 6–10pp NP
2 copies + 30 offprints Ill: line, h-t, b/w
Edit req: articles should contain
summary/résumé of about 15-20 lines

134 Afrika und Übersee – Sprachen, Kulturen

Dietrich Reimer Verlag, Unter
den Eichen 57,
D-1000 Berlin 45
(030) 8314081
1910– 2Yr Circ: n/a
Subs: DM115
Eds: Jürgen Zwernemann & Hilke
Meyer-Bahlburg
Afrikanisches Seminar,
Rothenbaumchaussee 5,
2000 Hamburg 13, Federal Republic of
Germany Book rev
Book rev ed: Hilke Meyer-Bahlburg
*'Articles mainly on African languages, on
history in connection with languages, on
traditional literature in connection with
languages'*
Contrib: African languages and
linguistics
L: 30pp NP 25 copies Ill: none

135 Aktueller Informationsdienst Afrika/Africa Current Affairs Information Service

Institut für Afrika-Kunde
Neuer Jungfernstieg 21, D-
2000 Hamburg 236
(040) 3562523
1974– 0342–0396 Biwk Circ: 200
Subs: DM195
Ed: Klaus Hemstedt
*'Reproduction of articles from ca.20
African newspapers published in English,
French and Portuguese and dealing with
social, economic and political conditions
and developments in Africa except Egypt
(covered by the Current Affairs Informa-
tion Service published by the Deutsches
Orient-Institut, Hamburg)*
No contrib

136 Internationales Afrikaforum

Weltforum Verlag,
Kriemhildenstr.38,
D-8000 München 19
(089) 175439
1964– 0020–9430 Qtly Circ: n/a
Subs: DM98
Ed: Hans-Gert Braun & Count Alois
von Waldburg-Zeil Book rev
*'Chronik: (45 pages) political, social,
economic, cultural development; essay section: forum for specialists and experts from
various schools of thought; literary review'*
Contrib: politics, social affairs, economics, occasionally history
L: 10–15 pp NP 5 copies Ill: graphs,
diagrams, author must supply camera-
ready artwork

137 Matatu. Zeitschrift für Afrikanische Kultur und Gesellschaft

In der Au 33, D-6000
Frankfurt am Main 90, Federal
Republic of Germany
(069) 786310
1987– 0932–9714 2Yr Circ: 400
Subs: DM45 inst DM28 indiv
Ed: Holger G. Ehling Book rev
Book rev eds: Holger G. Ehling &
Monika Trebert
*'Features all aspects of Black and African
cultural studies, with emphasis on litera-
ture. The second issue of each volume is a
focal issue. Recent and forthcoming issues
(focus): Contemporary Nigerian Literature
(1987), Culture and Resistance in South
Africa (1988), Tradition and the Black
Woman Writer (1989). English, French
and German languages'.*
Contrib: in areas above, all aspects of
Black and African studies
L: 15–20pp P: varies + 2 copies Ill:
photog, b/w drawings, lithographs
Edit req: MLA-Handbook style, summary of 10–15 lines, self-addressed
envelope

Italy

138 **Africa. Rivista Trimestrale di Studi e Documentazione†**
Istituto Italiano per l'Africa,
16 via Ulisse Aldrovani,
00197 Roma
1946– 0001–9747 Qtly Subs: L40,000
Ed: Teobaldo Filesi

139 **Nigrizia. Fatti e Problemi del Mondo Nero†**
Missionari Comboniani,
Vicolo Pozzo 1, 37129 Verona
1883– 0029–0173 Mon Subs:
L15,000/$18
Ed: Aurelio Boscaini

Netherlands

140 **Africa Tervuren†**
Musée Royal de l'Afrique
Centrale
13 Steenweg op Leuven, 1980
Tervuren
1955 0001–9879 Qtly Subs: BFr.650
Ed: J.-B. Cuypers

141 **Journal of African Languages and Linguistics†**
Vakgroep Afrikaanse
Taalkunde, Rijksuniversitet te
Leiden, Van Wijksplaats 4,
2311 BX Leiden
1979– 0167–6164 2Yr Subs: $49 inst $25 indiv
Ed: Thilo C. Schadeberg

142 **Journal of Religion in Africa**
E.J. Brill Publishers,
POB 9000, 2300 PA Leiden,
(0532) 333641 Tx: 556473 UNILDS
Fax: (0532) 336017
1967– 0022–4200 3Yr Circ: 2,000
Ed: Adrian Hastings, Department of
Theology and Religious Studies, The
University, Leeds LS2 9JT. Book rev
Book rev ed: Rosalind Shaw,
Department of Social Anthropology,
University of Edinburgh, George
Square, Edinburgh EH8 9LL, Scotland
*'Concerned impartially with all aspects,
present and past, of religion in Africa –
traditional, Christian, Islamic –
approached historically, anthropologically
or theoretically. Most issues are focused
upon one theme, e.g. on modern Islam'*
Contrib: in areas above
L: 4,000–8,000w NP 25 offprints Ill:
occasional photog, maps Edit req: two
copies, d-s

Portugal

143 **Revista Internacional de Estudos Africanos†**
Travessa das Aguas Livras
21–5 Esq., 1200 Lisboa
1985– [?] Qtly
Ed: Jill R. Dias

Spain

144 **Bulletin du CEEA/ECA Newsletter**
A/c Colegio Mayor
Universitario N.S. Africa,
Obispo Trejo 1, Ciudad
Universitaria, 28040 Madrid
1986– 2Yr Circ: 2,500
Subs: free to ECAS associations &
members, or on exchange basis
Ed: Luis Beltran Book rev
*'General information on Africanist activi-
ties (conferences, symposia, seminars, pub-
lications, etc.) in Europe and other
countries'*
Contrib: news and information on
Africanist activities, any scholarly
activity, any subject
NP 2 copies Ill: none

145 **Estudios Africanos**
Asociación Española de
Africanistas,
A/c Colegio Mayor Univ. N.S.
Africa,
Obispo Trejo 1, Cuidad
Universitaria, 28040 Madrid
1985– 2 Yr Circ: 1,000
Subs: Spain 2,000 Pts elswhere 2,500
pts
Ed: Carlos Gonzalez Echegaray
Book rev
*'African   studies,   specifically   social
sciences'*
Contrib: social sciences in general but
all areas considered
L: 20–25pp NP+ 5 copies Ill: photog,
maps, b/w
Edit req: d-s, a summary in English/
French

Sweden

146 **Development Dialogue.**
A Journal of International
Development Corporation†
The Dag Hammarskjöld
Centre, Ovre Slottsgatan 2,
S 752 20 Uppsala
1972– 0345-2328 2 Yr Subs: free
Eds: Sven Hamrell, Olle Nordberg

Switzerland

147 **Genève-Afrique. Journal of**
the Geneva Institute of
Development Studies and of
the Swiss Society of African
Studies
CP 136, CH-1211, Genève 21,
(022) 315940 Tx: 22810 IUED
Fax: (022) 384416
1962– 2 Yr Circ: 1,400
Subs: SFr 26 Stud: rates available on
request
Ed: Laurent Monnier Book rev
Book rev ed: Annie Jeanmonod
'Aims to promote dialogue and scientific

exchanges between Africa and Switzerland
and publishes articles in English and
French on African politics, economics,
history, sociology, anthropology and litera-
ture'
Contrib: in areas above
L: 10–25pp NP 30 offprints copies on
request Ill: ill, photog
Edit req: for 20pp or more, an abstract
of 10–15 lines

United Kingdom

148 **Africa**
International African
Institute, Lionel Robbins
Building, 10 Portugal Street,
London, WC2A 2HD
(01) 831 3068
1928– 0001-9720 Qtly Circ: 1,200
Subs: £70 inst £37.50 indiv (includes
Ann bibliography)
Ed: Murray Last Book rev
Book rev ed: Tom Young, Dept. of
Economics & Political Studies, SOAS,
Malet Street, London WC1E 7HP
'The study of African societies and cul-
tures: encourages an inter-disciplinary
approach, involving the social sciences,
languages and culture and actively seeks
out international scholarly contributions'
Contrib: social sciences, history, en-
vironmental   and   life   sciences,
languages and culture
L: 8,000w (excluding bibliography) NP
25 offprints Ill: line, h-t, photog
Edit req: two copies, d-s, A4, abstract
of not more than 400w

149 **Africa Analysist**
Orchard House,
167 Kensington High Street,
London W8 4PF
(01) 937 5500, (01) 937 7673
1986– 0950-902X 2Mon
Subs: £185/$345 inst £120/$220 indiv
Ed: Richard Hall

150 **Africa and the World**
Distribution Centre,
Blackhorse Road, Letchworth,
Herts. SG6 1HN
(0462) 67255 Fax: (0462) 480 947
EM: 84 BUR101
1987– 0950–0650 Qtly Circ: 2,500
Subs: £40/$60 inst £25/$40 indiv
Ed: Chuba Okadigbo
*'Analysis and opinion on African political,
social and economic affairs. In support of
Pan-Africanism'*
Contrib: on African political, social
and economic affairs
NP 1 copy
Edit req: two copies, d-s, A4, with 50w
note on author's current affiliation and
publications

151 **Africa Confidential**
Flat 5, 33 Rutland Gate,
London SW7 1PD
(01) 584 9141 Tx: 8951859 Fax: 581 3529
1960– 0044–6483 Biwk Circ: n/a
Ed: Stephen Ellis
Subs: UK £100 elsewhere £130/$250
Stud: £35/$60
*'Exclusive features on African politics and
economics, and relations between Africa
and the rest of the world; short 'pointers'
on similar subjects'*
No contrib

152 **Africa Economic Digest**
5–15 Cromer Street,
London WC1H 8LS
(01) 833 3661 Tx: 262505
Fax: (01) 833 4991
1980– 0144–8234 Wk Circ: 3,500
Subs: £200/$400
Ed: Richard Synge
*'Business and economic news on OAU
Africa'*
Contrib: commissioned only

153 **Africa Events**
55–57 Banner Street,
London EC1Y 8PX
(01) 253 4726, (01) 608 0205
Tx: 252028 Fax: (01) 608 0208

1984– 0267–6362 Mon Circ: 24,000
Subs: UK £16 Americas $48 elsewhere
$38
Ed: Abdilatif Abdalla Book rev
Contrib: current affairs, analytical,
economy, business, arts, sports,
environment
L: 1,000–2,000w P: £80 per 1,000w + 1
copy Ill: photog

154 **Africa Newsfile**
Euston House, 81–103 Euston
Street, London NW1 2ET
(01) 388 3111 exts. 2157/2218 Tx: 927946
AMFILE Fax: (01) 387 7324
1987– 0952–4290 Biwk Circ: n/a
Subs: £185/$350 inst £120/$220 indiv
Stud: £50/$90
Ed: Ikhenemho S. Okomilo Book rev
*'Insight and analytical briefing on busi-
ness, economics and political developments
in Africa; economic intelligence reports'*
Contrib: Africa development issues,
politics and the economy
L: 2,000w P: NUJ rates Ill: line, h-t

155 **Africa Research Bulletin†**
Africa Research Ltd., The Old
Rectory, Woolfardisworthy,
Devon EX17 4RX
(0392) 215655
1964– Series A: Political 0001–9844
Series B: Economic 0001–9852 Mon
Subs: £125/$250 per series
Ed: J.G.S. Drysdale

156 **African Affairs**
18 Northumberland Avenue,
London WC2N 5BJ
(01) 930 1661
1901– 0001–9909 Qtly Circ: 2,800
Subs: £38/$65
Eds: R. Hodder-Williams &
P. Woodward Book rev
Book rev ed: D Killingray, Dept of
Historical & Cultural Studies,
Goldsmiths' College, Univ of London,
New Cross, London SE14 6NW
*'Original articles on current or recent
social, economic and political developments
in Africa'*

Contrib: all areas concerned with Africa, written in style immediately accessible to non-specialists and specialists alike
L: 6,000w NP 25 offprints Ill: maps, photog
Edit req: style sheet available from eds

157 The African Book Publishing Record
Hans Zell Publishers, An imprint of the K.G. Saur division of Butterworths, POB 56, Oxford OX1 3EL
(0865) 511428 Tx: 94012872 ZELL
Fax: (0865) 310183 (for Zell)
1975– 0306–0322 Qtly Circ: 800
Subs: £75/$130
Eds: Hans M. Zell & Mary Jay
Book rev
Book rev eds: Gary Gorman, School of Information Studies, Charles Sturt University, POB 588, Wagga Wagga, NSW 2650, Australia; and, Mark DeLancey, Dept. of Government and International Studies, University of South Carolina, Columbia, SC 29208, USA
'Provides extensive bibliographic coverage of new and forthcoming African publications; also includes an extensive book review section and reviews of new African serials; plus news, reports, interviews, articles, etc. about African booktrade activities and developments'
Contrib: book reviews solicited only; articles welcomed on aspects of African publishing and the booktrade, and African librarianship L: 1,800–5,000w P: (major articles only) £50-£75+ 6 copies Ill: photog
Edit req: d-s, A4, refs with fn at end of articles; all book reviews to be submitted through joint book review editors above

158 African Business
Carlton House, 69 Great Queen Street, POB 261, London WC2B 5BN
(01) 404 4333 Tx: 8811757 ARABY
Fax: (01) 404 5336

1966– Mon Circ: 18,000
Subs: £30/$70 Stud: £20/$49 (new subs only)
Ed: Linda van Buren Book rev
'Covers all sectors; regular articles on agriculture, banking, finance, energy, mining, manufacturing technology, marketing and trade, transport and communications'
Contrib: anything on African economics and business L: 750w P: varies Ill: line, h-t, photog

159 The African Communist
POB 902, London N19 3YY
(01) 263 8417
1959– 0001–9976 Qtly Circ: 17,000
Subs: £5 (£10 air)
Ed: Brian Bunting Book rev
'Published in the interest of African solidarity and as a forum for Marxist-Leninist throught. Main emphasis on Southern Africa, particularly South Africa'
Contrib: commissioned only

160 African Concord Magazine
5–15 Cromer Street, London WC1H 8LS
(01) 833 3661–5 Tx: 262505
Fax: (01) 837 6028
1984– Wk Circ: 40,000
Subs: £38.50 Stud: £19.25
Ed: Lewis Obi (Lagos) & Tunde Agbabiaka (London) Book rev
Book rev ed: Jon Offei-Ansah
'African issues and events – politics, economics, culture and arts, ideas; events and issues as they affect African people in the diaspora, UK, USA, Canada and the Caribbean'
Contrib: opinions on African issues, special news features on African affairs and the diaspora
L: 1,000w P: £50–£100 Ill: photo, cartoons b/w & col
Nigerian office: Concord Press of Nigeria Ltd., POB 4483, Ikeja, Lagos State, Tel: 901010–9 Tx: 21138

161 **African Farming & Food Processing**
27 Wilfred Street,
London SW1
(01) 834 7676 Tx: 297165
Fax: (01) 821 7045
1979– 6Yr Circ: 9,000
Subs: £28/$48
Ed: Jonquil Phelan Book rev
'All aspects of African agriculture and food processing, including finance, appropriate technology, crops, livestock, irrigation, packaging, processing'
Contrib: commissioned only, in all areas above
L: 1,500w P: yes, + 6 copies Ill: photog b/w & col

162 **African Journal of Ecology**
Blackwell Scientific
Publications Ltd, Osney
Mead, Oxford OX2 0EL
(0865) 240201 Fax: (0865) 721205
1963– Qtly Circ: 600
Subs: £83 members of East African Wildlife Society £23
Ed: F.I.B. Kayanja Book rev
Book rev ed: S.K. Eltringham,
Department of Zoology, Downing Street, Cambridge
'Original scientific articles and book reviews'
Contrib: African ecology
L: 4,000w NP 50 copies Ill: line, photog (if essential)

163 **African Journal of Medicine & Medical Sciences†**
Blackwell Scientific
Publications Ltd., Osney
Mead, Oxford OX2 0EL
(0865) 240201
1970– 0309–3913 Qtly Subs: £55/$97.50
Ed: L.A. Salako

164 **African Languages and Cultures**
School of Oriental and African Studies, Thornhaugh Street, Russell Square, London WC1H 0XG
(01) 637 2388 Tx: 291829 SOASP
Fax: (01) 436 3844
1988– 0954–416X 2Yr Circ: n/a
Subs: £10/425
Ed: Graham Furniss
'Africa-oriented papers in descriptive linguistics, comparative linguistics and classification; oral literature, African writing in African and metropolitan languages; African art and music'
Contrib: in areas above
L: 25pp NP 10 offprints Ill: line, h-t
Edit req: d-s, A4, style sheet available from ed

165 **African Literature Today**
James Currey'Publishers,
54b Thornhill Square,
London N1 1BE
(01) 609 9026 Tx: 262433 W6327
Fax: (01) 609 9605
1968– 0–85255–5 Ann Circ: 4,000
Subs: £7.95 per vol
Eds: Eldred Durosimi Jones & Eustace Palmer, c/o Fourah Bay College, University of Sierra Leone, Freetown, Sierra Leone
'Each volume focuses on a special aspect of African literature, such as 'Women and African Literature', 'Poetry, Oral and Written', 'Drama', 'Prose', which is announced in advance'
Contrib: yes, provided they fit into the announced topic
L: 3,500w NP 1 copy
Edit req: d-s, A4, refs with fn at end of articles

166 African Research and Documentation
c/o The Library, Institute of Development Studies, University of Sussex, Falmer, Sussex BN1 9RE
(0273) 606261 Tx: 877997 IDSBTN
1962– 0305–826X 3Yr Circ: 400
Subs: £10/$25
Ed: Maureen Mahoney Book rev
'Articles and news items on all aspects of African studies, library and archive collections relating to Africa, and African bibliography'
Contrib: all aspects of African studies and documentation
L: 6,000–8,000w NP 6 offprints Ill: line, h-t, b/w

167 African Review of Business and Technology
27 Wilfred Street, London SW1
(01) 834 7676 Tx: 297165
Fax: (01) 821 7045
1964– Mon Circ: 19,000
Subs: £36/$66
Ed: Jonquil Phelan Book rev
'All aspects of business and technology in Black Africa including management, finance, construction, computers and development issues'
Contrib: commissioned only: interviews, telecommunications, manufacturing, computers
L: 1,500w P: yes, + 6 copies Ill: photog b/w & col

168 African Textiles
Alain Charles House, 27 Wilfred Street, London SW1E 6PR
(01) 834 7676 Tx: 297166
Fax: (01) 821 7045
1980– 0144–7521 6Yr Circ: 13,067
Subs: £28/$48
Ed: Zsa Tebbit Book rev
'Latest developments worldwide plus reports on market trends, general management skills and needs, projects, company

profiles and exhibition previews and reviews'
Cotnrib: in areas above
L: 1,000w P: £90 per 1,000w + variable number of free copies/offprints Ill: line, h-t, photog, b/w & col

169 African Times†
Hansib Publishing Ltd., Tower House, 139–149 Fonthill Road, London N4 3HF
(01) 281 1191
1984– Wk
Ed: Arif Ali

170 African Woman
London Women Centre, Wesley House, 4 Wild Court, London WC2B 5AU
1988– 0953–9816 Qtly Circ: 5,000
Subs: £12 Stud: Europe and USA £6
Ed: Working Group (Coordinator: Mabel Ikpoh) Book rev
'Produced and edited by African women, to articulate their needs, achievements and aspirations. Economics, politics, culture and development issues are all discussed from an African women's perspective. Includes features, interviews, news, and reviews from across the continent and the diaspora'
Contrib: women and development
L: 2,000w NP Ill: photog, maps

171 Bulletin of the School of Oriental and African Studies
School of Oriental and African Studies, Thronhaugh Street, Russell Square, London WC1H 0XG
(01) 637 2388 Tx: 291829 SOASP
Fax: (01) 436 3844
1917– 0041–977X 3Yr Circ: 1,000
Subs: £40/$75
Ed: editorial board Book rev
Book rev ed: Diana Matias
'Original scholarly articles on the languages, culture, history and archaeology, etc. of Africa, the Near and Middle East and Asia'

Contrib: in areas above
L: 15,000w NP 25 offprints Ill: line, h-t, photog, b/w
Edit req: d-s, single-sided, fn d-s at end

172 Computers in Africa and Telecoms Update
Africa File, 21 Mill Lane, London NW6 1NT
(01) 794 5308 Fax: (01) 435 1945
EM: 933524 GEOZ AFRICA-FILE
1987– 0953–3257 6Yr Circ: 5,500
Subs: Africa £32 elsewhere £38 (airmail, 2 years)
Ed: Sean Moroney Book rev
Computer industry news from Anglophone Africa; guidelines and important international computing trends; regular software and hardware reviews; detailed surveys of national computer markets; new products; computer applications of particular relevance to Africa; expert advice
Contrib: in areas above
L: 200–1,000w P: £60 per 1,000w + 1 copy Ill: line, photog b/w

173 EASA: Trade & Investment in Eastern and Southern Africa
Africa File, 21 Mill Lane, London NW6 1NT
(01) 794 5308 Fax: (01) 435 1945
EM: 933524 GEOZ AFRICA-FILE
1987– 17Yr Circ: 300
Subs: Africa £140 elsewhere £190 (airmail)
Ed: Sean Moroney Book rev
A business newsletter covering trade and investment opportunities in Eastern and Southern Africa, paying particular attention to intra-regional trade, SADCC and PTA projects, transport development and ports and shipping
Contrib: in areas above
P: £60 per 1,000w + 1 copy Ill: line drawings, maps

174 Index on Censorship
39c Highbury Place, London N5 1QP
(01) 359 0161 Fax: (01) 226 8666
1972– 0306–4220 10Yr Circ: 5,500

Subs: UK £18 elsewhere £20/$30 Stud: £11/$20
Ed: Sally Laird Book rev
As much as possible we like to publish the particular artists' banned material. Features on special artists/ journalists etc. welcome. Recent trends in a country where censorship has been tightened or loosened
Contrib: censorship of writers, journalists, musicians, artists, newspapers etc. around the world
L: 2,500w P: £42 per 1,000w + 2 or more copies Ill: photog
Edit req: in consultation with country researcher

175 Inter-Arts
Broughton House, 62 Broughton Street, Edinburgh EH1 3SA
(031) 557 4773
1986– 0951–0176 Qtly Circ: 1,000–1,500
Subs: UK £6 inst £4 indiv elsewhere £7 inst £5 indiv
Eds: Moussa Jogee, Colin Nicholson & Jenny Dawe Book rev
Book rev ed: Jenny Dawe
Each issue contains articles, reviews and poetry which fall into our broad remit of 'cultural connections'. We aim to widen the knowledge and broaden the perceptions of an intelligent readership
Contrib: Third World connections, original poetry, material from or about Africa – literary, economic, political, sociological
L: 2,500w NP 2 copies Ill: line

176 Journal of African Earth Sciences and the Middle East
Pergamon Press, Headington Hill Hall, Oxford OX3 0BW
(0865) 64881 Tx: 83177 EM: TOUR ONYX (10 rue Vandrezanne, 75013 Paris, France)
1983– 6Yr Circ: 1,000
Subs: DM650 (airmail) Stud: DM186
Ed: C.A. Kogbe Book rev
Book rev ed: C.A. Kogbe, Rock View International Tour Onyx, 10 rue Vandrezanne, 75013 Paris, France

Contrib: geology, mineral resources, energy resources and water resources – Africa and the Middle East
NP Ill: photog

177 Journal of African History
Cambridge University Press, The Edinburgh Building, Shaftesbury Road, Cambridge CB2 2RU
(0223) 312393 Tx: 817256
Fax: (0223) 315052
1960– 0021–8537 3Yr Circ: 1,750
Subs: £40/$89 (incl. airmail) inst £21/$31 indiv
Ed: David Anderson, Department of History, Birkbeck College, London WC1E 7HX (Ed from 1990–: David Robinson) Book rev
'Covers the history of the whole African continent, from prehistory to modern times, and includes articles on archaeology, ethnology and linguistics'
Contrib: as above; emphasis has recently been given to themes in economic history, labour history and the history of colonial rule
L: 4,000–6,000w NP 25 offprints Ill: line, h-t
Edit req: style sheet available from eds

178 Journal of African Marxists/ Journal des Marxistes Africains
23 Bevenden Street, London N1 6BH
1981– 263–2268 2Yr Circ: 3,000
Subs: Africa £8 Europe £14 elsewhere £16 inst Africa £5 Europe £8 elsewhere £9 indiv
'An independent forum for Marxist thought; discussion of the fundamentals of Marxism in the conditions of Africa; analysis of Africa's development problems from a Marxist perspective; critical discussion of various versions of Socialism in Africa; aims to facilitate the emergence of a systematic body of Marxist thought in Africa, written in the English, French, Portuguese or Arabic languages'
Contrib: current affairs or theoretical/

cultural issues on African from a non-sectarian Marxist standpoint L: 1,000–2,000w NP 1 copy Ill: line, photog b/w
Edit req: d-s, English, French, Portuguese or Arabic languages, no fn

179 The Journal of Commonwealth Literature
Hans Zell Publishers, An imprint of the K.G. Saur division of Butterworths, POB 56, Oxford OX1 3EL
(0865) 511428 Tx: 94012872 ZELL
Fax: (0865) 310183 (for Zell)
1965– 0021–9894 2Yr Circ: 1,000
Subs: £30/$52 inst £22/$38 indiv
Eds: Alastair Niven & Caroline Bundy
'Provides a focal-point for discussion of literature in English outside Britain and the USA. The first number of each volume consists of an issue of critical studies and essays; the second is the bibliography issue, containing an annual checklist of publications in each region of the Commonwealth'
Contrib: all areas of Commonwealth writing including African literatures; also bibliographic contributions and checklists on prominent authors
L: 2,500–5,000w P: NP for articles; payment is made to contributors of the bibliography issue (rates on application) 2 copies Ill: photog
Edit req: style sheet available from eds

180 The Journal of Modern African Studies
Huish, Mill Street, Chagford, Devon, TW13 8AR
(06473) 3569
1963– 0022–278X Qtly Circ: 2,000
Subs: UK £44 N. America $104 elsewhere £49 Stud: £21/$48
Ed: David Kimble Book rev
'Offers a quarterly survey of politics, economics, and related topics that is designed to promote a deeper understanding by both academics and practitioners of what is happening in Africa today'
Contrib: from all over the world as long as they are both scholarly and 'readable'

L: 5,000–7,000w, with exceptions up to 10,000w NP 1 copy per contributor, 25 offprints per author Ill: tables, diagrams
Edit req: one copy – not the original typescript

181 Journal of Southern African Studies
Oxford University Press,
Walton Street,
Oxford OX2 6DP
(0865) 56767
1974– 0305–7070 Qtly Circ: 500
Subs: UK £37 N. America $78 elsewhere £45 inst £18.50 indiv
Eds: Rob Turrell, Ian White & Colin Stoneman Book rev
Book rev ed: c/o eds, 21 St. Giles, Oxford OX1 3LA
'Interdisciplinary scope . . . draws important connections within the humanities and social sciences . . . charts the progress of southern African studies in all fields . . . committed to developing further links between theory and the reality . . . special issues on topics in depth'
Contrib: in areas above
L: 8,000w NP 1 copy, 25 offprints Ill: h-t, photog
Edit req: three copies, provision on IBM or Apple disk

182 Links
Third World First, 232 Cowley Road, Oxford OX4 1UH
(0865) 245678
1974– 0261–4014 Qtly Circ: 6,000
Subs: UK £15 inst £10 indiv elsewhere £2.50
Ed: Jenny Hammond
'Investigates the causes and continuance of under-development, especially the role played historically and now by the industrialised countries. Each issue concentrates on a single theme'
Contrib: n/a

183 Modern Africa
57/59 Whitechapel Road,
London E1 1DU
(01) 377 8413 Tx: 265871 ref.76: CJJ024
Fax: (01) 247 5407
1977– ISSN: n/a 6Yr Circ: 14,000
Subs: £36/$50
Ed: Patrick Smith
'Regional magazine for business people and government officials in sub-Saharan Africa. Articles cover manufacturing and processing, raw materials, energy, transportation, communications, construction, banking, new government projects etc. Also features on new technology, equipment and business developments in the industrialised countries; city reports and commodities monitor'
Contrib: in areas above
L: 600–800w P: £75 per 1000w 1 copy Ill: h-t, line, maps, charts, colour trannies

184 New African
69 Great Queen Street,
London WC2B 5BN
(01) 404 4333 Tx: 8811757 ARABY
Fax: (01) 404 5336
1966– Mon Circ: 35,581
Subs: £40/$70 (airmail) Stud: £15/$35 (airmail)
Ed: Alan Rake Book rev
'Surveys of countries, different economic sectors – banking, brewing, etc.'
Contrib: commissioned only Ill: line, h-t, photog, col

185 New Internationalist
42 Hythe Bridge Street,
Oxford OX1 2EP
(0865) 728181 Tx: 83147 NEWINT
Fax: (0865) 726753
1972– 0305–9529
Mon Circ: 65,000
Subs: £18/$30 (airmail)
Ed: Collective Book rev
Book rev ed: Chris Brazier
'Each issue is devoted to one subject of world significance – South Africa, Mozambique, conservation, food, women etc.'
Contrib: commissioned only
Ill: h-t

186 Newswatch
Lyntonia House
7–9 Praed Street,
London W2 1NJ
(01) 402 1319 Tx: 8953471 INTER
1985– Wk Circ: 150,000
Subs: UK £48 Americas $110 elsewhere
£65 Stud: £36, $82.50, £48.75
Ed: Ray Ekpu Book rev
Book rev ed: Kayode Soyinka
*Though concentrating on major political,
economic and social interest stories, this is
a general interest news magazine, report-
ing on Africa, with special interest on
Nigeria, and international affairs as they
affect Africa'*
Contrib: occasional, in any area
L: 1,000w P: NUJ rates + copies re-
quested
Ill: line, h-t, photog, col & b/w
Nigerian Office: 62 Oregun Road,
PMB 21499, Ikeja, Lagos State Tel:
960950, 962887 Tx: 27874 NEWCOM
Fax: 962887

187 PAL Platform. The Pan-
African Liberation Platform
111B Moray Road,
London N4 3LB
(01) 263 5225
1989– 0954–7959 Qtly Circ: 5,000
Subs: £12 inst £8 indiv
Ed: Ifi Amadiume Book rev
*A multi-disciplinary educational and
cultural publication, which focuses on the
African world. It is concerned with analysis, debate and dialogue in the development
of ideas, through the integration of race,
gender and class perspectives. Aims,
through a platform controlled by Africans
to contribute towards the development of
ideas for a progressive transformation and
self-reliant development of the African
world and to confront and challenge isola-
tionist tendencies in the growth of ideas'*
Contrib: viewpoints on development,
current theoretical development in
and outside Africa; current research,
new creative writing from Africa;
women's studies
L: 5,000w Ill: photog b/w NP 1 copy

Edit req: copy of typed ms, d-s, with
brief autobiographical note

188 Review of African Political
Economy
Regency House,
75–77 St. Mary's Road,
Sheffield S2 4AN
(0742) 752671 0305–6244 3Yr
Circ: 1,500
Subs: UK & Africa £12 elsewhere £16
Stud: £8.50
Ed: Doris Burgess (Managing) Book
rev
Book rev ed: Morris Szeftel
*Bridges the gap between academia and
political commitment, promoting scholarly
work but relating it to Africa's on-going
struggles for development and liberation.
Includes briefings, debates, book lists and
documents from movements in Africa'*
Contrib: the super-powers, migrant
population movements, grassroots
activities, education, the military, culture, religion and activities specifically
relating to women
L: articles 8,000w, briefings 3,000–
4,000w NP 2 copies Ill: line, h-t,
photog

189 South Magazine
1st Floor, Rex House,
4–12 Lower Regent Street,
London SW1Y 4PE
(01) 930 8411 Tx: 8814201 TRIMED
Fax: (01) 930 0980
1981– 0260–6976 Mon Circ: 80,000
Subs: UK £16 elsewhere $29 (airmail)
Ed: Raana Gauhar Book rev
Book rev ed: Janice Turner
*Business, politics, science & technology,
arts & leisure – looking at the world from a
Third World perspective'*
Contrib: in areas above
L: 1,000w or less P: varies + 1 copy
Ill: graphics, cartoons, photog b/w &
col

190 Southscan
POB 724, London N16 5RZ
(01) 800 7654 Tx: 933524 GEONET
(Box: GEOZ SOUTHNEWS)

Fax: (01) 800 7654
1986– 0952–7542 Wk Circ: n/a
Subs: £85/$150 inst £30/$50 indiv
Ed: n/a Book rev
'Weekly review of political and economic events concentrating on South Africa but taking in all of Southern Africa and based on correspondents in the field'
No contrib

191 **Southern African Review of Books**
25A Greencroft Gardens, London NW6 3LN

(01) 624 5700
1987– 0952–8040 6Yr Circ: 5,000
Subs: UK £15 inst £7.50 indiv elsewhere £18/$35 inst £10/$20 indiv
Ed: Kenneth Parker Book rev
'Tabloid review containing book reviews – review articles – on Southern Africa'
Contrib: in areas above
L: 2,000w P: £50 + 3 copies Ill: h-t

192 **Third World Quarterly**
13th floor, New Zealand House, 80 Haymarket, London SW1Y 4TS

(01) 930 8411 Tx: 8814207
Fax: (01) 930 0980 (Grp 3)
1978– 0143–6597 Qtly Circ: 4,000
Subs: £20/$30
Ed: Altaf Gauhar Book rev
Book rev ed: Maya Jaggi
'Detailed analysis of global affairs. Regular source of information on contemporary social, economic, and political issues. Coverage of the Asia/Pacific region, Latin America and the Caribbean, Africa and the Middle East, devoting an entire section to literature and including reviews of recent research'
Contrib: contemporary issues and events of importance to the Third World
L: 5,000–6,000w NP 8 copies Ill: author must supply camera-ready artwork
Edit req: d-s

193 **Third World Impact**
Hansib Publishing Ltd, Tower House, 139/149 Fonthill Road, London N4 3HF

(01) 281 1191 Fax: (01) 263 9656
1971– 2Yr Circ: 12,500
Subs: £17.95
Ed: Arif Ali
'Comprehensive work of reference regarding the presence of the visible minorities in all spheres of British life with a Who's Who and reference sections'
Contrib: most of areas above
L: 1,000w P: varies Ill: line, photog

194 **Third World Reports**
'Wild Acre', Plaw Hatch, Sharpthorne, West Sussex, RH19 4JL

(0324) 810875 Fax: (01) 390 5400
1983– 2Wk Subs: £75/$200
Ed: Colin Legum
'Privately published newsletter, averaging two reports a week. Its main interest focuses on Africa, but it regularly analyses developments affecting all Third World countries'
No contrib

195 **Wasafiri**
POB 195, Canterbury, Kent CT2 7XB

(0227) 764000
1984– 0269–0055 2Yr Circ: 500–600
Subs: UK £12 inst £8 indiv elsewhere £16/$35 inst £12/$25 indiv (airmail)
Ed: Susheila Nasta Book rev
Book rev eds: Louis James & Susheila Nasta
'Published by the Association for the Teaching of Caribbean, African Asian and Associated Literatures; critical coverage of new writing; a forum for current debate concerning the teaching of multicultural literature both at school and university level. Focus issues have been on the Caribbean, education and women'
Contrib: literature and education in Africa, the Caribbean, South-East

Asia, Black British writing, interviews with writers
L: 5,000w NP 2 copies Ill: line, photog
Edit req: two copies, MLA style sheet, d-s, typed, stamped addressed envelope

196 **West Africa**
   43–45 Coldharbour Lane,
   Camberwell,
   London SE5 9NR
(01) 737 2946 Tx: 892420
Fax: (01) 253 1629 Attn: West Africa
1917– Wk Circ: 24,000
Subs: UK £52 N. America $95 Africa £55 (airmail) Stud: 25% discount
Ed: Ad'Obe Obe Book rev
'Business and economy, political, social'
Contrib: in areas above
L: 1,000w P: £50 Ill: line, h-t, photog, b/w

United States

197 **Africa News**
   POB 3851, Durham, NC 27702
(919) 286 0747 Tx: 3772229
Fax: (919) 286 2614
EM: 800 345 1301 NEWSNET
1973– 0191–6521 Biwk Circ: 3,200
Subs: USA $48 inst $30 indiv elsewhere $62 inst $44 indiv
Ed: Tami Hultman Book rev
Book rev eds: Sally Banker & Tami Hultman
'Covers African politics, economy, culture and US policy and international issues affecting the continent. Special features include new publications section, bulletin board, exclusive interviews and articles on women, environment, wildlife and development'
Contrib: in areas above
L: n/a P: $10 + 1 copy Ill: 1, photog b/w

198 **Africa Report**
   833 United Nations Plaza,
   New York, NY 10017
(212) 949 5666 Tx: 666565
Fax: (212) 286 9493
1956– 0001–9836 6Yr Circ: 10,000

Subs: USA $24 elsewhere $30
Ed: Margaret A. Novicki Book rev
Book rev ed: Andre Astrow
'Provides in-depth analysis of African economic and political developments; includes 'Update' country profiles, book reviews, culture columns'
Contrib: political, economic, development
L: 1,500–2,000w NP 3 free copies Ill: photog, b/w
Edit req: journalistic not academic style, no fn

199 **Africa Today**
   c/o Graduate School of
   International Studies,
   University of Denver,
   Denver, CO 80208
(303) 871 3678
1954– Qtly Circ: 1,500
Subs: USA $33 inst $35 elsewhere
Stud: $12
Ed: Edward A. Hawley Book rev
'Thematically arranged scholarly articles on political, social or economic developments in or related to Africa. 'Africa Rights Monitor', a survey of human rights conditions on the continent, in each issue'
Contrib: all areas concerning contemporary Africa
L: 3,000–5,000w NP + 5 copies Ill: photog, b/w line
Edit req: style sheet available from ed

200 **African Arts**
   African Studies Center,
   University of California,
   Los Angeles, CA 90024
(213) 825 1218
1967– 0001–9933 Qtly Circ: 4,000
Subs: USA $28 elsewhere $34
Eds: Donald J. Cosentino, Doran H. Ross, John F. Povey; Amy E. Futa (executive) Book rev
Book rev ed: Marla C. Berns
'Covers all the art forms of Africa especially contemporary and traditional art but not excluding dance, film, theatre and popular decorative forms. Book and show reviews relating to the above and features on new

museum acquisitions and items of general interest. The African continent is the focus, rarely pieces on the diaspora if there is a strong African connection'
Contrib: any areas, generally relating to specific field work or research; predominantly academics and specialist scholars
L: 15–20 pp NP 2 copies Ill: line, h-t, photog, b/w & col
Edit req: d-s, glossy b/w and positive slides not negative prints

201 African Economic History
African Studies Center,
Boston University,
270 Bay State Road,
Boston, MA 02215, USA
(617) 353 7306 Tx: 9103501947 BUASC
1972– 0145–2258 Ann Circ: 350
Subs: $7 inst $12 indiv
Eds: Margaret Jean Hay, Allen Isaacman, Paul Lovejoy & Richard Roberts Book rev
Book rev ed: Margaret Jean Hay
'Focuses on recent economic change in Africa as well as the colonial and pre-colonial economic history of the continent'
Contrib: in any area of African economy history, in English and French
L: 30–40pp NP 10 free copies Ill: line
Edit req: two copies, d-s

202 African Farmer Magazine
The Hunger Project,
One Madison Avenue,
New York, NY 10010
(212) 532 4255 Tx: 4972126 THPI
Fax: (212) 532 9785
1988– Qtly Circ: 100,000
Subs: free
Ed: Kristin Helmore
'Dedicated to small-scale farmers of Africa, the intention of the magazine is to support the growing dialogue between the continent's farmers and those in a leadership position within Africa. We are committed to a partnership between those who formulate and implement policy and those whose lives are most directly impacted by those policies, the farmer'
Contrib: infrastructure, export crops, extension workers, farming techniques, articles by African journalists
L: 400w P: varies + copies Ill: photog

203 African Studies Review
c/o African Studies
Association, Credit Union
Building, Emory University,
Atlanta, GA 30322
(404) 329 6410
1957– 3Yr Circ: ASA members only
Subs: free to ASA members
Ed: Carol Thompson, Department of Political Science, VKC 327, University of Southern California, Los Angeles, CA 90089–0044, USA Book rev
Book rev ed: Mark DeLancey, Department of Government and International Studies, University of South Carolina, Columbia, SC 29208, USA
'Includes scholarly articles from an interdisciplinary perspective on African studies plus book reviews. Frequently features special thematic issues. Currently one issue per year includes research overview papers sponsored by Social Science Research Council'
Contrib: interdisciplinary African studies
L: 30–40pp NP 25 offprints Ill: author must supply camera-ready artwork
Edit req: d-s, Chicago Manual style

204 Africana Journal. A Bibliographic Library Journal and Review Annual†
Africana Publishing Co.,
Holmes & Meier Publishers
Inc., 30 Irving Place,
New York, NY 10003
(212) 254 4100
1970– 0095–1080 Ann Subs: $65 inst $35 indiv
Ed: David E. Gardinier

205 **Africana Libraries Newsletter**
Main Library E660,
Indiana University,
Bloomington, IN 47405
(812) 855 1481
1975– 0148–7868 Qtly Circ: 500
Subs: free (donations accepted for
airmail postage)
Ed: Nancy J. Schmidt
*'Newsletter of the Archives Libraries
Committee of the African Studies Associa-
tion USA. Includes minutes of committee
meetings and CAMP (Cooperative
Africana Microform Project) meetings,
short articles about Africana publications
and collections, announcements, new pub-
lications and articles to note'*
Contrib: areas of interest to African
studies librarians
L: 2pp NP 1 copy (to non-subscribers)
Ill: none
Edit req: d-s

206 **ASA News**
c/o African Studies
Association, Credit Union
Building, Emory University,
Atlanta, GA 30322
(404) 329 6410
1967– Qtly Circ: ASA members only
Subs: free to ASA members
Ed: Edna G. Bay
*'Reports current and future events of
interest to members and Africanists,
archives of the Association, bibliographical
and news notes, opinion editorials, and
significant correspondence'*
Contrib: announcements, letters,
notes on seminars and conferences,
short articles of interest to the
Africanist community
L: 5pp NP 1 copy Ill: author must
supply camera-ready artwork
Edit req: d-s

207 **Ba Shiru†**
Department of African
Languages and Literature,
University of Wisconsin,
866 Van Hise Hall,
Madison, WI 53706
(608) 263 3192
1970– 0045–1282 2Yr Subs: $16 inst $6
indiv
Ed: Margaret Brualdi

208 **The Black Scholar. Journal of
Black Studies and Research†**
Black World Foundation,
Box 2869, Oakland, CA 94609
(415) 547 6633
1969– 0006–4246 6Yr Subs: $35 inst $25
indiv
Ed: Robert Chrisman

209 **History in Africa**
David Henige, Memorial
Library, 728 State St.,
Madison, WI 53706
(608) 262 6397
1974– 03615413 Ann Circ: 400–500
Subs: $28
Ed: David Henige
*'Interested in problems of method, includ-
ing historiography, source analysis,
textual criticism, bibliography, and
epistemology. Also in comparative studies
relevant to understanding the African past'*
Contrib: in areas above; book review
essays
L: 30–40pp NP 20–25 offprints Ill: line
drawings, photog, b/w camera-ready
artwork required

210 **The International Journal of
African Historical Studies**
African Studies Center,
Boston University,
270 Bay State Road,
Boston, MA 02215
(617) 353 7306 Tx: 9103501947
1968– 0361–7882 Qtly Circ: 700
Subs: $55 inst $27 indiv
Ed: Norman R. Bennett Book rev
'Covers all aspects of the African past,

including interactions between Africa and the New World. Articles are accepted in English or French, and the publication of original source materials is encouraged'
Contrib: any area of African history
L: 30–40pp NP 10 offprints Ill: line, some h-t
Edit req: two copies, d-s

211 Issue: A Journal of Opinion
c/o African Studies Association, Credit Union Building, Emory University, Atlanta, GA 30322
(404) 329 6410
1970– 2Yr Circ: ASA members
Subs: free to ASA members
Ed: Harvey Glickman, Department of Political Science, Haverford College, Haverford, PA 19041, USA Book rev
'Edited by a member of the Association's Current Issues Committee, presents provocative and timely comment on events in Africa and on developments in African studies'
Contrib: political or policy-oriented questions relating to Africa or to African studies
L: 15–20 pp NP 1 copy Ill: author must supply camera-ready artwork

212 Journal of Black Studies†
Sage Publications Inc., 2111 West Hillcrest Drive, Newbury Park, CA 91320
(805) 499 0721
1970– 0021–9347 Qtly Subs: $72 inst $30 indiv
Ed: Molefi Kete Asante

213 Research in African Literatures
c/o Richard Bjornson, Ohio State University, POB 3509, Columbus, Ohio 43210–0509
1970– 0034–5210 Qtly Circ: 800
Subs: USA $32 inst $20 indiv elsewhere £36 inst $24 indiv
Ed: Richard Bjornson Book rev
'Publishes scholarly articles on all aspects of African oral and written literatures. Also includes bibliographies and institutional research reports'
Contrib: African oral and written literatures
L: 20–30pp NP 2 copies Ill: prints, photog, b/w artwork
Edit req: MLA style sheet

214 Sage: A Scholarly Journal on Black Women
SWEP/SAGE, POB 42741, Atlanta, GA 30311
(404) 681 3643 ext. 360
1984– 0741–8639 2Yr Circ: 2,000
Subs: USA $25 inst $15 indiv elsewhere $31 inst $21 indiv Stud: $10
Eds: Patricia Bell-Scott & Beverly Guy-Sheftall Book rev
Book rev ed: Miriam Willis
'Articles, critical essays, interviews, resource listings, documents, announcements, photographs relating to lives of Black Women (women of African descent) wherever they reside'
Contrib: in areas above
L: 25 pp NP 2 copies Ill: photog
Edit req: d-s, typed

215 Studies in African Linguistics
African Studies Center, University of California, 10244 Bunche Hall, Los Angeles, CA 90024–1310
(213) 825 3686
EM: imn6gs@uclamvs.bitnet
1920– 0039–3533 3Yr Circ: 350
Subs: $20 inst $12 indiv
Ed: Russell G. Schuh
'Descriptive, comparative, or theoretical linguistic articles in which the primary data source is languages native to the African continent'
Contrib: as above
L: 10–300pp NP 25 offprints Ill: line, h-t
Edit req: abstract of 100–200w; style sheet avail from ed

216 **Third World Resources.**
   A Quarterly Review of
   Resources from and about the
   Third World
   464 19th Street,
   Oakland, CA 94162
   (415) 536 1876/835 4692
   1985– 8755–8831 Qtly Circ: 1,500
   Subs: N. America $30 inst $30 (2 yrs)
   indiv elsewhere $42 inst $45 (2 yrs)
   indiv
   Eds: Thomas P. Fenton & Mary
   J. Heffron
   'Notices and descriptive listings of
   organizations and newly released print,
   audiovisual, and other educational re-
   sources on Third World regions and issues.
   Each issue contains a four-page insert with
   a comprehensive listing of resources of one
   particular region or subject'
   Contrib: n/a

217 **Transafrica Forum.**
   A Quarterly Journal of
   Opinion on Africa and the
   Caribbean†
   545 8th Street SE, Suite 200,
   Washington, DC 20003
   1982– 0730–8876 Qtly Subs: $35 inst
   $20 indiv
   Ed: Niikwao Akuetteh

218 **Ufahamu**
   African Studies Center,
   University of California,
   10244 Bunche Hall,
   Los Angeles, CA 90024
   (213) 825 6518
   1970– 0041–5715 3Yr Circ: 250
   Subs: $22 inst $16 indiv
   Ed: Ali Jimale Ahmed Book rev
   Book rev ed: Steven C. Rubert
   'Contributions from anyone interested in
   Africa and related subject areas. Contribu-
   tions may include political-economic analy-
   sis, commentaries, review articles, film
   and book reviews, and poetry'
   Contrib: as above
   L: 20–33pp NP 1 copy Ill: n/a
   Edit req: style sheet avail from ed

USSR

219 **Narody Azii i Afriki: Istoriya,**
   Ekonomika, Kultura†
   Izdatel'stvo Nauka,
   Profsoyuznaya 90, 117864
   GSP-7 Moscow V485
   1955 0120–6995 6Yr Subs: 50.70 Rub.
   Ed: A.A. Kutzenkov

AFRICA

Journals in Africa lead a precarious
existence, and many lag behind
their publication schedules by as
much as three or four years, others
are currently dormant; and for
new journals the mortality rate is
high, with many not publishing
beyond 'volume I, number 1'.
   This is a small selection of
African-published journals with a
record of fairly regular publication
in the past. It includes African
studies scholarly periodicals, as
well as a number of general
interest/current affairs and
literary/cultural magazines.
   For comprehensive coverage of
African serials, including
numerous specialist journals, see
The African Book World & Press: A
Directory/Répertoire du Livre et de la
Presse en Afrique (see **1**)

Cote d'Ivoire

220 **Revue de Littérature et**
   d'Esthétique Negro-
   Africaines†
   Les Nouvelles Editions
   Africaines
   01 BP 3525, Abidjan 01
   32 12 51, 32 16 22
   1983– Qtly Subs: CFA3,000
   Ed: N'Guessan Djangone Bi

Gabon

221 Muntu
BP 770 CICIBA, Libreville
76 12 71 Tx: 5689 GO
1984– 0768–9403 2Yr Circ: 2,000
Subs: Africa CFA8,000 elsewhere
CFA10,000
Ed: Th. Obenga Book rev
'Articles and features on Bantu civiliza-tions'
Contrib: linguistics, history, anthropology
P; 20 copies Ill: line, h-t, photog, b/w & col

Kenya

222 Transafrican Journal of History†
POB 10622, Nairobi
331135
1971– 0251–0391 Ann Subs: $28
Ed: Gideon S. Were

223 The Weekly Review†
POB 42271, Nairobi
26878, 23547
1975– Wk Subs: $160
Ed: Hilary Ng'weno

Malawi

224 Journal of Humanities
Faculty of Humanities,
Chancellor College,
University of Malawi,
POB 280, Zomba
522222 Tx: 44742 CHANCOL
1987– Ann Circ: n/a
Subs: Malawi K10 elsewhere $10 inst
Malawi K5 elsewhere $8 indiv (airmail)
Ed: Didier N. Kaphagawani Book rev
Book rev eds: Didier N. Kaphagawani
& Brighton Wedi-Kamanga
'Due to the diverse specialities in the Humanities in general, the contents and scope vary from issue to issue'
Contrib: classics, fine and performing arts, literature and orature, linguistics, theology and philosophy

L: 20pp NP 2 copies Ill: line, figures, photog
Edit req: two copies, d-s, refs & fn at end of articles

Nigeria

225 The African Guardian†
Guardian Magazines Ltd,
PMB 1217, Oshodi, Lagos,
Lagos State
524080, 542098 Tx: 23283 GUARDN
1985– 0794–2788 Wk Subs: £57/$120
Ed: Nduka Irabor

African Concord, *see* **160**

Newswatch, *see* **186**

226 Okike. An African Journal of New Writing
POB 53, Nsukka, Anambra State
1971– 0331–0566 3Yr Circ: 6,000
Subs: £12, $24, N30
Ed: Onuora Ossie Enekme Book rev
'Primarily a creative writing journal, featuring poetry, short fiction and short drama. Critical essays that give insight into the theory and practice of creative writing are valued'
Contrib: in fiction, poetry, drama, criticism, etc.
L: 15 quarto pp NP 1 copy Ill: photog, sketches, b/w
Edit req: d-s in duplicate, brief autobiographical note should accompany submissions

Senegal

227 Africa Development/Afrique et Développement
CODESRIA, BP 3304, Dakar
23 02 111 Tx: 61339 CODES
1976– 0850–3907 Qtly Circ: n/a
Subs: $35
Ed: Zenebeworke Tadesse Book rev
'Bi-lingual journal devoted to in-depth, comprehensive and accessible analysis of the complex social, economic and political issues of contemporary Africa'

Contrib: original contributions which should not be under consideration by another publication at the same time; any field in the social sciences focused on Africa, or a comparative analysis of Third World issues L: 30pp NP 20 offprints + 2 copies Ill: line
Edit req: d-s, with notes, fn, tables etc. on separate pages; CRC for maps, charts; abstract of 150–200w; author's name, academic status, current affiliation to be provided on separate covering page

228 **Ethiopiques.**
 Revue Trimestrielle de
 Culture Négro-Africaine
 Fondation Léopold Sédar Senghor, Rue El-Hadji Seydou Nourou Tall X René Ndiaye, BP 2035, Dakar
21 53 55
1975– 0850–2005 Qtly Circ: 3,000
Subs: CFA8,000/F160
Ed: Moustapha Tambadou Book rev
'Revue culturelle négro-africaine; lettres et arts dans leurs rapports avec le monde noire; revue d'études francophones'
Contrib: in above areas
L: 2,000–3,000w Ill: photog

South Africa

229 **African Studies**
 University of the Witwatersrand, PO WITS, Johannesburg 2050
(011) 716 2023 Tx: 4–27125
Fax: (011) 403 1926
1921– 0002–0184 6Yr Circ: 700
Subs: R35 inst R15 indiv
Ed: W.D. Hammond-Tooke Book rev
Book rev ed: N. Pines
'Scholarly articles on topics relevant to African anthropology, linguistics, sociology and related studies'
Contrib: in areas above
L: 10,000w NP 45 copies Ill: b/w

230 **Staffrider**
 Ravan Press, POB 31134, Braamfontein 2017
(403) 3925/6/7/8/9 Fax: 3392439
1978– 0258–7211 Qtly Circ: 6,000
Subs: $21
Ed: Andries Walter Oliphant Book rev
'Southern African poetry, fiction, photography, art, essays on culture, cultural reports, drama, interviews. Focus on culture and resistance'
Contrib: in areas above
L: 5,000–8,000w P: commissioned varies, non-commissioned 5 copies Ill: photog, graphics, b/w
Edit req: d-s, typed

Tanzania

231 **The African Review**
 Department of Political Science and Public Administration, University of Dar es Salaam, POB 35042, Dar es Salaam
(051) 48252/49192 ext. 2237
Tx: 41561 UNIVIP/41327 UNISCIE
1971– 0856–0056 2Yr Circ: 1,000
Subs: £14.50/$28
Ed: I.K. Bavu Book rev
Book rev ed: Jeannette Hartmann, Department of Sociology, University of Dar es Salaam, POB 35043, Dar es Salaam
'A journal of African politics, development and international affairs'
Contrib: African politics, African development, international affairs, social sciences and policy making
L: 25–30 pp NP 3 copies
Edit req: d-s, A4, fn at end

232 **Taamuli. A Political Science Forum**
 Department of Political Science and Public Administration, University of Dar es Salaam, POB 35042, Dar es Salaam
(051) 48252/49192 ext.2237
Tx: 41561 UNIVIP/41327 UNISCIE

1970– 0049–2817 2Yr Circ: 1,000
Subs: $15
Ed: Ruth Meena Book rev
Book rev ed: Jeannette Hartmann,
Department of Sociology, University
of Dar es Salaam, POB 35043, Dar es
Salaam
'The journal deals with articles on world politics in general, particularly in East Africa. Secondly, social sciences and political issues'
Contrib: political issues/social sciences
L:20–25pp NP 3 copies
Edit req: d-s, A4, fn at end

Zambia

233 African Social Research†
Publications Office,
University of Zambia,
POB 32379, Lusaka
213221
1944– 2Yr Subs: £8/$18
Ed: Chisepo J.J. Mphaisha

Zimbabwe

234 Journal of Social Development in Africa
P Bag 66022, Kopje, Harare
707414/5/6 Tx: 2390 GENSEC
1986– 1012–1080 2Yr Circ: 350
Subs: $30 inst $15 indiv
Ed: Brigid Willmore Book rev
'Social development issues, particular concern with Africa and the Third World, cross-disciplinarian, concerned with developing appropriate intervention strategies, and with issues of poor and marginalised'
Contrib: in areas above
L: equivalent of 12–14 10pt A5pp NP 1 copy, 10 offprints Ill: line-drawing diagrams
Edit req: two copies, single-sided A4 paper, d-s, author's details on separate sheet, a summary abstract of less than 100w, no fn

235 Moto Magazine†
Mambo Press,
94 Fife Avenue, POB UA320,
Harare
21854
1982– Mon Subs: Z$8.50

IV. MAJOR LIBRARIES AND DOCUMENTATION CENTRES

This section aims to identify the major libraries worldwide (outside Africa) with substantial Africana collections, *either* maintained as separate Africa-related collections, *or* with significant holdings of Africana material overall, although not separately maintained. Libraries in Africa are not included as they are extensively covered in another Hans Zell publication *The African Book World & Press: A Directory/ Répertoire du Livre et de la Presse en Afrique* (*see* **1**) which provides fully annotated listings of all the major university, college, public and national libraries in Africa, in addition to including details of several hundred special libraries.

Information for this chapter was collected by means of a questionnaire mailing. Approximately 80% of those approached responded; but a small number unfortunately could not apparently find the time to complete and return our questionnaires. Information on libraries which did not respond, but which are known to have significant collections relating to Africa, is nonetheless included. These entries are marked by a † dagger symbol, and information provided is inevitably incomplete; for these entries we have supplemented information by using short extracts from two existing resources published by Hans Zell Publishers: (1) for the UK and Europe, *The SCOLMA Directory of Libraries and Special Collections on Africa in the United Kingdom and Western Europe* (*see* **83**), attributed as 'SCOLMA Directory' with information current as at 1982; (2) for the United States, the *African Studies Information Resources Directory* (*see* **16**) compiled and edited by Jean E. Meeh Gosebrink, attributed as 'ASIRD', which contains information current as at approximately 1983/84. Indeed, much fuller descriptions of many libraries' special collections or holdings, or collection strength, etc. can be found in these two sources.

When questionnaires were duly completed and returned, the following information is given: full name and address, telephone, telex, fax numbers (and electronic mail address for some); the name of the person in charge of the African studies collection (where applicable); hours of opening; conditions of access; loan and reference/referral services or facilities; size of the African studies collection (number of books and current serials taken); on-line data base services provided and, if applicable, whether on-line catalogue is accessible to outside users; details of publications and find-aids issued; and a brief description of the collection, including any special features, or descriptions of major holdings of Africa-related manuscript and archival materials, or special audio-visual collections and collections of non-print media.

Note: university and public libraries are alphabetically arranged under names of towns, within each country.

Abbreviations used:

Acc	– Access [to the library collections]
AL/contact	– Africana or Collection development librarian (and/or other contact) in charge of African studies collections, or of collection in general
b	– books [number of books in collection]
Coll	– Collection [size of]
cs	– current serials [number of current serials taken]
fac	– facilities
H	– Hours of opening
Loan/ref fac	– Loan and reference/referral services and facilities provided
On-line cat	– On-line catalogue [indicates accessability of on-line catalogue to outside users, and access through what system]
On-line dbs	– On-line database services [details of systems, e.g. JANET, etc.]
Photocop fac	– Photocopying facilities [most libraries provide this, but it is not usually specifically stated]
Publs	– Publications and finding-aids issued/available
Spec feat	– Special features of the collection/s [i.e. collection strength; special archival and manuscript holdings or collections; collections of non-print media, etc.]

Australia

236 La Trobe University†
Borchardt Library, Bundoora,
Victoria 3083

(03) 3083

Note: the Borchardt Library of La Trobe University reportedly contains one of the most extensive monograph and research collections on Africa in Australia, particularly extensive in the fields of history, politics, economics, anthropology and education. No further information available, questionnaire not returned.

237 University of Sydney
Library, University of
Sydney, NSW 2006

(02) 692 2222 Tx: 20056 Fax: (02) 692 4593

AL/contact: Ian Duncan (Social Sciences Librarian)

H: Term – Mon-Thurs 08.00–22.00 (Fri to 20.00), Sat 09.00-17.00, Sun 13.00–17.00

Acc: open to the general public, but only members of the Univ. of Sydney and other university graduates may borrow

Loan/ref fac: multi-disciplinary ref service

Coll: ca.2,500b, ca.40cs

Spec feat: no specific African studies collection, material is shelved according to Dewey subject classification. Collection, while still small, is growing in response to increased academic interest. Holdings mainly in history, politics, government with some anthropology, economics, religion, African languages and literature (the last with a strong emphasis on new African writing).

238 University of Western Australia, Reid Library
Nedlands, WA 6009

(09) 380 2349 Tx: 92992

AL/contact: Penelope Hetherington

(Sen. Lecturer, African History,
History Dept)
H: Term – 08.30–22.00
Vacation – 08.30–18.00
Acc: open access
Loan/ref fac: for all members of library;
reference desk
Coll: ca.8–10,000b, ca.50–100cs
On-line dbs: ABN, URICA, DIALOG
etc,
On-line cat: URICA, shared with W.
Australia College of Advanced
Education (WACAE), and (probably)
with Murdoch Univ pending
amalgamation. Access to users of
WACAE
Publs: Dept of History library lists
Spec feat: one of the largest Africana
collections in Australia, mainly on
Southern African history, includes
microfilm copies of: Carter/Karis Col-
lection, A.B.Xuma Personal Papers,
Lutuli, A., Papers, ICU Yase Natal
Records, S.A. Dept. Justice Files selec-
ted by R. Edgar; I. Wallerstein collec-
tion; newspapers such as *Umsebenzi*,
Guardian, *Windhoek Advertiser*, *Drum*,
Umvikele Thebe, *Liberation*, *Fighting
Talk*; S.A. Parliamentary Papers and
Debates; also *Ethiopian New Times &
Ethiopian Observer* (full set); South
African Institute of Race Relations,
archives (45 reels, on African socio-
economic conditions); S.A. Native
Representative Council, Verbatim
Report of Proceedings 1937–1946 (4
reels); S.A. Miscellaneous Manu-
scripts 1911–1933 (1 reel); Papers of C.
Kadalie from Univ of Wits (fiche).
Some papers on Zaire, Zambia.
Monographs strong on South Africa,
particularly South African labour history, also Zimbabwe, Ethiopia, Kenya.
Also holds audio-visual material (8
videos, and numerous films – mainly
on South Africa); and growing reference collection.

Austria

239 **Universität Wien**
     Fachbibliothek für
     Afrikanistik, Doblhoffgasse
     5/9, A-1010 Wien
(1) 42 22 73 AL/contact: Erich René
Sommerauer H: Mon-Fri 10.00–12.00/
14.00–16.00 Acc: open to students and
faculty and the general public Loan/ref
fac: on request
Coll: 10,000b, 100cs
Spec feat: strong on African languages
and linguistics, history, politics, literature; maps; 170 microf, 330 cass; some
old rare books 16–19th century.

Belgium

240 **Bibliothèque Africaine**
     Place Royale 7,
     B-1000 Bruxelles
(02) 511 58 70 Tx: 21376, 23979
Fax: (02) 5143067
AL/contact: W. van Hemelrijck
H: Mon-Fri 09.00–12.00/13.30–16.45
Acc: n/a
Coll: 400,000b, 610cs
On-line dbs: BELINDIS (Belgian
Information and Dissemination
Service), available to outside users,
user manual available on request
Publs: monthly list of acquisitions
Spec feat: in addition to very complete
and exceptional collections of official
and unofficial documents on the
Congo and the former Belgian Congo,
the library's collection contains rare
books on Africa bought mainly by
King Leopold II for his personal
library.

241 **Koninklijk Museum voor
     Midden-Afrika/Musée Royal
     de l'Afrique Centrale**
     Steenweg op Leuven 13,
     B-1980 Tervuren
(02) 767 54 01 Tx: 27048 BUGEO
AL/contact: the director of the
Museum
H: 08.30–12.00/13.00–17.30

Acc: open access/no restrictions
Loan/ref fac: no loan fac; reading on the premises, photocop fac
Coll: 90,000b, 3,000cs
Publs: catalogue available on request
Spec feat: African varia in geology (samples, old maps, crystals); zoology (large collection of insects, fishes, amphibians, reptiles, birds, mammals, library on African zoology); cultural anthropology (large collection of artefacts, ethnic music records etc.); history (archival material on Belgian presence overseas before 1960, Stanley Archives).

242 State University of Ghent
Faculty of Arts and
Philosophy, Africa
Department, Rozier 44,
B-9000 Ghent

(091) 25 76 11 ext. 4129
AL/contact: Jacques Boucneau
H: Mon & Fri 09.00–12.00, Tue 13.30–16.00, Wed 09.00–12.00/13.30-17.00
Acc: free access
Loan/ref fac: loan fac
Coll: 20,000b, 50cs
Spec feat: African languages and literature, African history, traditional and modern African societies, anthropology

Canada

243 Carleton University†
University Library, Ottawa,
K1S5B6

(613) 564 3816
Coll: ca.12,000b, 250cs, 20,000 government documents
Note: no further information available, questionnaire not returned.

244 McGill University
McLennan Library, Reference
Dept, 3459 McTavish St,
Montreal PQ, H3A 1Y1

(514) 398 4735 Fax: (514) 398 7184
EM: PEB.QMM
AL/contact: n/a

H: Term – 08.30–23.00
Vacation – 09.00–18.00
Acc: open to serious scholars and university students
Loan/ref fac: full service to institutional clientele, reduced service to external patrons
Coll: medium size, not separately defined
On-line dbs: DIALOG, MINISIS/IDRC, Infoglobe, InfoMart, UTLAS
On-line cat: via UTLAS, off-site access to institutional patrons only
Spec feat: no special collections or holdings, concentration traditionally on anglophone West Africa and reference sources for the continent.

Denmark

245 Centre for Development Research
Library, Ny Kongensgade 9,
DK-1472 Copenhagen K

(33) 14 57 00
AL/contact: Ole Norgaard
H: Mon-Fri 09.00–16.00
Acc: n/a
Loan/ref fac: full loan and ref facilities
Coll: Africana not separately maintained
Publs: series of 'C-papers', mainly Library Accessions list, catalogues, and occasional bibliographies
Spec feat: n/a

246 Det Kongelige Bibliotek†
Christians Brygge 8,
DK-1219 Copenhagen

(1) 15 01 11 Tx: 15009
H: Mon-Sat 09.00–19.00
Acc: open to the public for reference purposes, and certain materials are available for home loan.
Coll: ca.16,000b, ca.170cs
Spec: feat: the whole of the African continent is covered and publications acquired in the humanities, the social sciences and theology.
[SCOLMA Directory]

247 Mellemfolkeligt Samvirke/ Danish Association for International Development

Borgergade 10–14,
DK-1300 Copenhagen
(2) 33 32 62 44 Tx: 15928 MS
AL/contact: Helle Leth-Møller
H: Mon-Wed, Fri 13.00–16.00, Thur 13.00–18.00
Acc: open access/no restrictions
Loan/ref fac: books 1 months, no lending for serials
Coll: 5,000b, 60cs
Publs: *MS Biblioteksnyt* (MS Library News); bibliographies, booklists
Spec feat: Third World affairs in general; special collection 'MS Indvandrerdokumentation' (MS Documentation Centre for Migration Questions in Denmark).

Finland

248 Helsinki University Library, Unioninkatu 36, POB 312, 00171 Helsinki

(358) 0 1911 Tx: 121538 HYK
AL/contact: Leena Parssinen
H: Mon-Fri 09.00–21.00 (in the summer to 18.00), Sat 09.00–18.00 (closed in July), Sun 12.00–18.00
Acc: open access for research purposes
Loan ref fac: African material available only in reading rooms, no interlibrary loans, copies of microfiches and of articles in serials are provided, photocop fac
Coll: Africana not separately maintained, ca.64cs
On-line dbs: DIALOG, Telesystems Questel
Spec feat: collection of printed Ovambo Literature (Northern Namibia), ca.400 vols to 1972; 19th century publications in the Ondonga languages, printed in Finland by the Finnish Missionary Society; several dialects in 20th century material; most printing since 1901 in Ovamboland, literature printed after 1972 is included in the National Library Collection of

the Library. The collection consists of religious books, school books and practical guides; part was microfiched in 1985 for the Namibian National Library, copies are in the Library. The Emil Liljeblad Collection is an ms. collection consisting of folklore of the Ovambo tribes of Northern Namibia.

France

249 Bibliothèque de Documentation Internationale Contemporaine

6 Allée de l'Université,
92001 Nanterre Cedex
47 21 40 22
AL/contact: none specific
H: Mon 12.30–18.00, Tue-Fri 10.00–18.00, Sat 10.00–18.00 (from 12.00 consultation only), reduced hours in August
Acc: public admission with card authorization, restricted access to documents
Loan/ref fac: materials not to be taken off the premises
Coll: ca.50,000b, ca.100cs
Spec feat: covers francophone, anglophone (particularly South Africa), hispanophone and lusophone; politics, economics and social sciences from an international viewpoint; colonies and decolonisation in the 20th century; the two world wars in Africa. Collection of the Bibliothèque Africaine et Malgache, papers of importance on the colonial period and the early years of independence; collection of German documents published before 1945 on the German colonies. Documents are primarily those emanating from Europe, the US and USSR; few from Africa, apart from official journals. Photograph collection on the Sudan. Material on the Algerian war.

250 **Bibliothèque Nationale**
58 rue Richelieu, 75084 Paris
Cedex 02

(1) 47 03 81 26 Tx: 211368 BIB NAT P
AL/contact: Paulette Lorderau
(acquisitions, bibliography)
H: Dept. des Imprimés Mon-Fri 09.00–
20.00 (closed in August)
Other departments 09.00–17/18.00
Acc: primarily to scholars and
students; others can apply for access
authorization
Loan/ref fac: for ref on premises only;
some photocop fac also photographs,
microfiches, microfilms
Coll: ca.100,000b, collection not
separately maintained
On-line dbs: GEAC-BNOPALE, CD-
ROM in preparation
On-line cat: available in reference
room only
Publs: *Littératures Africaines à la Bibliothèque Nationale, 1973–1983; Périodiques
Malgaches de la Bibliothèque Nationale;
Les Auteurs Afro-Americains, 1965–1982;
Les Publications en Série Editées au
Sénégal, 1856–1982*, and various
catalogues
Spec feat: the legal depository of the
colonial period to 1960 has a rich
collection on francophone countries; a
collection of works in the Malagasy
language; works in other African languages e.g. Fulani, Hausa, Kiswahili;
the library of SEGOU, the collection of
the Société de Géographie – voyages,
expeditions and explorations in Africa.
Current acquisitions are expanding
literature holdings, in French, English,
Portuguese and the African
languages.

251 **Centre d'Etude d'Afrique
Noire**
Institut d'Etudes Politiques,
Bibliothèque BP 101,
Domaine Universitaire,
33405 Talence Cedex
56 84 42 52
AL/contact: Françoise Meynard

H: Mon-Fri 09.00–12.00/14.00–17.00
Acc: restricted to students, researchers
and scholars
Loan/ref fac: loans on or off the
premises, inter-library loans,
photocop fac
Coll: ca.13,000b, ca.565cs
On-line dbs: document searching on
the information system of the Institute
On-line cat: via telephone 56 84 42 99
Publs: *Année Africaine* (Ann), *Travaux
et Documents de CEAN* (Qtly), *Multi-
graphiés du CEAN* (Ann), *Bibliographies
du CEAN* (2Yr), *Politique Africaine*
(Qtly, see **128**)
Spec feat: specialises on Africa south
of the Sahara; politics, economics,
international relations, society, contemporary African religions and history; the press; collection of African
newspapers and official journals of
francophone countries.

252 **Centre d'Etude et de
Documentation sur l'Afrique
et l'Outre-mer†**
La Documentation Française,
29–31 Quai Voltaire,
75340 Paris

(1) 40 15 7161 Tx: 204826 DOCFRAN
AL/contact: Agnès Lavagna
H: Mon-Fri 10.00–18.00
Coll: ca.65,000b, ca.550cs
Publs: *Afrique Contemporaine* (*see* **118**)
Spec feat: material is collected on all
regions of Africa; collection of 70,000
photographs; complete collection of
bulletins and gazettes issued by the
former French colonies in Africa; card
index to the legislation of francophone
African countries.
[SCOLMA Directory]

253 **Centre d'Etudes Africaines†**
Bibliothèque, 54 boulevard
Raspail, 75006 Paris

(1) 45 44 39 79
AL/contact: Olenka Darkowska-
Nidzgorska
H: Mon-Fri 10.00–12.30, 14.00–17.00
Coll: ca. 12,000b ca.400cs
Publs: *Cahiers d'Etudes Africaines; Biblio-*

graphie des Travaux en Langue Française sur l'Afrique au Sud du Sahara: Sciences Sociales et Humaines (Ann, *see* **103**); *Répertoire des Thèses Africanistes Françaises*
Spec feat: collections strong in anthropology, history, sociology, folklore, geography, economic and social development, and politics.
[SCOLMA Directory]

254 **Centre d'Etudes et de Recherches sur les Pays d'Afrique Noire Anglophone**
Bibliothèque, Université Paul-Valery, BP 5043, 34032 Montpellier
67 72 18 66
AL/contact: J.D. Sévry
H: Wed-Thurs 08.00–10.00
Acc: n/a
Coll: 500b, 40cs
Spec feat: mainly books on African literature and civilization; main areas covered are Nigeria, Kenya and Southern Africa. Also books on African history, and a collection of MAs written by students.

255 **Centre de Recherches Africaines**
Bibliothèque, 9 rue Malher, 75004 Paris
(1) 42 78 33 22
AL/contact: Liliane Daronian
H: Tue-Wed 14.00–18.00
Acc: researchers and students at masters and doctorate level
Coll: 12,000b, 450cs
Publs: *Cahiers du C.R.A.*
Spec feat: the library is linked with the Universities of Paris Panthéon-Sorbonne, Sorbonne-Nouvelle and René Descartes, and is multidisciplinary; covers the whole of the African continent; two distinct types of holdings – the first multidisciplinary on history, ethnology, sociology, linguistics, and geography, and the second primarily historical.

256 **Centre de Recherches et d'Etudes sur les Sociétés Méditerranéennes†**
Bibliothèque, Maison de la Méditerranée, 3 avenue Pasteur, 13100 Aix-en-Provence
23 03 86
AL/contact: Marie-Jose Bianquis
H: Tues-Fri 09.00–12.30, 13.30–17.00
Coll: ca.22,000b, ca.220cs
Spec feat: acquires material in the social sciences and humanities on Morocco, Algeria, Tunisia, Libya and the Sahara; especially extensive holdings in the fields of history, geography, economics, law, political science, arts, literature, sociology, anthropology and demography.
[SCOLMA Directory]

257 **Centre des Hautes Etudes sur l'Afrique et l'Asie Moderne†**
Bibliothèque, 13 rue du Four, 75006 Paris
(1) 43 26 96 90
AL/contact: Anne Malecot
H: Tues, Wed, Fri 09.00–12.30, 14.00–17.30
Coll: ca.10,000b ca.300cs
Publs: *Mémoires du CHEAM*
Spec feat: special emphasis on francophone West Africa, Ethiopia, Djibouti and Somalia; subject areas in which the Centre specialises are ethnology, politics, economics, and religion, especially Islam.
[SCOLMA Directory]

258 **Musée de l'Homme†**
Bibliothèque, Place du Trocadéro, 75116 Paris
(1) 47 04 53 94
AL/contact: Françoise Weil
H: Mon, Tues, Sat 13.00–17.00, Wed, Fri 10.00–17.00
Acc: open to the public for reference purposes
Spec feat: collects anthropological material on a worldwide basis; African coverage particularly strong for

francophone countries. The Library also houses the collection of the Société des Africanistes.
[SCOLMA Directory]

Germany (Federal Republic)

259 **Arnold-Bergstraesser Institut für Kulturwissenschaftliche Forschung†**
Bibliothek, Windaustrasse 16, D-7800 Freiburg
(0761) 85091 Tx: 0772527
AL/contact: Stephanie Gerum
Coll: ca.50,000b, 400cs
Spec feat: particularly strong collections in the fields of education and administration; extensive collections of 'grey literature' and of African development plans.
[SCOLMA Directory]

260 **Bayerische Staatsbibliothek**
Ludwigstrasse 26, 8000 München 22
Postal address: Postfach 340150, D-8000 München 34
(089) 21981 Tx: 897248 BSB Fax: (089) 2809284
AL/contact: none specific
H: Mon-Fri 09.00–20.00 (Sat to 17.00)
Acc: closed access
Loan/ref fac: full loan and ref fac
Coll: ca.40,000b
On-line dbs: ZBSB via HOST DBJ Berlin
Spec feat: African collections not separately maintained; strong on African history, African-European relations, travel and exploration; substantial holdings of early (16th-19th century) literature.

261 **Freie Universität Berlin†**
Bibliothek des Fachbereichs Politische Wissenschaft (Otto Suhr Institut), Ihnestrasse 21, D-1000 Berlin 33
(030) 8382307
AL/contact: Hans-Werbin Köhler

H: Reading room – Mon-Fri 09.00–20.00
Lending – Mon-Wed 09.00–16.30, Thur-Fri 09.00–15.00
Acc: free access for graduate and postgraduate study and research at all academic levels
Coll: ca.30,000b, ca.270cs
Spec feat: collects material on the whole continent of Africa, with particular reference to colonial history, economics, development, sociology, and international affairs; a great deal of material is obtained in microform.
[SCOLMA Directory]

262 **Staats-und Universitätsbibliothek Bremen**
Postfach 33 01 60, D-2800 Bremen 33
(0421) 2182601/2602 Tx: 245811
AL/contact: none specific
H: Mon-Fri 09.00–16.30
Acc: n/a
Loan/ref fac: full loan and ref fac
Coll: 3,000–4,000b,
On-line dbs: yes, to external hosts worldwide
On-line cat: no; off-line cat on microfiches
Spec feat: 2,000 books entitled 'Black Writings', from the collection of Janheinz Jahn.

263 **Deutsches Institut für Entwicklungspolitik†**
Bibliothek, Frauenhoferstrasse 33–36, D-1000 Berlin 10
(030) 3418071
Coll: ca.40,000b, ca.300cs
Spec feat: major collections on development policy and planning, international trade, monetary policy, debt problems, regional planning, and industrialization.

264 **Stadt-und
     Universitätsbibliothek**
     Bockenheimer Landstrasse
     134–138, Frankfurt am Main
     D-6000
     (069) 7907 246/247 Tx: 414024 STUB
     AL/contacts: Irmtraud Wolcke-Renk,
     Anne Kasper
     H: Mon-Fri 08.30–16.30
     Acc: open access
     Loan/ref fac: reading-room for ref
     books, interlibrary loan
     Coll: ca.100,000b
     Publs: *Neuerwerbungen Afrika; Fachkata-
     log Afrika* (11 vols), *Current Contents
     Africa* (*see* **105**)
     Spec feat: has the responsibility,
     assigned by the Deutsche Forschungs-
     gemeinschaft in 1964, for maintaining
     a special collection for Africa south of
     the Sahara; its aim is to provide a
     collection of all relevant literature as
     completely as possible, with materials
     being made available for lending pur-
     poses. All subjects except law, econo-
     mics and natural science.

265 **Niedersächsische Staats-und
     Universitätsbibliothek
     Göttingen**
     Postfach 2932,
     Prinzenstrasse 1,
     D-3400 Göttingen
     (0551) 395231
     AL/contacts: Drs. Klaer, Kiefert &
     Schwartz
     H: Mon-Fri 09.00–20.00, Sat 09.30–
     14.00
     Acc: n/a
     Loan/ref fac: full loan and ref fac
     Coll: ca.20,000b, ca.100cs
     On-line dbs: several
     On-line cat: yes, admission necessary
     Publs: on-line databases
     Spec feat: no specific Africa-related
     collections; comprehensive collections
     in all subjects, rare book collections

266 **Ifo-Institut für
     Wirtschaftsforschung†**
     Abteilung
     Entwicklungsländer,
     Bibliothek,
     Poschingerstrasse 5,
     Postfach 86 04 60,
     D-8000 München 86
     (089) 92241 Tx: 522269
     H: Mon-Fri 09.00–16.00 (Fri to 14.00)
     Acc: for reference purposes only
     Coll: ca.15,000b, ca.100cs
     Spec feat: collects material on the
     whole of Africa in the fields of econo-
     mics, development, and the social
     sciences.
     [SCOLMA Directory]

267 **Institut für Afrika-Kunde**
     Bibliothek, Neuer
     Jungfernstieg 21,
     D-2000 Hamburg 36
     (040) 3562526/3562519
     AL/contact: Gertrud Wellmann
     (Librarian)
     H: 09.00–12.30/13.30–17.00
     Acc: open to the public
     Loan/ref fac: ref only
     Coll: 34,000b, 462cs
     On-line dbs: on request
     Publs: *Neuerwerbungen der Bibliothek*
     (Accessions Lists)
     Spec feat: supported by the Deutsche
     Forschungsgemeinschaft, the library
     collects 'Report Literature' from sub-
     Saharan Africa; collection of 25 daily or
     weekly newspapers from Africa, cut-
     tings from which are published fort-
     nightly in *Aktueller Informationsdienst
     Afrika* (*see* **135**); collection of govern-
     ment gazettes from 25 African coun-
     tries which are regularly indexed in
     Afrika Spectrum (*see* **133**). All acquisi-
     tions are indexed, annotated and fed
     into the database of the 'Übersee
     Dokumentation' (ÜD), Hamburg. The
     ÜD, through its Africa unit, publishes
     the quarterly *Select Bibliography of
     Recent Literature* and special biblio-
     graphies.

268 **Institüt für Afrikanistik**
Bibliothek, D-5000 Köln 41
(0221)4703885
AL/contact: Eithe Carlin
H: 09.00–13.00
Acc: n/a
Loan/ref fac: on the premises only
Coll: 15,500b, 100cs
On-line cat: yes
Spec feat: oriented towards African linguistics, particularly East Africa (Nilotic, Cuslitic language), Mande, Bantu, Creole, Khoisan.

269 **Institut für Auslandsbeziehungen**
Bibliothek und Dokumentation,
Charlottenplatz 17,
D-7000 Stuttgart 1
(0711) 2225147 Tx: 0723772
Fax: (0711) 224346
AL/contact: n/a
H: Mon, Tue, Fri 10.00–16.00 (Wed & Fri to 21.00, Sat to 12.00)
Acc: n/a
Loan/ref fac: national and international inter-library loan
Coll: 10,500b, 250cs
Publs: Biannual report, *Zeitschrift für Kulturaustausch; Materialien zum Internationalen Kulturaustausch*
Spec feat: foreign countries, cultural relations with foreign countries, cultural theory, ethnic stereotypes, research on exchanges, developing areas and problems of technical assistance and educational training, history of emigration and migration, ethnic minorities.

270 **Institut für Ethnologie und Afrika-Studien**
Bibliothek, Johannes Gutenberg-Universität,
D-6500 Mainz
(06131) 392798
AL/contact: Margarete Krotky (Librarian), Ulla Schild (African Literature)
H: by appointment

Acc: by appointment only
Loan/ref fac: no loans
Coll: 25,000b, 218cs
Spec feat: in addition to the general Africana collection, the institute houses the 'Janheinz Jahn-Bibliothek', a collection of African literature, including literature in European and African languages, children's literature, popular literature and comics, literary journals – 10,000 titles and 173 journals.

271 **Institut für Weltwirtschaft**
Bibliothek, Postfach 4309/
Düsternbrooker Weg 120,
D-2300 Kiel 1
(0431) 884383/498 Tx: 292479 WELTW
Fax: (431) 85853
AL/contact: J. Köhli
H: Mon-Thur 08.00–18.00 (Fri to 16.30)
Acc: n/a
Loan/ref fac: lending library, inter-library loan, catalog and on-line searching service based on written enquiries, selective dissemination of information, photocop services
Coll: ca.73,000b, ca.3,000cs
On-line dbs: ECONIS (Economics Information System), 8000 records referring to Africa
On-line cat: in preparation
Publs: *Bibliographie der Wirtschaftswissenschaften* (Bibliography of Economics, and a catalogue of journals relating to Africa)
Spec feat: strong on economic statistics, commercial and trade literature, official publications, and publications from public authorities, banks, trade unions, and political parties.

272 **Staatsbibliothek Preussischer Kulturbesitz**
Orientabteilung, Potsdamer Strasse 33, Postfach 1407,
D-1000 Berlin 30
(030) 266 2489 Tx: 183160 STAAB
AL/contact: Kurt Sollfrank
H: Staatsbibliothek Mon-Fri 09.00–21.00 (Sat to 17.00) Orientabteilung Mon-Fri 09.00–17.00 (Sat to 13.00)

Acc: open access
Loan/ref fac: full loan and ref fac; inter-library loan; photocop and microfilm fac
Coll: 15,000b, 80cs
Spec feat: no specific Africa-related collections; collection development mainly in the areas of literature, languages and linguistics, history, politics, sociology and geography.

273 Universitätsbibliothek Tübingen
Orientabteilung, Postfach 2620, Wilhelmstrasse 32, D-7400 Tübingen
(07071) 292577/293430/292852
AL/contact: Walter Werkmeister
H: Mon-Fri 08.30–21.00 (during vacation to 19.00) Sat 08.30–16.00 (during vacation to 12.00)
Acc: open public access
Loan/ref fac: national and international interlibrary loan; loan facilities only for members of the University (students and staff) and for residents of Tübingen; special reading room for Oriental Studies (card subject catalogue)
Coll: ca.60,000b, ca.300cs
On-line dbs: in preparation
On-line cat: in preparation
Publs: *Neuerwerbungen Vorderer Orient* (Accessions List Near and Middle East)
Spec feat: African studies collection is part of the larger collection of books from and about the Near and Middle East; thus the relevant section contains literature pertaining to the countries of North and Northeast Africa – Morocco, Algeria, Tunisia, Libya, Egypt, Northern Sudan, Ethiopia, Horn of Africa.

274 Völkerkundliche Bibliothek
c/o Frobenius-Institut, Liebigstrasse 41, D-6000 Frankfurt am Main
(069) 721012
AL/contact: Siegfried Seyfarth
H: Mon-Thur 14.00–17.30 Fri 09.00–12.00

Acc: open to research workers, scholars and the interested public
Loan/ref fac: some restrictions on lending
Coll: ca.20,000v, ca.100cs
Spec feat: mainly ethnology and non-European prehistory worldwide, including Africa; also holds 55 non-current journals relating to Africa.

India

275 Centre of East African Studies
Library, University of Bombay, Bombay 400 098
(22) 6120841–5, 6127021, 6127062–5
AL/contact: The Librarian, Jawaharlal Nehru Library, University of Bombay, Bombay 98
H: 09.00–19.00
Acc: open access
Loan/ref fac: n/a
Coll: 10,000b, ca.50cs
On-line dbs: special bibliographies; Current Awareness Service (new journals received) to faculty members & research scholars working in the University
Spec feat: primary and secondary source material on Africa; covers all Africa but especially Eastern and Western; primarily social sciences, holdings are substantial in history, political science, economics, sociology, geography and literature etc; reference works; 78 US doctoral dissertations in African studies; some primary source materials available on microfiche and microfilm.

Italy

276 Biblioteca Nazionale†
Palazzo Reale, 80132 Napoli
(081) 40 28 42, 41 62 12
AL/contact: Sergio Riccio
H: Mon-Fri 09.00–20.00 (Sat to 14.00)
Spec feat: no special African collections, but substantial amount of African material spread over the collection as a whole; special holdings of

travel books from the 17th to the 19th centuries; large collection of photographs.
[SCOLMA Directory]

277 Curia Generalizia dei Missionari d'Africa (Padri Bianchi)
Biblioteca, Via Surelia 269, 00165 Roma
(06) 632314/632318 Tx: 626258 PABIA
AL/contact: H. Maurier
H: 09.00–12.00/15.00–18.00
Acc: open access
Loan/ref fac: ref only, no loans, photocop fac
Coll: ca.8,000b, 34cs
Spec feat: African collection started in 1868; intended primarily as a resource for those for whom the organization is responsible, and its students; holdings concentrate on subjects of interest to missionaries e.g. history, ethnography, archaeology, sociology, Islam, African religions, African philosophy and theology, development, and African literature; most holdings in English and French, but some in German, Italian and Portuguese.

278 Istituto Italo-Africano
Biblioteca, Via Ulisse Aldrovandi 16, 00197 Roma
(06) 3216712/3221258
AL/contact: Carla Ghezzi
H: Mon-Fri 08.00–14.00 (Thur also 15.00–17.00)
Acc: by means of identification
Loan/ref fac: ref only, no loans; photocop fac
Coll: 65,000b, 200cs
Publs: *La Letteratura Africana Nella Biblioteca dell'Istituto Italo-Africano*
Spec feat: the library inherited the fund of the library of the Ministero per l'Africa Italiana, which ceased in 1953; unique material on Ethiopia, Libya and Somalia.

279 Istituto per le Relazioni tra l'Italia e i Paesi dell'Africa, America Latina e Medio Oriente
Biblioteca, Viale Tritone 62/9, 00187 Roma
(06) 6792321/6792311 Tx: 621594
H: Mon-Fri 09.00–13.00 and Thur-Fri 14.30–16.30
Acc: open access
Loan/ref fac: n/a
Coll: 3,000b
Publs: *Politica Internazionale*
Spec feat: n/a

280 Istituto Universitario Orientale
Biblioteca del Dipartimento di Studi e Ricerche su Africa e Paesi Arabi, Piazza San Giovanni Maggiore 30, 80134 Napoli
(81) 207462/285206
AL/contact: Enrico Catemario
H: Sun-Fri 09.00–14.30
Acc: to university students and other persons with guaranty
Loan/ref fac: loan to university students, no special referral service
Coll: ca.20,000b, ca.300cs
Spec feat: collections on African history, linguistics, Egyptology, Ethopian studies; rare books on Berber studies; increasing collection on Arab studies, including the Maghreb and the Near East.

Japan

281 Institute for the Study of Languages and Cultures of Asia and Africa
Tokyo University of Foreign Studies, Library, 4–51–21 Nishigahara, Kitakt, Tokyo 114
(03) 917 6111 Fax: (03) 910 0613 EM: Gengobunka Tokyo
AL/contact: n/a
H: Mon-Fri 09.30–17.00 (Sat to 12.00)
Acc: researchers of the Institute,

teaching staff of Tokyo University of
Foreign Studies; for others,
applications in writing to the Director
Loan/ref fac: loans limited, reference
open to the public
Coll: 3–4,000b, ca.105cs
Spec feat: n/a

282 **Institute of Development
     Economies**
     Library, 42 Ichigaya-
     Hommura-cho, Shinjuku-ku,
     Tokyo 162
(03) 353 4231 Tx: 32473 AJIKEN
Fax: (03) 226 8475
AL/contact: Yasuko Tanno, Susumu
Imura
H: 09.45–16.45
Acc: open access
Loan/ref fac: loan service to members
of Institute
Coll: 20,000b (on Africa) 90cs
On-line dbs: NIKKEI-Telecom & Atlas
Publs: *Ajia Keizai Shiryo Geppo*
(Library Bulletin, partly in English)
Spec feat: focus on social sciences of
modern Africa; economics, develop-
ment, sociology, politics, agriculture,
industry. The Institute maintains a
separate collection of statistics on Africa
(1,762 titles, 12,300 vols, including
monographs, annuals, serials.)

Netherlands

283 **Afrika-Studiecentrum**
     The Library, Wassenaarseweg
     52, POB 9555, 2300 RB Leiden
(071) 273354
AL/contact: J. van der Meulen
H: Mon-Fri 09.00–13.00, 14.00–17.00
Acc: open access
Loan/ref fac: loan fac restricted to
books; reading room, microfiche/film
reader, photocop fac
Coll: 32,000b, 600cs
Publs: *Documentatieblad* (Abstracts
journal of the African Studies Centre
Leiden); acquisitions lists
Spec feat: collections emphasizing
cultural anthropology, history, law,
literature, politics, religion, and social
and economic development.

284 **University of Amsterdam**
     Library, P.C. Hoofthuis
     Section Dutch/Afrikaans,
     Spuistraat 134,
     1012 VB Amsterdam
(020) 5254532
AL/contact: E. van Hulsteijn
H: Mon, Wed, Fri 09.00–17.00 (Tue &
Thur to 22.00)
Acc: in principle for students and
faculty of the Faculty of Arts of the
University, but others are admitted
Loan/ref fac: loans for students and
faculty, others need special
permission
Coll: ca.515b
On-line dbs: central system of the
University Library
On-line cat: at local terminals (PC
Hoofthuis and University Library);
outside access on application
Spec feat: although officially restricted
to Afrikaans, the collection is intended
not to be racially biased; thus a limited
number of books are held on South
African history and current social and
political affairs, together with holdings
in current and past languages of South
Africa.

285 **Koninklijke Bibliotheek**
     Prins Willem Alexanderhof 5,
     Postbus 90407, 2509 LK
     s'Gravenhage
(070) 140911 Tx: 34402
Fax: (070) 140450
AL/contact: none specific
H: Mon-Fri 09.00–17.00 (Sat to 12.00),
and 15 Sept-15 June 19.30-22.00
Acc: open to all with a borrower's card
Loan/ref fac: loans with a borrower's
card: in person, by letter and by
telephone; photocop fac
Coll: ca.13,000b, ca.133cs
On-line dbs: on-line public access
catalogue
Publs: union catalogue of periodicals,
bibliographies, literature lists, *Koninklijke Bibliotheek: Gids voor Gebruikers*
(user guide)
Spec feat: mainly humanities and the
social sciences; depository library;

covers all countries and regions, strongest representation being South Africa, Egypt, Zaire, Algeria, Morocco and Ghana; 40% of collection is history, 30% geography, and 30% other disciplines e.g. literature, linguistics and sociology; 275 titles published pre-1800, and 3,000 between 1800–1945.

286 **Royal Tropical Institute**
Central Library,
Mauritskade 63,
1092 AD Amsterdam
(020) 5688245/462 Tx: 15080 KIT
Fax: (020) 6684579
AL/contact: A. van der Wal
H: Mon-Fri 10.00–16.45
Acc: closed access/by arrangement
Loan/ref fac: loan and inter-library loan fac; photocop fac, information and bibliographical services by phone and by post
Coll: ca.35,000b, ca.1,600cs
Publs: accessions list
Spec feat: general collection, but emphasis is given to socio-economic affairs, agriculture, anthropology, geography, and history; UN collection; depository of World Bank.

New Zealand

287 **National Library of New Zealand**
POB 1467, Wellington
7743 000 Tx: 30076 NATLIB
Fax: 743 035
AL/contacts: C. Keyse (Head of Ref Services), S. Dell (Keeper of Collections, Alexander Turnbull Library)
H: Mon-Fri 09.00–17.00 (Sat to 13.00)
Acc: open access
Loan/ref fac: full reference & referral service; no loans to public exept non-ref publications on interlibrary loan; archives consulted only in the reading rooms of the Alexander Turnbull Library
Coll: 5,000b, 100cs
On-line dbs: NZBN – multidisciplinary, records from NZ

libraries and some overseas countries
On-line cat: yes, both on-line and microfiche
Spec feat: African studies collection not separately maintained. The Alexander Turnbull Library, a division of the National Library, holds manuscript material relating to the South African War (1899–1902): diaries, letters and papers by members of the New Zealand Contingents in SA; records of the South African War Veterans Assoc 1937–1980 (also separate collections of the Waikato, Northland, Levin and Wellington branches); records of the Auckland Peace Association 1899–1906; and *O'er Veldt and Kopje, an Account of the Operations of the New Zealand Contingents in the Boer War* by James Arthur Shand, unpublished, ca.1931.

Norway

288 **Universitetsbiblioteket i Bergen**
Mohlenprisbakken 1,
N 5007 Bergen
(05) 212500 Tx: 42690 UBB
Fax: (05) 320666
AL/contact: Tom Johnsen
H: Mon-Fri 08.00–15.45
Acc: open access
Loan/ref fac: available
Coll: ca.7,000b, ca.50cs
On-line dbs: BIBSYS – Norwegian University Library on-line catalog, DIALOG and other international and national dbs
Spec feat: an important centre for Sudanese, Middle Eastern, Islamic and development studies; material held on other African countries also; national and UN depository library.

289 **Chr. Michelsen Institute**
Department of Social Science and Development Library,
Fantoftvegen 38, 5036 Fantoft
(05) 284410 Tx: 40006 CMI
Fax: (05) 285613

AL/contact: Kirsti Hagen Andersen
H: Mon-Fri 08.00–15.00
Acc: open
Loan/ref fac: loan for books, not
periodicals; photocop fac for articles
Coll: 10,000b, 450cs
On-line dbs: catalogue is
computerized; on-line access to
international databases, service only
Publs: *DERAP Publications, DERAP
Working Papers, Human Rights Pro-
gramme Publications & Working Papers*,
Norwegian Development Research
Catalogue (every 3rd year)
Spec feat: the collection of Africa
material is best on publications on
Norwegian main cooperating coun-
tries: Eastern and Southern Africa;
95% of publications are in English;
social sciences (economics, political
science, anthropology).

Portugal

290 **Arquivo Historico
Ultramarino†**
Calcada da Boa-Hora 30,
1300 Lisboa
(01) 63 80 19 Tx: 630498
AL/contact: Isau Santos
Spec feat: extensive holdings of documentary material relating to the
former Portuguese colonies.
Note: no further information available,
questionnaire not returned.

Spain

291 **Biblioteca Nacional**
Sección de Africa y Mundo
Arabe, PO de Recoletos 20,
28001 Madrid
(01) 2756800 ext.122
AL/contact: Asunción Fernandez de
Aviles Delgado
H: 09.00–21.00
Acc: researchers
Loan/ref fac: reading on the premises;
specialist bibliographic ref services
available; interlibrary loan
Coll: 41,500b, 2,000cs

Publs: *Nuevos Ingresos* (Qtly); *Guía de
Bibliotecas y Centros de Documentación
especializados*, a guide to the Sección,
inventory of photographs
Spec feat: 634 volumes of miscellaneous papers and transcriptions of
archival documents; personal archives
of Garcia Figueras, Guillermo
Ritwagen and Juan Fontan Lobé. Collections of the writings and correspondence of El Raisuni. Extensive
collection of photographs on Africa.

Sweden

292 **Scandinavian Institute of
African Studies/Nordiska
Afrikainstitutet**
POB 1703, 751 47 Uppsala
(018) 155480 Tx: 8195077
Fax: (018) 695629
AL/contact: Birgitta Fahlander
H: Mon & Thurs 10.00–19.00 (Tue,
Wed & Fri to 15.00)
Acc: open access
Loan/ref fac: loans for books but not
newspapers, journals or government
documents; ref lists; photocop fac
Coll: 34,000b, 600cs
On-line dbs: LIBRIS, DIALOG,
QUESTEL, IBISCUS; own database
containing acquisitions since 1967
Publs: *Africana i Nordiska Afrikainsti-
tutets Bibliotek* (Ann, new acquisitions),
Att Studera Afrika (Studying Africa)
Spec feat: collection of current govern-
ment documents and publications
from the African countries, and docu-
ments from the UN Economic Commission for Africa. The only library in
Nordic countries specializing in contemporary post-1945 Africa.

Switzerland

293 **Institut Universitaire
d'Etudes du Développement**
24 Rue Rothschild,
CH-1211 Genève 21
(022) 731 25 21 Tx: 22810 IUED
AL/contact: René Barbey

H: 09.00–18.00
Acc: open access
Loan/ref fac: n/a
Coll: 35,000b, 300cs
Spec feat: n/a

294 International Labour Office
Central Library and
Documentation Branch,
CH-1211 Genève 22

(022) 799 86 82 Tx: 415647 BIT
Fax: (022) 7988685
AL/contact: Kate Wild
H: 09.00–17.00
Acc: open access
Loan/ref fac: documents, except those
in ref collection, are available on loan
to ILO officials, ILO Branch Offices
and on interlibrary loan to other users;
microfiches of texts of journal articles;
photocop fac
Coll: 13,705b, 440cs
On-line dbs: LABORDOC
On-line cat: via ESA-IRS, HRIN and
ORBIT; Pergamon ORBIT Infoline
Publs: *International Labour Documentation* (Mon, current awareness and
abstracting bulletin), *ILO Thesaurus:
Labour, Employment and Training Ter-
minology* (trilingual: English, French,
Spanish)
Spec feat: materials are in a multitude
of languages, with English represent-
ing ca.60%, French 20% and Spanish
10%; main subjects are industrial relations, labour law, employment and
working conditions, social security,
vocational training, labour related
aspects of economics, social development, rural development, techno-
logical change, etc.

295 Stadtbibliothek Winterthur
Museumstrasse 52, Postfach,
CH-8401 Winterthur

(052) 84 51 45
AL/contacts: Peter Sulzer
(Eggenzahnstrasse 1, CH-8400
Winterthur; former dir of library);
Verena Amberg
H: Mon-Fri 08.00–16.30
Acc: open access

Loan/ref fac: home loans – one month,
reading & study room
Coll: ca.5,000b, 128cs
Publs: *Africana-Sammlung und Africana-
Katalog in der Stadtbibliothek Winterthur*
(2 vols, 1977, 1982)
Spec feat: African languages and literatures: linguistics, preference is given
to dictionaries and grammar books;
various forms of oral tradition – tales,
myths, praise-songs, proverbs, either
edited in books or recorded on discs;
new African literature in African and
European languages; literary history,
criticism and sociology.

296 United Nations Library at Geneva
Palais des Nations,
CH-1211 Genève 10

(022) 734 6011 ext 4181
AL/contact: General Reference
Librarian, UN Documents Librarian
Acc: Masters, PhD level, with a
referral letter from university
professor, company or public library
Loan/ref fac: yes, on production of
referral letter
Coll: 1,000,000b, 12,000cs (total library
collection)
On-line dbs: UN Bibliographic
Information System
Publs: *UNDOC: Current Index, Monthly
Bibliography* Part I books, government
documents, serials Part II periodical
articles
Spec feat: Africana not separately
maintained; specialized material in the
fields of economics, finance, law and
politics; collection includes a very
complete collection of general reference works; definitive collection of
works on international, constitutional
and administrative law; international
collection on economics, finance,
social questions, atomic energy;
archives of the League of Nations and
complete collection of UN documents;
maps and geographical works; 300,000
government publications.

297 **Zentralbibliothek Zürich**
Zähringerplatz 6, Postfach,
CH-8025 Zürich

(01) 261 72 72
AL/contacts: Hans-Peter Hohener,
R. Mathys
H: n/a
Acc: open access
Loan/ref fac: n/a
Coll: ca.20,000b
Spec feat: central library of the University of Zürich; Africana not separately maintained; on average some 500 new titles on Africa acquired every year.

United Kingdom

298 **University of Birmingham**
Main Library, PO Box 363,
Birmingham B15 2TT

(021) 414 5816 Tx: 338938
Fax: (021) 471 4691 EM: 79:LEI 1024
AL/contact: Tom French
H: Term – Mon-Fri 09.00–21.00 (Sat to 12.30)
Vacation – Mon-Fri 09.00–19.00
(except Aug, when open Mon-Fri 09.00–17.00 only)
Acc: visitors welcome; prior written application preferred, especially if access to special collections is sought
Loan/ref fac: loan fac only to registered members of the University and to registered external borrowers, but are usually available on inter-library loan; ref fac available to all visitors
Coll: ca.25,000, ca.200cs
On-line dbs: Dialog, ORBIT, ESA-IRS, DATASTAR, BLAISE, STN
On-line cat: access through JANET
Publs: *Library Guide, Select Basic Sources for West African Studies* (1986)
Spec feat: systematic acquisition of Africana since 1963; extensive holdings of material from anglophone West Africa; also from Francophone West African countries (which constitute the Library's specialization under the SCOLMA scheme). The collection includes some 500 17th, 18th and 19th century monographs; theses from the Centre of West African Studies; a collection of pamphlets, mainly from Nigeria, including market literature; the papers of the Church Missionary Society, the Cadbury Papers, and those of the British Cotton Growing Association.

299 **British Library**
Humanities and Social
Sciences, Great Russell Street,
London WC1B 3DG

(01) 323 7676 Tx: 21462
AL/contact: Carole Holden
H: Mon, Fri & Sat 09.00–17.00 (Official publications & Social Sciences 09.30–17.00); Tues-Thurs 09.00–21.00 (Official publications & Social Sciences 09.30–19.00)
Acc: by readers ticket
Loan/ref fac: collections available for reading on the premises; some books and serials available for inter-library loan through the Document Supply Centre (*see* **300**)
Coll: no separate collection, material dispersed throughout library
On-line dbs: BLAISE
On-line cat: access to subscribers and through JANET
Publs: readers guides on the use of the catalogue etc., *African Studies. Papers presented at a colloquium at the British Library, 7–9 January 1985* (*see* **91**)
Spec feat: extensive African holdings including material of interest in the map, music, philatelic, manuscript and newspaper collections; a substantial collection of books, serials and newspapers were received by colonial copyright deposit between the later 19th and mid-20th centuries from South Africa in particular, but also from Mauritius, Sierra Leone, East Africa, Gambia and Ghana; holdings of official publications from African countries are also strong, especially for those countries formerly under British control.

300 **British Library Document Supply Centre**
Boston Spa, Wetherby,
West Yorkshire LS23 7BQ
(0937) 843434 Tx: 557381
Fax: (0937) 546333
Loan/ref fac: document supply service available to registered customers
Coll: ca.5,000b, ca.500cs
Spec feat: mainly academic monographs and journals in English; emphasis on material from South Africa.

301 **British Library of Political and Economic Science**
10 Portugal Street,
London WC2A 2HD
(01) 405 7686 Tx: 24655 BLPES
AL/contact: n/a
H: Mon-Fri 09.30–21.20 (July-Sept to 17.00)
Sat 10.00–17.00 (closed July-Sept and Christmas vac)
Acc: by arrangement (by scholars and research workers)
Loan/ref fac: individual loans to members of London School of Economics only; national back-up library in inter-library loans scheme; reference and referral; photocop fac
Coll: several thousand books, ca.300cs
On-line dbs: the Library subscribes to a wide range of databases in the fields of the social sciences
On-line cat: access through JANET
Publs: *Guide to the Library, A London Bibliography of the Social Sciences*
Spec feat: extensive collections of government documents, especially from Anglophone Africa. Statistical publications (except those on education) are collected as fully as possible and particular attention is paid to census reports, statistical year books and trade returns. Annual reports of relevant ministries are acquired whenever possible, and the library attempts to obtain all five-year plans and associated planning documents.

302 **University of Cambridge**
African Studies Centre
Library, Free School Lane,
Cambridge CB2 3RQ
(0223) 33 4398 Tx: 81240 CAMSPL
Fax: (0223) 33 4748 EM: ASC11 @ UK.AC.CAM.PHX
AL/contact: L. de Decker (Ms)
H: Mon-Fri 09.00–17.30
Acc: by arrangement (by scholars and research workers)
Loan/ref fac: n/a
Coll: ca.20,000b, ca.100cs
Spec feat: supplements the holdings of other Cambridge libraries, but is particularly concerned with political, social, economic, and developmental literature. Meyers Fortes Ashanti Social Survey Collection.

303 **Commonwealth Secretariat Library**
10 Carlton House Terrace,
London SW1Y 5AH
(01) 839 3411 ext. 5013 Tx: 27678
Fax: (01) 930 0827
AL/contact: Eileen Hurtagh
H: Mon-Thurs 09.15–17.30 Fri 09.15–17.15
Acc: by appointment, with permission from the Librarian
Loan/ref fac: for reference only
Coll: substantial
Publs: extensive, on various aspects of Commonwealth production (by Commonwealth Secretariat); also periodicals – *International Development Policies, Commonwealth Law Bulletin, Commonwealth Currents*, etc.
Spec feat: over 4,000 serials currently received including official statistical publications, development plans and publications from international organizations; emphasis is on current Commonwealth development; subjects include trade, agriculture, economics, statistics, industry, politics, education, women and development, and youth and health.

304 **University of Durham†**
University Library,
Palace Green,
Durham DH1 3RN
(0385) 61262/3, 64971 ext. 669 or 722
(Oriental section)
Tx: 537351
AL/contact: Agnes M. McAulay
(Librarian), Lesley E. Forbes (Keeper
of Oriental Books)
H: Term – Mon-Fri 08.45–17.30 (Sat
09.00–12.30)
Vacation – Mon-Fri 09.00–13.00,
14.00–17.00 (Sat to 12.30)
Spec feat: collections on medieval and
modern North Africa and on Islamic
Africa; the civilizations of ancient and
Christian Egypt and Ethiopia are
covered extensively. The Sudan
Archive, a collection of the papers of
the former officials, soldiers, missionaries, businessmen, and individuals
who served or lived in the Sudan
during the Anglo-Egyptian Condo-
minium period (1899–1956) was begun
in 1957.
[SCOLMA Directory]

305 **Edinburgh University
Library**
George Square,
Edinburgh EH8 9LJ
(031) 667 1011 ext. 6602
Tx: 727442 UNIVED
Fax: (031) 667 7938 EM: JANET address
is LIBRARY @ UK.AC. EDINBURGH
AL/contact: Brenda E. Moon
(University Librarian)
H: Term – Mon-Fri 09.00–22.00 (Fri to
17.00, Sat to 12.30)
Vacation – Mon-Fri 09.00–17.00; hours
vary in different sections on different
sites
Acc: non-members of the University
are asked to write in advance to the
University Librarian
Loan/ref fac: ref fac normally free of
charge; other services including
borrowing available on subscriptions
or fee
Coll: n/a

On-line dbs: access to all usual
services via the Reference Service for a
fee
On-line cat: yes
Publs: *A Miscellany of Africana* (exhibition catalogue)
Spec feat: African materials are integrated with the general and special
collections of the 400-year old, large
and decentralized library system, and
their size and extent cannot be quanti-
fied. The Library acquired material
published in Malawi and Zambia as
part of the SCOLMA Area Specialization Scheme. The Centre of African
Studies Library is held in the Main
Library. New College Library is rich in
material on Christian missions in
Africa and on non-Christian religion
as is the Centre for the Study of
Christianity in the non-Western
world. The Centre of Tropical Veterinary Medicine Library has good collections on veterinary and allied topics in
Africa.

306 **Foreign and Commonwealth
Office Library**
Cornwall House,
Stamford Street,
London SE1 9NS
(01) 217 2007/2008 Fax: (01) 928 2917
AL/contact: Margaret Cousins
H: Mon-Fri 09.30–17.30
Acc: open to the public for reference
purposes
Loan/ref fac: loans to other libraries
only; photocop fac
Coll: n/a
Spec feat: extensive collection, mainly
on Anglophone Africa, especially on
pre-independence period; early works
on travel and exploration; treaty col-
lections; comprehensive and indexed
collection of legislation of Common-
wealth countries in Africa.

307 **Institute of Commonwealth Studies Library**
27–28 Russell Square,
London WC1B 5DS
(01) 580 5876
AL/contact: Patricia Larby
H: Term – Mon-Wed 10.00–19.00 (Thurs & Fri to 18.00) Vacation – Mon-Fri 10.00–17.30
Acc: University staff, post-graduate students; individuals undertaking advanced level research on the Commonwealth
Loan/ref fac: ref only
Coll: total number of all items 30,000
Publs: *Accessions List* (Qtly), *Theses in Progress in Commonwealth Studies* (Ann), *The Southern African Materials Project, 1973–1976.*
Spec feat: covers the Commonwealth countries of Africa with particular emphasis on official materials, research publications and bibliographies. Materials from Sierra Leone and Gambia are collected under the SCOLMA Area Specialization Scheme. Special collections include political ephemera issued by political parties, trade unions and pressure groups; a set of Foreign Office confidential prints to the year 1904 and a microfilm set of Colonial Office confidential prints to 1916. Among the microfilm holdings are the Archival Records of the Trade Union Council of South Africa; The Carter-Karis Collection of South African Political Materials; the manuscripts collection includes the papers of Sir Keith Hancock on the Buganda constitutional crisis of 1954–55.

308 **Institute of Development Studies Library**
University of Sussex, Falmer, Brighton BN1 9RE
(0273) 616261 Tx: 877997 IDS BTN
AL/contact: Maureen Mahoney
H: Mon-Fri 09.00–17.30
Acc: n/a
Loan/ref fac: ref and inquiry services

operate from 10.00–18.15; loans for inter-library users via inter-library loan
Coll: 200,000b, 6,000cs (size of whole collection, including African studies)
On-line dbs: searching through major commercial hosts
On-line cat: to be provided shortly, probably via dial-up facilities
Spec feat: concentrates on African publications, of relevance to economic and social development, from both official and non-official sources within African countries. Material concerning African countries issued within the developed world is collected as far as is possible. Few items are in indigenous languages, the concentration being on European language publications. Specific areas of subject interest include amongst others, health, education, communication, industrial development, debt and adjustment, population studies, development theory, women and political development. IDS is a UN depository library.

309 **Institute of Education Library**
University of London,
11–13 Ridgmount Street,
London WC1E 7AH
(01) 637 0846
AL/contact: Comparative Education Librarian
H: Term – Mon-Thurs 09.30–20.00 (Fri to 19.00, Sat to 12.30)
Vacation – hours are shorter
Acc: open to the general public, on production of proof of identity
Loan/ref fac: loans only to members of the Library; inter-library loans; otherwise ref only
Coll: number of books not known, 22cs
On-line dbs: DIALOG-hosted databases, particularly in education and psychology
On-line cat: the computerized issue system (covering nearly all recent additions) can be used as a catalogue, and access through JANET
Publs: *Education Libraries Bulletin,*

Accessions List, Catalogue of the Comparative Education Library, 6 vols, (1971 + supplement, 1974)
Spec feat: extensive collection of offical reports and statistics on education

310 International Development Centre Library†
Queen Elizabeth House,
University of Oxford,
21 St. Giles, Oxford OX1 3LA
(0865) 273600/273590
Tx: 83147 attn. QEH
AL/contact: Sheila Allcock
H: Term – Mon-Fri 09.00–13.00, 14.00–19.00 (Sat to 12.30)
Vacation – Mon-Fri 09.00–13.00, 14.00–17.00
Acc: open to the public, with the majority of books available for loan; some material restricted
Publs: *Accessions List*
Spec feat: books, pamphlets, newspapers, periodicals and official publications relating to current economic and political developments in the whole of Africa. Special collection of African and Caribbean literature. Files of newspaper clippings taken from the main English dailies and some other newspapers. The library also includes the collections (strong on agricultural statistics, land economics and population with particular reference to food supply) of the former Institute of Agricultural Economics, University of Oxford (see note below).
[SCOLMA Directory]
Note: formerly the Institute of Commonwealth Studies, which ceased to exist in July 1986, when it was merged, with the Institute of Agricultural Economics, into the International Development Centre.

311 University of Leeds†
The Brotherton Library,
Leeds LS2 9JT
(0532) 31751
AL/contact: D. Cox (Librarian and Keeper of the Brotherton Collection)

H: Term – Mon-Fri 09.00–22.00 (Sat to 13.00)
Vacation – Mon-Fri 09.00–21.00 (to 17.00 long vacation, Sat to 13.00, 12.30 long vacation)
Spec feat: general collections on Africa in the fields of literature, history, geography, sociology, politics, economics, law and education, including official documents. The Library acquires publications from the Zaire Republic, Rwanda, Burundi and Zimbabwe under the SCOLMA Area Specialization Scheme.
[SCOLMA Directory]

312 University of Manchester†
John Rylands University Library, Oxford Road, Manchester M13 9PP
(061) 273 3333 Tx: 668932
AL/contact: Hector Blackhurst
H: Term – Mon-Fri 09.00–21.30 (Sat to 13.00)
Vacation – Mon-Fri 09.30–17.30 (Sat to 13.00)
Publs: *Africa Bibliography* (*see* **97**)
Spec feat: comprehensive general collection of African material covering all subject areas, but with particular emphasis on North Africa and Ethiopia, African anthropology and Arabic/Near Eastern studies. Two important special collections: the library of the International African Institute, especially strong in ethnography, sociology and linguistics; and the Development Documentation Centre, which holds current material from developing countries in the form of government documents, periodicals, and newspapers.
[SCOLMA Directory]

313 Overseas Surveys Directorate
Technical Information & Support Services Ordnance Survey, Romsey Road, Southampton SO9 4DH
(0703) 792236 Tx: 477843
Fax: (0703) 792404
AL/contact: R.T. Porter

H: Mon-Fri 09.00–16.30
Acc: bona fide researchers,
developers, consultants
Loan/ref fac: ref only, but published
maps on sale
Coll: ca.4,000b, ca.60cs, ca.40,000
maps, ca.500,000 air photographs,
ca.5,000 files
Publs: *Data & Information Sheet*, list of
OSD mapping
Spec feat: maps, air photographs, survey data; and documents on international boundaries, on land legislation, and on Survey legislation; mainly
for the developing Commonwealth
countries plus Liberia, Ethiopia,
Sudan. Maps include all published
DOS/OSD mapping plus many sheets
produced by national survey organizations of the countries concerned; air
photographs are vertical, black &
white, scales usallly 1:10,000–1:70,000,
used for map making, not for sale
without country's permission; Survey
data is mainly manuscript trigono-
metrical observations, descriptions,
coordinates, not copyable without
country's permission.

314 **Overseas Development Natural Resources Institute**
Central Avenue,
Chatham Maritime, Chatham,
Kent ME4 4TB
(0634) 880088 Fax: (0634) 880066/880077
AL/contact: John Wright
H: Mon-Fri 10.00–17.00
Acc: by appointment
Loan/ref fac: reference, enquiry, loans
through inter-library loan, limited
photocop fac
Coll: 250,000b, 2,500cs – size of whole
collection, including African studies
On-line dbs: in-house computer
system – CAIRS on a Microvax II;
TRAIS (Tropical Agriculture
Information Service), for ODA/ODNRI
staff only, searching of specialised
external dbs e.g. Agris, Agricola,
CABI,
Publs: *Accessions Bulletin* (Mon)
Spec feat: specialises in the literature

of tropical agriculture in the context of
aid development and is recognised as
a major world resource in this field.
ODNRI is a scientific unit of the
Foreign & Commonwealth Office
Overseas Development Administration, and is an amalgamation of the
former Tropical Products Institute, the
Centre for Overseas Pest Research and
the Land Resources Development
Centre.

315 **Rhodes House Library**
South Parks Road,
Oxford OX1 3RG
(0865) 270909 Tx: 83656
Fax: (0865) 277182
AL/contact: A.S. Bell (Librarian)
H: Term – Mon-Fri 09.00–19.00 (Sat to
13.00
Vacation – Mon-Fri 09.00–17.00 (Sat to
13.00)
Acc: open to all members of the
University of Oxford and to those
holding a Bodleian Library reader's
ticket
Loan/ref fac: reference only; books are
lent to other libraries for use in those
libraries
Coll: ca.125,000, ca.220cs
Publs: *Manuscript Collections* (excluding Africana), *Manuscript Collections of
Africana*, *Manuscript Collections of
Africana: supplement*, *Manuscript Collections* (Africana and non-Africana)
Spec feat: specializes in the social,
political and economic history of the
Commonwealth, the United States
and sub-Saharan Africa. As a department of the Bodleian Library, it
receives British copyright publications;
foreign books and periodicals are pur-
chased. Commonwealth government
publications are available in long runs.
The Library is strong in manuscript
material relating to British colonial
administration. It holds the papers of
Cecil Rhodes, of Arthur Creech Jones,
of the Fabian Colonial Bureau and of
the Africa Bureau, and it has collected
the papers of many former colonial
officials.

316 **Royal Commonwealth
   Society Library**
   Commonwealth House,
   18 Northumberland Avenue,
   London WC2N 5BJ
(01) 930 6733 Fax: (01) 930 9705
AL/contact: Miss T.A. Barringer
H: Mon-Fri 10.00–17.30
Acc: access to collections by members
and accredited students
Loan/ref fac: loans to members;
photocop fac; copies of photographs
by arrangement
Coll: ca.15,000b, 73cs
Publs: *Subject Catalogue of the Royal
Empire Society*, vol. 1, (1930, repr. 1967)
*Subject Catalogue of the Library of the
Royal Commonwealth Solciety*, vols. 3–4
(1971); *Biography Catalogue* (1961),
Manuscript Catalogue (1975), *RCS
Photograph Collection* (Microfilm collection, with printed guide, 1988);
Library Notes with List of Accessions (6Yr)
Spec feat: The Library has major collections on all African Commonwealth
countries and on South Africa, and
extensive material on the former
colonial territories of other European
countries. There are numerous
original collections of works on
African exploration, and there is a
substantial pamphlet collection on the
slave trade. Long runs of older periodicals have been extensively catalogued, and there is much official
material. The manuscript collection,
through not large, has important historical material, and there are some
20,000 photographs of Africa, catalogued in detail.

317 **Royal Institute of
   International Affairs**
   10 St. James's Square,
   London SW1Y 4LE
(01) 930 2233 Tx: 896691 RIIA
Fax: (01) 389 3593
AL/contact: n/a
H: Mon-Wed 10.00–18.00 (Thurs to
19.00), Fri closed
Acc: to members and research staff of
the Institute, bona fide post-graduate

researchers
Loan/ref fac: to members only,
through BLDSC
Coll: ca.14,000b, ca.45cs
Publs: *Index to Periodical Articles 1950–
1978 in the Library of the RIIA* (2 vols
and 2 supplements), *Classified Cata-
logue of the Library of the RIIA. An
Introduction* (1981)
Spec feat: n/a

318 **School of Oriental and
   African Studies**
   University of London,
   Thornhaugh Street,
   Russell Square,
   London WC1H 0XG
(01) 637 2388 Tx: 291829 SOASP
Fax: (01) 436 3844
AL/contact: Barbara Turfan
H: Term & Easter vacation – Mon-
Thurs 09.00–20.00 (Fri to 18.30), Sat
09.30–12.30
Christmas & Summer vacation – Mon-
Fri 09.00–17.00, Sat 09.30-12.30
Acc: to staff and students of the School
and to anyone else by application
Loan/ref fac: most monograph
materials available for loan; rare
books, manuscripts, serials and
materials designated 'Reference'
restricted to the Library
Coll: ca.50,000b, ca.600cs
Publs: *Library Guide*. Subject guides for
each region and for the archives and
manuscripts collection
Spec feat: collects material on and
from the whole of Africa in the
humanities and social sciences, and is
particularly strong in its coverage of
African languages and their literatures. In addition to published monographs and periodicals, holdings include maps, photographs, slides,
sound recordings and microforms as
well as a number of important collections of archives and private
papers, and manuscripts in European
and African languages. The Society for
Libyan Studies collection is held on
permanent loan. Under the SCOLMA
Area Specialization Scheme, SOAS

undertakes responsibility for the acquisitions of the publications of Somalia, Djibouti, Ethiopia, Tunisia, Algeria, Morocco, Mauritania, Liberia, Botswana, Lesotho and Swaziland.

319 University of York
J.B. Morrell Library,
Heslington, York YO1 5DD
(0904) 433867 Tx: 57933 YORKUL
Fax: (0904) 433433
EM: UK.AC.YORK.LIBRARY
AL/contact: Jane Henley
H: Term – Mon-Fri 09.00–22.00 (Sat to 17.15)
Vacation – Mon-Fri 09.00–21.00 (July-Sept 09.00–17.15)
Acc: open to all bona fide enquirers
Loan/ref fac: ref use only for non-members of the University; material may be borrowed through the Inter-Library Loans Services. Photocop and photographic fac
Coll: no separate collection, material dispersed throughout library according to subject, ca.70cs
On-line dbs: yes, charged at cost
On-line cat: access through JANET and PSS. JANET name UK.AC.YORK.LIBRARY Numeric address 00000610001240
Publs: *University of York Library; Southern African Studies: Guides to Literature Searching, York University. Centre for Southern African Studies. A Guide to the Southern African Archives in the University of York, Guide to the Tanganyikan Papers of Marian Lady Chesham*
Spec feat: the collection covers all aspects of Southern Africa (Angola, Botswana, Lesotho, Malawi, Mozambique, Namibia, South Africa, Swaziland, Zambia and Zimbabwe). There is a good collection of bibliographical guides to the area and a wide selection of official publications. The substantial archive collection is held at the Borthwick Institute of Historical Research, University of York, St. Anthony's Hall, Peasholme Green, York YO1 2PW (0904) 437233.

United States

320 Boston University
African Studies Library,
771 Commonwealth Avenue,
Boston, MA 02215
(617) 353 3726
AL/contact: Gretchen Walsh (Head), David Westley (Bibliographer)
H: Term (Sept-May) – Mon-Thurs 09.00–20.00 (Fri-Sat to 17.00)
Vacation – Mon-Fri 09.00–17.00
Acc: open to all scholars (in-house privileges only); write or call to make arrangements
Loan/ref fac: interlibrary loan
Coll: 120,000b, 500cs
On-line dbs: commercial databases available in main library
On-line cat: using a 1200 band modern dial (617) 353 9601 at a› connect library
Publs: *A Guide to African Language Materials in the Boston University Libraries*
Spec feat: particularly strong in publications of African national governments, regional and international agencies. Collects for the entire continent, with strength in sub-Saharan Africa. The social sciences and economics are emphasized, although the collection includes all academic disciplines.

321 University of California at Berkeley
The Library, Berkeley,
California 94720
(415) 643 9999 (Africana (415) 642 0956
Tx: TWX9103667114UC BERK
Fax: (415) 643 7891
AL/contact: Phyllis B. Bischof
H: Term – Mon-Thurs 09.00–22.00 (Fri and Sat to 17.00), Sun 13.00–17.00
Vacation (semester breaks and summer) – shorter hours; branch library hours vary
Acc: open access; purchase of a card possible at cost of $50.00 for one year, but card is unnecessary in order to use the collections
Loan/ref fac: ref/referral, literature

searches, interlibrary loan (for a fee), photocop fac
Coll: 72,500b, 1,000cs
On-line dbs: subscribe to the main database services, including DIALOG, BRS, DATATIMES, LEXIS, OCLC, WESTLAW, MILSONLINE, and RLIN
On-line cat: both Berkeley's GLADIS and the UC Systemwide MELVYL catalogues are available on a no-cost basis – for assistance call (415) 643 9999
Publs: *University of California Union Catalog of Monographs Catalogued by the Nine Campuses from 1963 through 1967* (47 vols)
Spec feat: extensive runs of serials and of foreign, domestic, and international government publications. Main Library collects social sciences and humanities, including economics, geography, linguistics, political science, sociology, and African history well documented by secondary sources. Excellent reference collection. Literary works by African writers collected in depth. Branch libraries collecting Africana include Anthropology, Biology, Business/Social Sciences, Entomology, Forestry, Music, Moffitt Undergraduate, Earth Sciences, Education-Psychology, Environmental Design, Natural Resources, and Public Health Libraries. Maps and atlases present on a continent-wide basis. Fine collection of Mauritian books; pre-eminent Yoruba collection. Rare books collection includes early voyages and travels.

322 **University of California at Los Angeles**
University Research Library, Los Angeles, CA 90024–1575
(213) 825 1518
AL/contact: Joseph J. Lauer
H: Mon-Thurs 08.00–23.00 (Fri to 18.00), Sat 09.00–17.00, Sun 13.00–23.00
Acc: open access
Coll: 145,000b (75,000 titles), ca.900cs
On-line cat: listed on OCLC, MELVYL (Univ of California system), and

ORION via access to campus Office of Academic Computing
Spec feat: special strengths are the collection of maps, government documents, publications in African languages (including Arabic and Amharic), newspapers and manuscripts (including archival materials on microfilm). Geographical areas of strength are East Africa, West Africa, and Northern Africa (which is covered by the Near Eastern bibliographer).

323 **Columbia University Libraries**
New York, NY 10027
(212) 854 2271 (library information service), (212) 854 8045 (African bibliographer) EM: @CUNIXE
AL/contact: Elizabeth A. Widenmann
H: vary from dept to dept and according to academic calendar
Acc: visiting readers must apply to Library Information Office, Columbia University, 234 Butler Library, New York, NY 10027
Loan/ref fac: interlibrary loan; specialized reference assistance on topics relating to Africa south of the Sahara. Orientation lectures and tours are also arranged.
Coll: ca.40,000b
On-line cat: no, but Columbia machine-readable cataloging is in the RLIN Publs: *Use of the Columbia University Libraries: Visiting Readers*
Spec feat: collections on Africa south of the Sahara emphasize the arts, economic development, geography, history, law, literature, political science, sociology and anthropology. Some materials are acquired in Arabic and African languages. Over 1,000 maps of Africa.

324 **Cornell University†**
Africana Studies and Research Center Library, 310 Triphammer Road, Ithaca, NY 14853
(607) 256 3822
Coll: ca.8,000b, ca.300cs

Spec feat: the collection on Africa, black America and the Caribbean concentrates on culture and history, social, economic and political development.
[ASIRD]

325 Dartmouth College†
Baker Library, Hanover, NH 03755

(603) 646 2868 Fax: (603) 646 2167
AL/contact: Gregory A. Finnegan
Acc: open access; library users who are not members of the College community or fee-paying guest borrowers must use materials in the library
Coll: ca.6,000b, ca.200cs
Spec feat: disciplines emphasized in collection development are art, anthropology, government, history, music and literature; the geographic emphasis has been placed on West Africa, but the scope of the collection has been expanded to encompass increasing interest in Southern Africa and East Africa.
[ASIRD]

326 University of Delaware Library†
Newark, Delaware 19711

(302) 451 2231
AL/contact: Maidel Cason (?)
Acc: open access; borrowing materials is restricted to the faculty, students and staff of the University.
Spec feat: the Africana collections place particular emphasis on West and Central Africa and give extensive coverage to Liberia. Angola, Mozambique and Guinea-Bissau are also represented in more than superficial collections.
[ASIRD]

327 Duke University
William R. Perkins Library, Durham, NC 27706

(919) 684 3009 (information), (919) 684 2373 (reference)
Fax: (919) 684 2855
AL/contact: Helene Baumann (Bibliographer, Collection Development)
H: Mon-Thurs 08.00–24.00, Fri-Sat 08.00–22.00, Sun 10.00–24.00
Acc: open access to the public; visiting researchers must use materials within the library
Loan/ref fac: interlibrary loan, photocop fac
Coll: ca.44,000b, ca.3,180cs
On-line dbs: numerous CD-ROM (including Sociofile and PAIS); and DIALOG, BRS, VUTEXT, etc.
On-line cat: for access (919) 681 8822.
Publs: Reference Dept. issues a variety of finding aids on many subjects
Spec feat: collection emphasis is on Anglophone Africa. Subject strengths include history, economics, political science, women and development studies; also numerous government documents. Close cooperation with the University of North Carolina at Chapel Hill (includes a common on-line catalog), whose Africana collection focuses on Franco- and Lusophone Africa, and the North Carolina State University, which collects technical and agricultural African materials. Aside from a collection of Swahili texts to support language teaching, materials collected are primarily in European languages. Strong manuscript holdings in British colonial history, the slave trade and nineteenth century European travellers' accounts.

328 Emory University†
General Libraries, Robert W. Woodruff Library, Atlanta, GA 30322

(404) 329 6861
AL/contact: Elizabeth A. McBride (African Studies Selector)
Acc: open access; monographs may be circulated but use of periodicals is limited to the library
Spec feat: Emory University libraries hold Africa-related materials in the Special Collections Department of the Robert W. Woodruff Library, and in

the Pitts Theology Library of its Candler School of Theology (*see* separate entry **329**)
[ASIRD]

329 Emory University
Pitts Theology Library, Atlanta, Georgia 30322

(404) 727 4166 EM: EMUVM I
AL/contact: Channing R. Jeschke (Librarian)
H: Mon-Thurs 07.45–23.00 (Fri to 17.00), Sat 09.00–17.00, Sun 14.00–23.00
Acc: open access
Loan/ref fac: interlibrary loan
Coll: 2,722b, 547cs
On-line dbs: OCLC
Publs: finding aids available for 3 ms collections: Mss.no.1 *Independent Orthodox Churches of South Africa. Archives, 1880–1974*; Mss.no.31 *Johnson, Joseph, Morgan, Cartoons, Rhodesia, 1965–1974*; Mss.no.83 *Megill, Esther L. Papers, Sierra Leone, ca.1950s.*
Spec feat: A union list of African religious periodicals is being prepared for publication. Records for 844 titles from a dozen libraries in Europe, Africa and the US are electronically stored. Titles are both current and ceased from 45 countries in about 20 languages. A printout is available at cost.

330 Fisk University Library
Special Collections, Fisk University, Nashville, Tennessee 37203

(615) 329 8730
AL/contact: Ann Allen Shockley
H: n/a
Acc: special collections may be used by bona fide scholars and researchers; advance arrangements preferred.
Coll: n/a
Publs: *Dictionary Catalog of the Negro Collection of the Fisk University Library*, 6 vols
Spec feat: Africana is dispersed by Library of Congress numbers within the Special Collections which house books by and about blacks nationally and internationally.

331 University of Florida Libraries†
116 Library West, Gainesville, FL 32611

(904) 392 0341
AL/contact: Peter Malanchuk
Acc: open access, no restrictions
Coll: ca.55,200b, ca.500cs
Spec feat: broad Africa-related collection, consisting mainly of materials dealing with the social sciences and the humanities, although there are extensive holdings on tropical agriculture; strong collections particularly on Southern Africa and the Žaire Republic; specialized holdings in the area of rural development.
[ASIRD]

332 Harvard College Library
Department of Collection Development, Cambridge, MA 02138

(617) 495 2401
AL/contact: Roberta G. Sellek (Book Selection Specialist)
H/Acc/Loan and ref fac, etc.: n/a
Note: questionnaire not completed; readers referred to *African Studies Information Resources Directory* (*see* **17**), 'Information there is essentially unchanged'.

333 Hoover Institution
Africa Collection, Stanford, CA 94305

(415) 725 3505 Fax: (415) 723 1687
EM: RLIN
AL/contact: Peter Duignan (Curator), Karen Fung (Deputy Curator)
H: Mon-Fri 08.00–17.00, Sat closed (main Library Sat 09.00–17.00)
Acc: open access to the public for on-site use, library stacks are closed, loan privileges to Stanford students, faculty and staff only
Loan/ref fac: interlibrary loan, General Reference (415) 725 3424, photocop fac

on pay machines
Coll: ca.60,000b, ca.540cs
On-line dbs: RLIN
Publs: *History of the Library and Archives of the Hoover Institution, Guide to the Hoover Institution Archives*
Spec feat: strengths: colonial history, political ephemera (election material, broadsheets, posters, etc.), African newspapers, Southern Africa, Nigeria, Zaire (Belgian Congo). ca.90 special/archival collections. Collections of Jay Lovestone, Herbert Weiss, William H. Friedland, L. Gray Cowan, S. Herbert Frankel, L.H. Gann, Harvey Glickman, Ernest W. Lefever, Rene Lemarchand, Paul Lubeck, Robert K. Middlemas, Frederick Quinn, Claude E. Welch.

334 Howard University
Moorland Springarn Research Centre, Washington, DC 20059

(202) 636 7260
AL/contact: D.M. Hull
H: Mon-Thurs 09.00–20.00 (Fri-Sat to 17.00)
Acc: closed stacks, patrons are welcome to use facilities
Loan/ref fac: non-circulation of materials
Coll: 65,000b, 70cs
Publs: *African Newspapers in the MSRC*, in-house acquisition lists
Spec feat: a wealth of information on the history and culture of black people in Africa, the Caribbean and US. Includes ca.1,600 books and pamphlets on slavery, unique collection of black authors in 20 languages, a teaching museum, archives, oral history, music department and prints and photographic unit. Undertakes a global acquisitions program.

335 University of Illinois Library
Africana, Room 328,
1408 W. Gregory Drive,
Urbana, IL 61801

(217) 333 6519 Fax: (217) 244 0398/6649
AL/contact: Yvette Scheven

H: Mon-Fri 09.00–17.00
Acc: open access to Illinois residents; visiting scholars are welcome and may obtain building and stacks use permits upon application
Loan/ref fac: full loan and ref fac; interlibrary loan service includes both lending and photocop fac; participates in international interlibrary loan
Coll: ca.60,000b, 1,000cs
On-line dbs: searches from a wide variety of on-line databases are performed which incur telecommunications costs; numerous CD-ROM products are also available throughout the library, and can be searched without cost. On-line cat: author, title, and subject searches are available to users throughout the state of Illinois through their local libraries; the Library's holdings are also included in the OLCL database.
Publs: *Africana: Library Access by Visiting Scholars* (basic information on facilities throughout the Library as well as in Africana); *Africana in the University of Illinois Library* (brochure describing the collection and services); *Selected Africana Acquisitions* (3Yr). All are free on request from Africana.
Spec feat: strong subject holdings include agriculture, anthropology, art history, economic and social development, education, geography, geology, history, law, library science, linguistics, literature, music, and political science. Over 200 African languages are represented, and about 45,000 African maps. A fine collection of nineteenth century geographical journals and general publications of the European colonial powers, as well as current journals, development plans, censuses, and statistical materials from African countries. Fifteen collections in the University Archives include the American Library Association archives and the Avery Brundage Collection, as well as University of Illinois programs in Sierra Leone, Malawi, and Kenya.

336 **University of Iowa Libraries**
    Iowa City, IA 52242
(319) 335 5885
AL/contact: John Bruce Howell
H: 07.30–16.00
Acc: n/a
Coll: 14,000b, 70cs
On-line dbs: DIALOG, BRS,
QUESTEL, CD-ROM for CIS, DAI,
ERIC, LEPAC, Medline, Newsbank,
NTIS, Psych,Lit., PAHO (USAID)
On-line cat: through (319) 335 3999
(see the Library's *Remote Access to the
OASIS Online Catalog* for details on
compatible hardware, etc., available
from the University of Iowa Library
Automation Project, University of
Iowa Libraries, Iowa City, IA 52242)
Publs: *Third World/Iowa: Books, Jour-
nals, Maps, and Microforms about 138
Developing Countries Acquired by the
University of Iowa Libraries 1980–1986*
vol.1 *Africa* (includes bibliographic
citations to 7,400 titles with online
records)
Spec feat: half of the African collection
includes Egypt, South Africa, Nigeria
and Algeria, with the remaining half
covering the rest of the continent.
Current emphasis is on titles from and
about Kenya, Tanzania, Nigeria and
South Africa.

337 **Indiana University Libraries**
    Bloomington, Indiana 47405
(812) 855 8020, (812) 855 8229
Fax: (812) 855 9134
AL/contact: Nancy J. Schmidt
H: Term – Mon-Fri 08.15–24.00 (Sat
from 10.00, Sun from 11.00)
Summer sessions and intersessions –
shorter hours
Acc: open access to the public
Loan/ref fac: Indiana University
students and staff and residents of
Indiana with proper identification may
borrow books. Periodicals, media, rare
books, microforms and manuscripts
do not circulate. Reference,
Interlibrary loan, photocop fac
Coll: 90,000b, 1,000cs
On-line dbs: 30 CD-ROM databases

may be searched by users free of
charge, online catalog searches done
free of charge, database searches done
for a fee by Reference Department
Publs: *African Music and Oral Data: A
Catalog of Field Recordings 1902–1975,
African Studies Periodicals and Other
Serials Currently on Subscription, Bibliography of Africana in the Institute for Sex
Research, Bibliography of Africana in the
Lilly Library*
Spec feat: in addition to books and
current serials, holds 25,000 uncatalogued government publications and
50,000 uncatalogued pamphlets,
newsletters and reprints. Main
strength of holdings is sub-Saharan
Africa: humanities, social sciences and
African language materials. Boxer
travel literature collection and manuscripts in Lilly Library; over 5,000
music and language recordings in the
Archives of Traditional Music, uncatalogued photographs and slides in the
Fine Arts Library; uncatalogued maps
in the Geography/Map Library;
Human Relations Area Files; films in
Audio-Visual Services Department.

338 **Library of Congress**
    African Section, African and
    Middle Eastern Division,
    Adams Building,
    Room 1026A,
    Washington DC 20540
(202) 707 5528 Tx: 710 822 0185 (main
Library no.) Fax: (202) 707 9199 (main
Library no.)
AL/contact: Beverly Gray
H: Mon-Fri 08.30–17.00
General Reading Rooms – Mon-Fri
08.30–21.30 (Sat to 17.00), Sun 13.00–
17.00
Acc: open access to anyone over high
school age
Loan/ref fac: reference, photocop fac,
microform duplication, interlibrary
loan
Coll: n/a, holdings dispersed primarily
by subject
On-line dbs: in-house use of online

catalog is accessible to users: MUMS, SCORPIO
On-line cat: indirectly through vendors (e.g. DIALOG) and machine-readable catalog (MARC) tapes are available for purchase through the Library's Cataloging Distribution Service
Publs: information about recent publications is available in the brochures: *The African Section in the Library of Congress, La Section Africaine de la Bibliothèque du Congrès*
Spec feat: pre-eminent collections on sub-Saharan African encompassing all geographic areas and every major field of study except technical agriculture and clinical medicine, which are under the jurisdiction of the National Agricultural Library and the National Library of Medicine, respectively. Holdings in economics, history, linguistics, and literature are especially strong. Most of the materials are housed in the Library's general book and periodical collections. Impressive holdings may also be found in special collections of legal publications, manuscripts, maps, microforms, music, newspapers, prints, photographs and films in the various custodial divisions of the Library. In addition, an uncatalogued pamphlet collection of some 20,000 items is housed in the African Section.

339 **University of Maryland Baltimore County**, Albin O. Kuhn Library and Gallery, 5401 Wilkens Avenue, Baltimore, MD 21228
(301) 455 2232
AL/contact: none specific; Simmona E. Simmons for bibliographies and liaison with Afro-American Studies Dept.
H: Mon-Thurs 08.00–24.00 (Fri to 18.00), Sat 12.00–18.00., Sun 12.00–24.00
Acc: open access
Loan/ref fac: circulating material through interlibrary loan
Coll: n/a, ca.60cs including Afro-

American
On-line-cat: available to persons on the University of Maryland campuses and by local dial-up access
Publs: in-house bibliographies
Spec feat: several special collections on microfilm. There are ca.579 reels of microfilm of materials from the Schomburg collection. There are 181 reels of microfilm for the books from the Black culture collection from Atlanta University. This collection emphasizes material about African art, folklore and literature. Other miscellaneous collections on microfilm include the Black Workers (selected years) during the era of the Great Migration, Black Abolitionist papers and some early papers of the NAACP.

340 **University of Michigan†**
University Libraries, Hatcher Graduate Library, Ann Arbor, MI 48109
(313) 764 9356
AL/contact: John A. Eilts (?)
Acc: open access; materials in the special collections must be used on the premises
Spec feat: substantial collections on Africa, covering the humanities and the social sciences; particularly strong holdings on classical, medieval and modern North Africa.
[ASIRD]

341 **Michigan State University Libraries**
Africana Library, W312–6 East Lansing, MI 48824–1048
(517) 355 2366 Fax: (517) 353 9606
EM: ALA 1048
AL/contact: Onuma U. Ezera (Head), Joseph J. Lauer (Africana Bibliographer)
H: Mon-Fri 08.00–12.00, 13.00–17.00
Acc: open access
Loan/ref fac: interlibrary loan, ref. and database systems
Coll: 104,200b, 3,200cs

On-line dbs: BRS, DIALOG
On-line cat: OCLC, MAGIC via MSU
net or MERIT – dial (517) 353 8500
Publs: *Africana: Select Recent Acquisitions* (Qtly), *Africana in Microfilm in the Michigan State University Library, Notes on the Use of MSU's Library Resources in African Studies*
Spec feat: most of the Africana holdings are integrated into the general research collections. The Africana Area Files, a large collection of pamphlets and fugitive material, is housed in the Africana Library. Sahel Documentation Center: collects and disseminates information dealing with various aspects of socio-economic development in the Sahel. (The Center's activities were reported in *Sahel Bibliographic Bulletin 1976–1985*). Congo Collection: consists of de Ryck's (a former governor of Belgian Congo) private library. There are more than 10,000 volumes including periodical titles, maps and about nine linear feet of manuscript material pertaining to Zaire, Burundi and Rwanda from 1880–1962. The Audio, Maps and Microforms, Special collections, Government Documents and Voice Library also have strong Africana content.

342 National Museum of African Art Branch Library
Smithsonian Institution Libraries, 950 Independence Avenue, SW, Washington, DC 20560
(202) 357 4875
AL/contact: Janet L. Stanley
H: Mon-Fri 09.00–17.15
Acc: open to the public by appointment
Loan/ref fac: full range of ref services, interlibrary loan, literature searching
Coll: 20,000b, 250cs
Publs: *Library Acquisitions List* (Mon)
Spec feat: the collections emphasize the visual arts, performing arts, ethnography, religion, oral traditions, and history. They also include materials on

African retentions in the New World. The Library maintains extensive vertical files on aspects of African art, history and culture. The Eliot Elisofon Photographic Archive at the National Museum of African Art houses more than 150,000 colour slides, 70,000 black and white photographs, and 120,000 feet of unedited film footage. (Contact Judith Luskey. Photo Archivist, (202) 357 4654).

343 State University of New York at Buffalo
Lockwood Memorial Library, Buffalo, New York, NY 14260
(716) 636 2817
AL/contact: Dorothy C. Woodson
H: Mon-Thurs 08.00–22.45 (Fri to 21.00), Sat 09.00–17.00, Sun 12.00–22.45
Acc: open access
Coll: ca.20,000b, ca12,500cs (SUNY/ Buffalo Univ Libraries total collection = 2.2m.b)
On-line dbs: all DIALOG and BRS databases, numerous CD-ROM databases
On-line cat: in 1990
Publs: *African Studies Resources in Lockwood Memorial Library*; wide range of reference and finding aids
Spec feat: extensive collection of secondary source material, no appreciable primary source materials.

344 State University College of New York at New Paltz†
Sojourner Truth Library, New Paltz, NY 12561
(914) 257 2139
AL/contact: Corinne Nyquist
(Coordinator, World Study Collection)
Acc: open access
Coll: ca.22,000b, ca.100cs
Spec feat: the World Study Collection of SUNY collects materials on the entire continent of Africa, in all subjects, but social science materials dominate. The collection is strongest on Eastern and Southern Africa, and in the fields of anthropology, educa-

tion, geography, history, music and politics.
[ASIRD]

345 Northwestern University Library,

Melville J. Herskovits Library of African Studies, Evanston, IL 60208–2300
(708) 491 7684 Fax: (708) 491 5685
AL/contact: Hans E. Panofsky
H: Mon-Fri 08.30–17.00, other times by special arrangement
Acc: open access
Loan/ref fac: interlibrary loan, all aspects of ref and referral service
Coll: 165,000b, 2,500cs
On-line dbs: (708) 491 3070
On-line cat: access through Northwestern Univ Lib's LUIS; LUIS can be used from any terminal wired to ACNS, terminals on Northwestern campus with an NTS DIU or AILU
Publs: *Africana File Listing as of April 1988, Joint Acquisitions List of Africana* (6Yr, *see* **107**); 1978–1983 microfiche index (microfiche index to vertical file); various bibliographies, guides, and finding aids issued.
Spec feat: largest separate Africana collection in the world, scope is continent-wide, and subject matter ranges from art, history, literature, music, and religion to communications, management, and cooking. The collection focuses primarily on the social sciences and humanities, with major geographic emphasis on sub-Saharan Africa. Also included are some materials from North Africa, mostly in French. Holdings include a rare book collection of more than 3,000 titles, including early accounts of European exploration; and a large collection – much of it unique – of uncatalogued material covering statistical publications, development plans, commission reports, censuses, laws, and debates, pamphlet materials from trade unions, political parties, and national liberation movements. Ca. 9,000 publications in some 300 African languages. Materials from and about Africa also exist elsewhere in Northwestern's library system: African maps are in the Map Collection; publications from the United States government and from international agencies are located in Government Publications; tapes and taped interviews with African authors are in the Poetry/Listening Facility; most newspaper and microform material is in the Newspaper/Microtext Room; sound recordings and some books on African music are in the Music Library; the Seeley G. Mudd Science and Engineering Library, the Geology Library, and the Transportation Library all contain some African material; Africana archives related to Northwestern University are in the University Archives; language tapes are available in the Language Laboratory (Kresge Hall).

346 Ohio University Library†

Athens, OH 45701
(614) 594 5240
Acc: open access
Coll: ca.31,000b, ca.160cs
Spec feat: essentially a general collection, but focusing on Southern and Eastern Africa; collection is strongest in history and economic development, but the subjects of geography, political science, education, art, literature and linguistics are also emphasized; strong map collections; African art collection.
[ASIRD]

347 Schomburg Center for Research in Black Culture†

515 Lenox Avenue, New York, NY 10037
(212) 283 5317 Fax: (212) 491 6760
AL/contact: Valerie Sandoval Mwalilino (?)
Acc: materials do not circulate; admission to collections after completion of admission forms detailing research needs
Coll: ca.85,000b, ca.500cs
Spec feat: The Schomburg Center for

Research in Black Culture is one of the world's largest and most comprehensive collection of records documenting the experiences of peoples of African origin and descent. The collections (which include extensive holdings of audiovisual materials, and prints, posters, paintings, sculptures, clippings, newspapers, pamphlet and sheet music, microfilms, archival records, etc.) are strongest in three areas: Afro-Americana throughout the Western hemisphere; sub-Saharan Africa; and Afro-Caribbeana. Since 1972 Schomburg's emphasis has been placed in the humanities, including art and art objects, and the social sciences.
[ASIRD]

348 Syracuse University†
E.S. Bird Library,
222 Waverly Avenue,
Syracuse, NY 13210
(315) 423 2575
AL/contact: Ann Bierstecker
Acc: open access; borrowing privileges by arrangement
Coll: ca.16,000b, ca.275cs
Publs: *Africana Microfilms at the E.S. Bird Library, Syracuse University: An Annotated Guide; A Guide to the Kenya National Archives*
Spec feat: collection strength is in materials relating to Eastern Africa, but there are also considerable holdings on Southern and West Africa.
Spec coll: Kenya National Archives microfilmed materials; Sir Richard Francis Burton papers; Francis G. Hall papers; the Laubach collection.
[ASIRD]

349 University of Texas at Austin†
The General Libraries,
Box P, Austin, TX 78712
(512) 471 3811
Acc: open access
Spec feat: Africa-related holdings are substantial in anthropology, geography, political science, African

languages and literatures. The Harry Ransom Humanities Research Center holds original and published material mostly relating to the literature of South and Southern Africa, including books, manuscripts, and original portraits of authors. The Population Research Center Library has extensive collections of African population census publications and demographic surveys.
[ASIRD]

350 United Nations†
Dag Hammarskjöld Library,
United Nations Plaza,
New York, NY 10017
(212) 754 7412
Acc: open to delegations, permanent missions to the UN and authorized users. Qualified researchers must obtain permission to use the collection
Coll: 400,000 (total coll), 4,000cs (total cs)
Publs: *UNDOC: Current Index* (10Yr), *Index to Proceedings . . . of the General Assembly; Current Bibliographical Information* (10Yr)
Spec feat: specialized international library which combines the functions of an international affairs bureau with those of a research library in the social sciences. Maintains complete collection of all the documents and publications of the United Nations, its affiliated bodies and specialized agencies, as well as those of the League of Nations. Government documents and official publications from African countries are held.
[ASIRD]

351 University of Virginia
Alderman Library,
Charlottesville,
VA 22903–2498
(804) 924 4989 Fax: (804) 924 4337
EM: MAK@VIRGINIA
AL/contact: Mary Alice Kraehe
H: Mon-Thurs 08.00–24.00 (Fri to

22.00), Sat 09.00–18.00, Sun 12.00–24.00

Acc: materials in general collections circulate to card holders

Loan/ref fac: full range of interlibrary loan services (contact (804) 924 3875); full range of reference services available to the general public

Coll: 30,000b, 384cs

On-line dbs: BRS, DIALOG, OCLC, PAIS on CD-ROM. Services available in-house

On-line cat: yes, contact Library for instructions on accessing; Library has NOTIS

Publs: *African Languages, A Guide to the Library Collection of the University of Virginia* (1986); *Africana Related Periodicals and Serials Currently Received at Alderman Library, University of Virginia* (1988)

Spec feat: pamphlets, predominantly government publications and departmental reports from East and South Africa during the period 1930–1960 (1,000). African language dictionaries, grammars and language learning aids, some with audio cassettes (1,000). Human Relations Area Files on microfiche. The Special Collections Department houses 42 collections containing material on Africa: particularly the Vieira correspondence regarding the Angolan grain trade, 1942–1943; the Dillar Family Papers, 1923–38, regarding various educational missions; the Stettinius Papers regarding records of the Liberia Company, 1946–1949; and the Terrell & Cocke Collections of letters, 1834–1865 to former masters from freed men settled in Liberia.

352 University of Wisconsin
Memorial Library,
728 State St, Madison,
WI 53706

(608) 262 6397

AL/contact: David Henige

H: Sun-Thurs 08.00–24.00, Fri-Sat 10.00–22.00

Acc: all materials are in general stacks and freely accessible, though entry to general library requires pass available on presentation of reasonable ID

Loan/ ref fac: semester loans available to all citizens of Wisconsin and staff of CIC universities; large ref dept open same hours as above

Coll: 60,000b, 500–600cs

On-line dbs: BRS, ERIC, DAI, etc.

On-line cat: some available; specific arrangements to be made either with General Reference dept in Memorial Library or relevant branch libraries (over 20)

Publs: specialized guides (e.g. Africana in microform) issued from time to time; the General Library System as well as Memorial Library have several guides to holdings, hours, conditions of use, etc.

Spec feat: particularly strong in Zaire, Central Africa (esp. Francophone CA), Nigeria, and Zimbabwe, and on materials published before ca.1960. Archival materials held by both Memorial Library and the library of the State Historical Society of Wisconsin.

353 Yale University Library
African Collection,
120 High St, New Haven,
CT 06520–7429

(203) 432 1882/3 Tx: 9102508365 YALE UNIVERSITY Fax: (203) 432 9652

EM: RLG-RLIN WYLBUR per Inter-Library Loan office

AL/contact: Moore Crossey

H: 08.30–17.30

Acc: RLG member institutions with ID (including undergraduates); graduate students, faculty (academic staff), other adult researchers with campus ID and/or driving licence or passport; non-RLG undergraduates require letter from their library stating need

Coll: ca.90,000b, ca.3,000cs

On-line dbs: ORBIT (on-line cat), DIALOG, MEDLINE etc.; CD-ROM eds of PAIS, *Dissertation Abstracts, MLA Bibliography, Psych. Abstracts* etc.

On-line cat: access by ca.1991
Publs: *Guide to Library Resources for the
Study of Southern Africa*, general guides
from the Reference Department, etc.
Spec feat: concentrated in the Sterling
Memorial (main) Library, the Seeley
Mudd (storage) Library, and in the
Divinity, Law, Medical, Kline Science,
Social Science, and other special
libraries. There are extensive collections in all languages (including
African languages and Arabic) in all
humanities and social science disciplines, and less extensive coverage on
the biological sciences, geology,
education, medicine, agriculture (technical), criminology, etc. Coverage of
anglophone West and Southern Africa
nears comprehensiveness in some
subject fields. Special collections include: Economic Growth Center Collection (in the Social Science Library),
statistics, development plans, bud-
gets, etc; the Day Missions Collection
in the Divinity Library; South African
law in the Law Library; tropical
forestry and ecology in the Forestry
Library; Historical Medical Library in
the Medical Library; the Garvan Sport-
ing Books Collection – big game hunt-
ing – in the Seeley Mudd Library. Ms.
collections in the Department of
Manuscripts and Archives has a
strong concentration of original and
microform mss. on Southern and
Western Africa – also postcards,
photographs, political ephemera; the
Map and Atlas Collection has good
holdings of modern maps and old
maps of South Africa.

V. PUBLISHERS WITH AFRICAN STUDIES LISTS

The information provided for this section was collected by means of a questionnaire, and attempts to list all the major publishers with significant African studies lists.

Not all publishers responded to our questionnaire mailing, despite at least one reminder/chaser sent to each. All such entries are indicated with a † dagger symbol, and entries are confined to a listing of name and address, telephone number, ISBN prefix, and name of chief executive/contact where known.

When questionnaires were duly completed and returned, a full entry includes: name and address, telephone, telex, fax numbers; ISBN prefix, year founded; names of chief executive and editor/contact person for African studies list; details of approximate number of titles published annually and in-print in the African studies field; series published in African studies; areas of specialization in African (or Third World) studies; information regarding areas/levels in which manuscript submissions are invited and preferred length of manuscripts, and details of any editorial or other requirements concerning manuscript submissions; and finally, details of US distributors of European publishers, or vice-versa European/UK distributors of US publishers, are given where the information was provided.

Abbreviations used:

ann	– annually [number of titles]
AS contact	– African studies contact person/editor
AS titles	– African studies titles [published]
Chief exec	– Chief executive
CRC	– Camera-ready copy
d-s	– double spaced
Edit req	– editorial requirements [for manuscript submissions]
Found	– year founded
ip	– in print [number of African studies titles]
ISBN prefix	– International Standard Book Number prefix(es)
Ms L	– manuscript length [preferred length]
Ms subm	– manuscript submissions [areas/levels in which invited]
Ser	– series [published in African studies]
UK distr.	– United Kingdom and/or European distributors
w	– words [number of]

EUROPE AND NORTH AMERICA

France

354 L'Harmattan, Edition
7, rue de l'Ecole
Polytechnique, 75005 Paris
(1) 43260452, 43547910
Found: 1975 ISBN prefix: n/a
Chief exec and contact: Denis Pryen
AS titles: 120 ip

355 Karthala Edition-Diffusion
22–24 boulevard Arago,
75013 Paris
(1) 43311559 Tx: 250303 PUBLIC
Found: 1980 ISBN Prefix: 2–86537
Chief exec and contact: Robert
Ageneau
AS titles: 30 ann, 250 ip
Ser: 'Les Afriques', 'Politique
Africaine', 'Reliu', 'Contes et
legendes'
Spec: essays on current social and
political issues, economic and political
studies, technical works (agronomy,
health etc.), oral literature, history,
languages
Ms subm: commissioned; direct submissions also considered

356 Editions Pélissier
Montamets, 78630 Orgeval
39757265
Found: 1978 ISBN prefix: 2–902804
Chief exec: René Pélissier
AS titles: 9 ip
Ser: 'Ibero-Africana'
Spec: Lusophone Africa; Spanish-
speaking Africa; history, politics,
bibliography, travel literature

357 Présence Africaine†
25bis rue des Ecoles,
75005 Paris
(1) 354 15 88 Tx: 200891 AFRISAC
Chief execs: Geoffrey Jones, Yande
Christianne Diop

358 UNESCO
United Nations Educational,
Scientific and Cultural
Organization,
7 Place de Fontenoy,
75700 Paris
(1) 45681000 Tx: 204461, 270602
Fax: 45671690
Found: 1946 ISBN prefix: 92–3
Chief exec: F. Mayor
AS titles: 8 ann, 60 ip
Spec: history, culture, communi-
cation, education, arts, apartheid
Ms subm: commissioned only

Germany (Federal Republic)

359 Institut für Afrika-Kunde
Neuer Jungfernstieg 21,
2000 Hamburg 36
(040) 356523
Found: 1963 ISBN prefix: 3–923519
Chief exec and contact: Rolf Hofmeier
AS titles: 6–8 ann, 90 ip
Ser: 'Hamburger Beiträge zur Afrika-
Kunde', 'Arbeiten aus dem Institut für
Afrika-Kunde'
Spec: social sciences (contemporary
political, economic and social develop-
ment) in Africa (except Egypt, covered
by the series published by the
Deutsches Orient-Institut, Hamburg)
Ms L: minimum 100pp
Edit req: ms in German language; ms
in English accepted in exceptional
cases only

360 K.G. Saur Verlag
Heilmannstrasse 17,
Postfach 71 10 09,
D-8000 München 71
(89) 791040 Tx: 5212067 SAUR
Fax: (89) 7910499
Found: 1974 ISBN prefix: 3–598
Chief exec: Klaus G. Saur
Note: distributor in Continental
Europe of the Hans Zell Publishers
list, *see* **391** for full entry.

Netherlands

361 E.J. Brill Publishing Company
POB 9000, 2300 PA Leiden
(071) 312624 Tx: 39296
Fax: (071) 317532
Found: 1683 ISBN prefix: 90–04
Chief exec: n/a
AS contact: M.G. Elisabeth Venekamp
AS titles: 10 ann 39 ip
Ser: 'Studies on Religion in Africa'
Ms subm: post-doctoral level
Ms L: 60,000w

Sweden

362 Scandinavian Institute of African Studies
POB 1703, S-751 47 Uppsala
(46) 18155480 Tx: 819077
Fax: (46) 18695629
Found: 1962 ISBN prefix: 91–7106
Chief exec: Anders Hjort
AS contact: Karl Eric Ericson
AS titles: 10–15 ann, 300 ip
Ser: 'Research Reports', 'Discussion Papers', 'Seminar Proceedings'
Spec: social science, arid lands, refugees, southern Africa
Ms subm: social and political science
Ms L: 100–150 pp
NA distr: Holmes & Meier Publishers Inc, 30 Irving Place, New York, NY 10003 (*see* **394**)

United Kingdom

363 Cambridge University Press
The Edinburgh Building, Shaftesbury Road, Cambridge CB2 2RU
(0223) 312393 Tx: 817256
Fax: (0223) 315052
Found: 1584 ISBN prefix: 0–521
Chief exec: Geoffrey Cass
AS contact: Jessica Kuper
AS titles: 3–4 ann, 110 ip
Ser: 'African Studies Series', 'Fontes Historiae Africaniae', 'Cambridge History of Africa', 'African Society Today'
Spec: none specific
Ms Subm: Post PhD, not PhD theses; history, sociology, anthropology, politics, economics
Ms L: up to 100,000w
Edit req: typed clean copy
NA distr: Cambridge University Press, 32 East 57th Street, New York, NY 10022; Tel: (212) 688 8885

364 Frank Cass & Co. Ltd.†
Gainsborough House, 11 Gainsborough Road, London E11 1RS
(01) 530 4226 Tx: 897719 Cass
ISBN prefix: 0–7146
Chief exec: Frank Cass

365 Catholic Institute for International Relations
22 Coleman Fields, London N1 7AF
(01) 354 0883 Tx: 21118 CIIR
Fax: (01) 359 0017
Found: 1940 ISBN prefix: 0–946848 & 1–852870
Chief exec: Ian Linden
AS contact: Stephen Gray
AS titles: 6 ann, 28 ip
Ser: 'Future for Namibia'
Spec: Southern Africa, politics, theology, development
Ms subm: commissioned only
NA distr: Novalis (Canada)

366 Centre for Research in Ethnic Relations
University of Warwick, Coventry CV4 7AL
(0203) 523523
Chief exec: Robin Cohen
AS contacts: Brenda Layton, Charlotte Wellington
AS titles: operates special book club in which books written by those associated with the Centre but published by independent publishers are offered for sale at discounted prices; list covers Africa, Asia and the Caribbean

367 **Clio Press Ltd**
     55 St. Thomas Street,
     Oxford OX1 1JG
(0865) 250333 Fax: (0865) 790358
Found: 1971 ISBN prefix: n/a
Chief exec: John Durrant
AS contact: Bob Neville
AS titles: 15 ip
Ser: 'World Bibliographical Series'
Spec: bibliographies
NA distr: ABC-Clio, POB 1911, Santa
Barbara, CA 93116–1911 (*see* **392**)

368 **Rex Collings Ltd.†**
     38 King Street,
     London WC2E 8JS
(01) 836 8634 Tx: 337340
ISBN prefix: 0–86036, 0–901720
Chief exec: Rex Collings

369 **James Currey Publishers Ltd**
     54 Thornhill Square,
     Islington, London N1 1BE
(01) 609 9026 Tx: 262433 W6327
Fax: (01) 609 9605
Found: 1985 ISBN prefix: 0–609–9605
Chief exec: James Currey
AS contact: James Currey or Alison
Hill
AS titles: 16 ann, 50 ip
Ser: 'Eastern African Studies',
'Apartheid and Society', 'African
Literature Today'
Spec: Eastern and Southern African
studies in history, politics, economics,
especially the relationship between
Apartheid and Southern African
society; study and criticism of African
literature in English; economic
development in the Third World;
Caribbean history and literature;
slavery studies
Ms subm: scholarly works and mono-
graphs in all above areas; also works in
the area of contemporary affairs, politics and government, in South Africa
especially
Ms L: between 36,000 and 150,000w
Edit req: typescripts only, unless there
are very special circumstances

370 **Earthscan Publications Ltd**
     3 Endsleigh Street,
     London WC1H 0DD
(01) 388 2117 Tx: 261681 EASCAN
Fax: (01) 388 2826
Found: 1987 ISBN prefix: 1–85383
Chief exec and contact: Neil Middleton
AS titles: 6–12 ann, 12 ip
Spec: feminism, economics, urban
studies, agriculture (arid, semi-arid
and wetland), industry, social studies,
geography, health studies, develop-
ment studies
Ms subm: all above
Ms L: not less than 35,000w
Edit req: typed scripts only, d-s; all
floppy discs to be IBM compatible and,
where possible, in Word Perfect

371 **Ethnographica Limited
     Publishers†**
     19 Westbourne Road,
     London N7 8AN
(01) 607 4074 ISBN prefix: 0–905788
Chief exec: Stuart Hamilton

372 **Hansib Publishing Ltd†**
     Tower House,
     139–149 Fonthill Road,
     London N4 3HG
(01) 281 1191 ISBN prefix: 1–870518

373 **Heinemann International**
     Halley Court, Jordon Hill,
     Oxford OX2 8ET
(0865) 311366 Tx: 837929 HEBOK
Fax: (0865) 310479
Found: 1890 ISBN prefix: 0–435
Chief exec: Ian Irving
AS contact: Vicky Unwin
AS titles: 10–12 ann, 275 ip (200
'African Writers Series', 75 general)
Ser: 'African Writers Series',
'UNESCO History of Africa'
Spec: Literature
Ms subm: fiction and poetry
Ms L: 200–250pp A4
Edit req: typed scripts, d-s; author
must retain copy of ms. as not respon-
sible for loss or damage NA distr:

Heinemann Educational Books Inc, 70 Court Street, Portsmouth, NH 03801 (*see* **399**)

374 Hurst & Co Publishers
38 King Street,
London WC2E 8JT

(01) 240 2666
Found: 1967 ISBN prefix: 1–85065, 0–905838, 0–903983
Chief exec: Christopher Hurst
AS contacts: Christopher Hurst, Michael Dwyer
AS titles: 4 ann, 55 ip
Spec: history, politics, social studies, neocolonialism, autobiography; also Asia: southwest, south, south east, east and Soviet central
Ms subm: research, tertiary
Ms L: no preference
Edit req: no ms submissions before synopsis has been submitted and approved

375 IC Publications†
69 Great Queen Street,
London WC2B 5BN

(01) 404 4333 Tx: 8811757
Fax: (01) 404 5336
ISBN prefix: 0–905268
Chief exec: Afif Ben Yedder

376 Institute for African Alternatives
23 Bevenden Street,
London N1 6BH

(01) 251 1503 Tx: 923 753 W 6019
Found: 1986 ISBN prefix: 1–870425–05
Chief exec and contact: Ben Turok
AS titles: 6 ann, 12 ip
Ser: yes, unspecified
Spec: general Africa
Ms subm: monographs
Ms L: 10,000w

377 Intermediate Technology Publications
103–105 Southampton Row,
London WC1B 4HH

(01) 436 9761 Fax: (01) 436 2013
Found: 1967 ISBN prefix: 1–85339,

0–946688
Chief exec and contact: Neal Burton
AS titles: 180 ip
Spec: appropriate technology, and the technical and economic aspects of development studies
Ms subm: in areas above: practical manuals, case studies of technical development, economic assessment of technical assistance
Ms L: maximum 80,000w
Edit req: authors should provide information about target audience for whom they are writing, and what the practical objectives of the book are; and confirm that ms. is not a unique copy

378 Karnak House
300 Westbourne Park Road,
London W11 1EH

(01) 221 6490
Found: 1975 ISBN prefix: 0–907015
Chief exec and contact: Amon Saba Saakana
AS titles: 5 ann, 13 ip
Ser: 'Ancient Afrikan History/ Civilization'
Spec: African-American, Afro-Caribbean, Africa; religion, history, linguistics, literature, children's books, anthropology, sociology, art, folk tales, proverbs, African languages, ancient Egypt, women's studies
Ms subm: all areas above, academic and general
Ms L: 50,000w; poetry minimum 60pp
Edit req: covering letter, biographical note, prepaid international coupon with name and address
NA distr: Red Sea Press, 556 Bellevue Avenue, Trenton, NJ 08618 (*see* **393**)

379 Kegan Paul International†
PO Box 256,
118 Bedford Court Mansions,
Bedford Avenue,
London WC1B 3SW

(01) 580 5511 Tx: 261771 KEGANP
Fax: (01) 436 0899
ISBN prefix: 0–7103
Chief exec: Peter Hopkins

US distr: Routledge, Chapman and Hall Inc. 29 West 35th Street, New York NY 10001; Tel: (212) 563 2269

380 **Longman Group Ltd**
Burnt Mill, Harlow,
Essex CM20 2JE
(0279) 26721 Tx: 81259 LONGMAN
Fax: (0279) 31059
Found: 1724 ISBN prefix: 0–582
AS contact: Catherine Menage
AS titles: 6 ann, 200 ip
Ser: 'Longman African Writers'
Spec: African history, African literature, undergraduate textbooks for African universities
Ms subm: fiction, undergraduate (first year) level textbooks
Edit req: typed copy of ms
US distr: Longman Inc., 95 Church Street, White Plains, NY 100601–1505, Tel: (914) 993 5000

381 **Macmillan Publishers Ltd**
Houndmills, Basingstoke,
Hants RG21 2XS
(0256) 29242 Tx: 858493
Fax: (0256) 479985
Found: n/a ISBN prefix: 0–333
Chief exec: Chris Harrison
AS contact: Frank Slater
AS titles: 20–30 ann, 100 ip
Ser: 'Sociology of Developing Societies', 'Macmillan Development Studies'
Spec: sociology of developing societies, sociology of development, international and development economics, political development, anthropology
Ms subm: secondary school material, in accordance with syllabi of country concerned; tertiary, preferably first-year undergraduate level
Edit req: typed, d-s ms

382 **Manchester University Press**
Oxford Road,
Manchester M13 9PL
(061) 273 5539 Tx: 668932
Fax: (061) 274 3346
Found: 1903 ISBN prefix: 0–7190
Chief exec: Francis Brooke

AS contact: Ray Offord
AS titles: 4 ann, 12 ip
Ser: 'International African Seminars', 'International African Library', 'Africa Bibliography'
Spec: anthropology, history, economics, politics
Ms subm: politics, economics, history
Ms L: 80,000w
NA distr: St. Martin's Press Inc, 1975 Fifth Avenue, New York, NY 10010 (*see* **410**)

383 **New Beacon Books†**
76 Stroud Green Road,
London N4 3EN
(01) 272 4889 ISBN prefix: 0–901241
Chief exec: Michael la Rose

384 **Oxford University Press**
Walton Street,
Oxford OX2 6DP
(0865) 56767 Tx: 837330 OXPRES
Fax: (0865) 56646
Found: 1478 ISBN prefix: 0–19
Chief exec: Sir Roger Elliott
AS contact: Henry Hardy
AS titles: 17 ip (series)
Ser: 'Oxford Studies in African Affairs'
Spec: politics, history, development studies, geography, economics
Ms subm: all areas, tertiary level
US distr: Oxford University Press Inc, 200 Madison Avenue, New York, NY 10016; Tel: (212) 679 7300

385 **Pathfinder Press**
47 The Cut, London SE1 8LL
(01) 261 1354
Found: 1970 ISBN prefix: 087348, 0913460, 0947083
Chief exec and contact: Alan Harris
AS titles: 1 ann, 7 ip
Spec: current political situation – Cuba, Caribbean, Central America, South Africa

386 **Pinter Publishers**
25 Floral Street,
London WC2E 9DS
(01) 240 9233 Tx: 912881 AH PIN

Fax: (01) 379 5553
Found: 1973 ISBN prefix: 0–86187
Chief exec: Frances Pinter
AS contact: Iain Stevenson
AS titles: 3–5 ann, 30 ip
Spec: economics, political economy, international relations, agriculture
Ms subm: as above
Ms L: maximum 80,000w
Edit req: outline and c.v. to be sent initially

387 Pluto Publishing
11–21 Northdown Street, London N1 9BN

(01) 837 4014 Tx: 262 433
Fax: (01) 278 1677
Found: n/a ISBN prefix: 07453
Chief exec and contact: Roger van Zwanenberg
AS titles: 5–10 ann, 13 ip
Ser: 'Africa and the Caribbean'
Spec: all aspects of political economy broadly defined, from African cultural studies e.g. music and art, to African women's studies, African history, society and politics
Ms subm: undergraduate, graduate, popular political analysis
Ms L: minimum 60,000w
Edit req: d-s, send return postage if ms is sent or send table of contents and two or three page outline

388 Routledge, Chapman and Hall
11 New Fetter Lane, London EC4P 4EE

(01) 583 9855 Tx: 263398
Fax: (01) 583 0701
ISBN prefix: 0–416
Chief exec: David Croom
AS contact: Tristan Palmer
AS titles: 2–5 ann, 12 ip
Ser: 'Routledge Introductions to Development', 'Development and Underdevelopment'
Spec: rural, urban, economic, environment, women, industrialization, political, development
Ms subm: all areas to do with Third World, mainly tertiary – undergraduate and above, plus a few A-level and professional level
Ms L: 100,000w (range 80,000–120,000s)
Edit req: a proposal consisting of an overview (2–4pp outline of book), list of contents, list of tables, maps, diagrams etc. (a rough indication of how many), a letter explaining why the book is being written, a description of the level and what market book is aimed at; what, if any, access to word processors, laser printers etc. with description of type and make, length of ms, date of expected delivery
NA distr: Routledge, Chapman and Hall, Inc. 29 West 35th Street, New York NY 10001; Tel: (212) 244 3336

389 Sage Publications Ltd†
28 Banner Street, London EC1Y 8QE

(01) 253 1516 Tx: 292607 SAGE
ISBN prefix: 0–8039
Chief exec: David Hill
US distr: Sage Publications Inc, 275 South Beverly Drive, Beverly Hills, CA 90212; Tel: (213) 274 8003

390 School of Oriental and African Studies
University of London, Thornhaugh Street, Russell Square London WC1H 0XG

(01) 637 2388 Tx: 291829 SOASP
Fax: (01) 436 3844
Found: 1917 ISBN prefix: n/a
Chief exec: C.D. Cowan
AS contact: M.J. Daly
AS titles: 2–3 ann, 55 ip
Spec: principally language, literature, history
Ms subm: normally only publishes for staff or close associates of the School

391 **Hans Zell Publishers**
An imprint of the K.G. Saur
division of Butterworths,
POB 56, Oxford OX1 3EL;
also at Shropshire House,
2–10 Capper Street,
London WC1E 6JA
(0865) 511428 (editorial only)
Tx: 94012872 ZELL
Fax: (0865) 310183 (Zell)
Chief execs: W. Gordon Graham,
Klaus G. Saur, Shane O'Neill
AS contact: Hans M. Zell
AS titles: 6–10 ann, 35 ip
Ser: 'New Perspectives in African
Literature', 'African Discourse'
(Oxford Centre for African Studies)
'Bibliographical Research in African
Written Literatures', 'Documentary
Research in African Written
Literatures'
Spec: all areas of African/Third World
studies, with an emphasis on refer-
ence sources Ms subm: reference
works annotated, or at least partially
annotated in all areas of African/Third
World studies; also full-length studies
on African literature; monographs in
the African social sciences and the
arts; agriculture and the environment;
mass media and communication
Ms L: for monographs ca.100,000–
120,000w, for reference works at least
200 pp
Edit req: outline/synopsis of scope and
contents must be submitted with
sample chapters/specimen pages and
indication of relationship to existing or
competing works, and proposed
length; special author proposal form
available on request
NA distr: K.G. Saur Inc, 245 West 17th
Street, New York, NY 10011; Tel: (212)
337 7023
Europe distr: K.G. Saur Verlag,
Heilmanstrasse 17, Postfach 71 10 09,
D-8000 München 71, Fed. Rep. of
Germany; Tel: (89) 791040
In UK orders to: Butterworths & Co.
(Publishers) Ltd, Borough Green,
Sevenoaks, Kent TN15 8PH; Tel:
(0732) 884567

United States

392 **ABC-CLIO**
POB 1911, Santa Barbara,
CA 93116–1911
(805) 968 1911, (800) 422 2546
Fax: (805) 685 9685
Found: 1955 ISBN prefix: 87436
Chief exec: Ronald J. Boehm
AS titles: 15 ip
Spec: historical bibliography, area
studies bibliographies UK distr: Clio
Press Ltd, 55 St. Thomas Street,
Oxford OX1 1JG (*see* 367)

393 **Africa World Press, Inc.†**
556 Bellevue Avenue,
POB 1892, Trenton, NJ 08607
(609) 695 3766, (609) 695–3402
Tx: 3794256 AFRIC
ISBN prefix: 0–86543, 870101
Chief exec: Kassahun Checole
Note: also trades as The Red Sea Press,
Inc.

394 **Africana Publishing
Company†**
Holmes & Meier Publishers
Inc. 30 Irving Place,
New York NY 10003
(212) 254 4100 ISBN prefix: 0–8419
Chief exec: Max Holmes

395 **Lilian Barber Press**
POB 232, New York NY 10163
(212) 874 2678
Found: 1980 ISBN prefix: 0–936508
Chief exec and contact: Terence Walz
AS titles: 5 ann, 25 ip
Spec: Africa, general (history);
Northern and Northeast Africa; social
anthropology (all regions) Ms subm:
as above, and also economics, archi-
tecture, politics, women's studies
Ms L: 180,000w
Edit req: inquiry by letter before sub-
mission of ms; perfectly typed ms in
two copies if submission approved;
publisher encourages word processed
submissions
UK distr: Lilian Barber Press, POB 109,
Gravesend, Kent DA11 7QR

396 **Crossroads Press**
  African Studies Association,
  Credit Union Building,
  Emory University,
  Atlanta, GA 30322
(404) 329 6410
Found: n/a ISBN prefix: 0–918456
Chief exec and contact: Edna G. Bay
AS titles: 2–3 ann, 35 ip
Spec: development, bibliographies, medical studies, history, humanities
Ms subm: all areas above
Ms L: not specified
Edit req: ms. must be submitted with review from two scholars, preferably members of the ASA. Author must be prepared to underwrite all necessary revisions, editing, and to prepare the ms camera-ready
Note: this is publishing arm of African Studies Association (*see* **585**)

397 **Garland Publishing Inc**
  136 Madison Avenue,
  New York, NY 10016
(212) 686 7492 Tx: 424588
Fax: (212) 889 9399
Found: 1969 ISBN prefix: 0–8240
Chief exec: Gavin Borden
AS contact: Phyllis Korper
AS titles: 5 ann, 35 ip
Ser: 'Critical Studies in Black Life and Culture'
Spec: literature, the arts, education, women's studies
Ms subm: all areas above
Ms L: 250–400pp
Edit req: prospectus, sample chapters
Europe distr: Garland Publishing, 10 Storey's Gate, London SW1P 3AY; Tel: (01) 493 7642

398 **Greenwood Press Inc**
  88 Post Road West, POB 5007,
  Westport, OT 06881
(203) 226 3571 Tx: 710 457 3586
Fax: (203) 222 1502
Found: 1967 ISBN prefix: 0–313, 0–275 (Praeger)
Chief exec: Robert Hagelstein
AS contact: James T. Sabin

AS titles: 20–25 ann, 500 ip
Ser: 'Contributions in Afro-American and African Studies', 'Bibliographies and Indexes in Afro-American and African Studies', 'African Special Bibliographical Series'
Spec: the spectrum from literary criticism to behavioural sciences, with an emphasis on political and economic affairs and military studies
Ms subm: all areas above on a university level
Ms L: 350pp, or less, d-s
Edit req: prefer to see a prospectus and vita prior to actual ms submissions; the prospectus should indicate scope, organization and length of the project and if or when a completed ms is available
UK & Europe distr: Westport Publications Ltd, 3 Henrietta Street, London WC2E 8LT; Tel: (01) 240 1003

399 **Heinemann Educational Books Inc**
  70 Court Street,
  Portsmouth, NH 03801
(603) 431 7894 Tx: (WUI) 6971447
Fax: (603) 431 7840
Chief exec and contact: John C. Watson
AS titles: 12 ann, 20 ann
Ser: 'Social History of Africa Series', 'Studies in African Literature'
Spec: social history, literature and literary criticism, development studies, women's studies, political science
Ms subm: college level texts, specialist monographs
Edit req: prefer synopses, contents lists, sample chapters in first instance
UK distr: Heinemann International (*see* **373**), James Currey Publishers Ltd (*see* **369**)

Holmes & Meier, see Africana Publishing Co, **394**

400 Howard University Press
2900 Van Ness Street,
Washington, DC 20008
(202) 686 6696
Found: 1972 ISBN prefix: 0–88258
Chief exec: O. Rudolph Aggrey
AS contact: Ruby Essien
AS titles: 11 ip
Spec: African diaspora studies
Ms subm: nutrition, environment, educational policy, women's studies, governmental policy
Ms L: 300–600pp, d-s

401 Humanities Press International Inc
171 First Avenue,
Atlantic Highlands,
NJ 07716–1289
(201) 872 1441 Tx: 752233 HILARIOUS
Fax: (201) 872 0717
ISBN prefix: various imprints
Chief exec: Keith Ashfield
Note: firm is largely distributor for several UK publishers

402 Indiana University Press
Bloomington, Indiana 47405
(812) 335 4773
Found: 1950 ISBN prefix: 0–253
Chief exec and contact: John Gallman
AS titles: 8–10 ann, 70 ip
Ser: 'African Systems of Thought'
Spec: history, politics, anthropology, folklore
Ms subm: scholarly books, upper division texts
Ms L: 75,000w
Edit req: initial enquiry by letter; all mss to be typed, d-s

403 The Edwin Mellen Press†
240 Portage Road,
Lewiston, NY 14092
(716) 754 2788 ISBN prefix: 0–88946
Chief exec: Herbert Richardson

404 Monthly Review Press
122 West 27th Street,
New York NY, 10001
(212) 691 2555

Found: 1951 ISBN prefix: 0–85345
Chief execs: Paul Sweezy, Harry Magdoff
AS contact: Frank Sheed
AS titles: 2 ann, 25 ip
Spec: socialist development, anti-apartheid movement, socialist theory
Ms subm: as above
Ms L: n/a
UK distr: Central Books Third World Publications (*see* **470**), Biblios Distributors

405 Ohio University Press
Scott Quadrangle,
Athens, OH 45701
(614) 593 1155
Found: 1964 ISBN prefix: 0–8214
Chief exec: Duane Schneider
AS contact: Holly Panich
AS titles: 10 ann, 50 ip
Ser: 'Eastern African Series', 'Ohio University Center for International Studies African Series'
Spec: eastern and southern Africa
Ms subm: scholarly manuscripts of interest to university scholars and libraries
Ms L: 250–500 manuscript pages
Edit req: typed, d-s, one side only
UK distr: Academic University Publishers Group Ltd, 1 Gower Street, London WC1E 6HA; Tel: (01) 580 3994

406 Orbis Books†
The Maryknoll Fathers,
Walsh Building,
Maryknoll, NY 10545
(914) 941 7590 ISBN prefix: 0–88344
Chief exec: John Eagleson

Red Sea Press, *see* Africa World Press
393

407 Reference Publications Inc
POB 344, Algonac, MI 48001
(313) 794 5722 Fax: (313) 794 7463
Found: 1975 ISBN prefix: n/a
Chief exec and contact: Keith Irvine
AS titles: 10 ip
Ser: 'Encyclopaedia Africana-Dictionary of African Biography'

Spec: biography, botany, encyclo-
paedias and references works
Ms subm: commissioned only

408 Lynne Rienner Publishers Inc
1800 30th Street, Suite 314,
Boulder, Colorado 80301

(303) 444 6684 Tx: 710 1111401
Fax: (303) 449 7605
Found: 1984 ISBN prefix: 0–931477,
1–55587
Chief exec and contact: Lynne Rienner
As titles: 32 ip
Ser: 'Food in Africa'
Spec: all areas except language, literature and art
Ms subm: tertiary through post-
doctoral work in history, social
sciences (including economics), and
agriculture
Edit req: prefer letter of enquiry (with
cv) including proposed outline or table
of contents, estimated length and
completion date, and intended market

409 Norman Ross Publishing Inc
1995 Broadway,
New York, NY 10023

(212) 873 2100 Tx: 237334 CPC UR
Fax: (212) 873–3796
Found: 1972 (as Clearwater
Publishing) ISBN prefix: n/a
Chief exec and contact: Norman A.
Ross
Spec: clearing house for microfilms
and microfiche worldwide, selling
primarily to libraries in the US and
Canada; represents major publishers
of Africana materials in microform
such as Inter Documentation
Company (IDC), Microform Academic
Publishers, World Microforms etc; a
line of bibliographies in print form on
Africana subjects is being developed
Ms subm: ms in the form of biblio-
graphies and other types of reference
works, and ideas for microform collections, whether the original materials to
be filmed are in the US, Africa, Europe
or elsewhere
Edit req: submissions should be made

(or at least available) in machine-
readable format

410 St. Martin's Press Inc
175 Fifth Avenue,
New York, NY 10010

(212) 674 5151 Tx: 7105810331
SMARTPRESS
Fax: (212) 420 9314
Found: 1952 ISBN prefix: 0–312
Chief exec: Thomas McCormack
AS contact: Kermit Hummel
AS titles: 10–15 ann, 100 ip
Spec: politics, history, economics
Ms subm: upper division
undergraduate/graduate level
Ms L: 80,000–100,000w

411 K.G. Saur/R.R. Bowker Co
245 West 17th Street,
New York NY 10011

(212) 337 7023, (212) 645 9700
Tx: 127703
Fax: (212) 242 6781
Found: 1872 ISBN prefix: 0–8352
(Bowker) 0–905450 (Hans Zell
Publishers)
Chief exec: Ira T. Siegel (Exec: K.G.
Saur/Hans Zell Publishers: Carol
Cooper)
Note: distributor in North America of
the Hans Zell Publishers list, *see* **391**
for full entry

412 Scarecrow Press
52 Liberty Street, POB 4167,
Metuchen, NJ 08840

(201) 548 8600, (1–800) 537 7107
Found: 1950 ISBN prefix: 0–8108
Chief exec: Albert W. Daub
AS contact: Jon Woronoff
AS titles: 8 ann, 60 ip
Ser: 'African Historical Dictionaries'
Spec: reference materials; a few mono-
graphs on librarianship, language,
literature
Ms subm: historical dictionaries or
other reference materials
Ms L: minimum 250 ms pages
Edit req: d-s, typed, one recognised
style to be followed (Chicago, APA,
MLA); if a bibliography, annotations

preferred; appropriate indexes, chronologies, or bibliographies are invited
UK distr: Bailey Bros & Swinfen Ltd, Warner House, Folkestone, Kent CT19 6PH; Tel: (0303) 56501

413 Three Continents Press Inc
1525 Wilson Blvd, Suite 621, Arlington, VA 22209
(202) 332 3885 Tx: 904059 WSH
Found: 1973 ISBN prefix: 0–914478, 0–89410
Chief exec and contact: Donald E. Herdeck
AS titles: 6–8 ann, 80 ip
Ser: 'Critical Perspectives', 'African Literature Association Annuals'
Spec: creative literature (prose, short stories, poetry), literary criticism, some cultural studies, music, architecture, other humanities; books in these areas from the non-Western: world: Africa, the Caribbean/Latin America, the Middle East (Morocco to Iran), Asia and the Pacific Islands
Ms subm: as above, primarily university level but original fiction and poetry also for high-school and below
Ms L: 250–400 manuscript pp i.e. 125–250 page books
Edit req: enquire first, do not send ms unless requested, ms to be as polished as possible; if a translation (from French, Arabic etc) submitted by translator, an introduction is requested by the translator placing the author in literary/cultural context, with some discussion of biographical material and particular work being presented; a brief bibliography and glossary may also be requested; if a critical work, a substantial bibliography, which the author is often requested to compile and index, is essential
UK distr: Forest Books, 20 Forest View, Chingford, London E4 7AY; Tel: (01) 529 0384/8470

414 University of California Press
2120 Berkeley Way, Berkeley, CA 94720
(415) 642 4247 Tx: 6502959492
Fax: (415) 643 7127
Found: 1893 ISBN prefix: 0–520
Chief exec: James H. Clark
AS contacts: William McClung, Alain Henon
AS titles: 10 ann, 100 ip
Ser: 'African Studies Center' series (monographs), 'Marcus Garvey and Universal Negro Improvement Assn. Papers', 'Perspectives on Southern Africa', 'UNESCO General History of Africa'
Ms subm: all areas and levels
UK distr: University of California Press, 15A Epsom Road, Guildford, Surrey GU1 3JT; Tel: (0483) 68364

415 University of Wisconsin Press†
114 North Murray Street, Madison, WI 53715
(608) 262 4928 Tx: 265452
ISBN prefix: 0–299
Chief exec: Allen N. Fitchen

416 University Press of America
4720A Boston Way, Lanham, Maryland 20706
(301) 459 3366 Fax: (301) 459 2118
Found: 1974 ISBN prefix: 0–8191
Chief exec and contact: James Lyons
AS titles: 5 ann, 30 ip
Ser: 'Dalhousie African Studies Series'
Spec: comparative government, language studies
Ms subm: as above, upper-level university
Ms L: 250–300pp
Edit req: send xerox non-returnable copy for review; laser or CRC ms for publication
UK distr: Eurospan Ltd, 3 Henrietta Street, London WC2E 8LU; Tel: (01) 240 0856

417 **The Victoria Corporation†**
222 Forest Avenue,
New Rochelle, NY 10804
(914) 636 6498
Chief exec: Joseph Okpaku

418 **Waveland Press Inc**
POB 400, Prospect Heights,
Ill 60070
(312) 634 0081; (708) 634 0081 (from Nov.89)
Found: 1975 ISBN prefix: 0–917974, 0–88133
Chief exec: Neil J. Rower
AS contact: Thomas J. Curtin
AS titles: 4 ann, 20 ip
Spec: college/university level text-books and supplements
Ms subm: as above
Edit req: submit contents and prospectus initially

419 **Westview Press**
5500 Central Avenue,
Boulder, CO 80301
(303) 444 3541 Tx: 23947
Fax: (303) 449 3356
Found: 1975 ISBN prefix: 0–8133
Chief exec: Frederick A. Praeger
AS contact: Dean Birkenkamp
AS titles: 20 ann
Ser: 'African Modernization and Development', 'Monographs in Development Anthropology'
Spec: history, politics-society, international relations, regional security, development, anthropology
Ms subm: as above
Edit req: full guidelines for authors available on request
UK distr: Jessica Kingsley

AFRICA

This is a highly selective listing of some of the more important, active publishers on the African continent, and who may consider manuscript proposals from scholars in Europe and North America.

For more comprehensive details of African publishers, including research institutions with publishing programmes, consult *The African Book World & Press: a Directory/Répertoire du Livre et de la Presse en Afrique, see **1**.*

Côte d'Ivoire

420 **Les Nouvelles Editions Africaines†**
1 boulevard de Marseille,
BP 3525, 01 Abidjan
32 12 51, 32 16 22 Tx: 22564
ISBN prefix: 27236
Chief exec: K.L. Liguer-Laubhouet

Ghana

421 **Ghana Publishing Corporation†**
Head Office,
Off Barnes Road, POB 4348,
Accra
812921 ISBN prefix: 9964–1
Chief exec: Kwame Nyarko

422 **Ghana Universities Press†**
POB 2419, Accra
225032 ISBN prefix:
Chief exec: A.S.K. Atsu

Kenya

423 **Heinemann Kenya Ltd†**
POB 45314, Nairobi
22144, 28949 ISBN prefix: 9966–46
Chief exec: Henry Chakava
UK and NA distr: African Books Collective, The Jam Factory, 27 Park End Street, Oxford OX1 1HU, England (*see* **448**)

Nigeria

**424 Fourth Dimension
     Publishing Co Ltd**
     Plot 64A City Layout,
     PMB 01164 Enugu,
     Anambra State
(042) 339969, 256765
Tx: 51319 FDPUBS
Found: 1976 ISBN prefix: 978–156
Chief exec and contact: Victor
Nwankwo
AS titles: 30 ann, 15 ip
Ser: 'Nsukka Studies in African
Literature'
Spec: African view points
Ms subm: scholarly works in law,
literature, African history, social
studies, medicine, physical sciences,
technology and children's literature
Ms L: 200–300pp
Edit req: ms must be typed d-s, and
bound
NA & UK distr: African Books Collective, The Jam Factory, 27 Park End
Street, Oxford OX1 1HU, England (*see*
448)

425 Ibadan University Press†
     Publishing House,
     University of Ibadan,
     Ibadan, Oyo State
400550–400614, exts. 1244, 1042/43
ISBN prefix: 978–121
Chief exec: Ayo Bamgbose (Chairman,
Publications Committee)
UK & NA distr: African Books
Collective, The Jam Factory, 27 Park
End Street, Oxford OX1 1HU, England
(*see* **448**)

**426 Obafemi Awolowo
     University Press**
     Obafemi Awolowo
     University, Ile-Ife, Oyo State
(036) 2302909
Found: 1968
Chief exec: Akin Fatokun
AS contact: A. Osadolor
AS titles: 6 ann, 10 ip
Ser: 'Ife History Series'

Spec: African and Third World history
and culture
Ms subm: areas above, tertiary level
Ms L: 200–350 manuscript pp
Edit req: clearly typed, d-s, on quarto
paper, left-hand 7cm margin, submitted in duplicate
UK & NA distr: African Books Collective, The Jam Factory, 27 Park End
Street, Oxford OX1 1HU (*see* **448**)

427 Spectrum Books†
     Sunshine House,
     2nd Commercial Road,
     Oluyole Estate, PMB 5612,
     Ibadan, Oyo State
310058, 311215 Tx: 31588 SPECTA
ISBN prefix: 978 2265
Chief exec: Joop Berkhout
UK distr: Safari Books (Export) Ltd.,
Le Cerisier St. Saviour, Jersey,
Tel: (0534) 32299

428 University of Lagos Press
     PO Box 132,
     University of Lagos Post
     Office, Akoka, Lagos, Nigeria
820311 ext. 409 Tx: 21210
Found: 1978 ISBN prefix: 978–2264
Chief exec: S. Bodunde Bankole
AS contact: Dayo Balogun
AS titles: 45 ip
Spec: Africana, economics, education,
law, business, medicine, language
Ms subm: tertiary level
Edit req: typed on A4, d-s, unbound,
author responsibility to obtain written
permission from copyright owner, if
extensively quotes from a copyrighted
work
UK & NA distr: African Books Collective, The Jam Factory, 27 Park End
Street, Oxford OX1 1HU (*see* **448**)

429 University Press Ltd.†
     Three Crowns Building,
     Jericho, PMB 5095, Ibadan,
     Oyo State
411356, 412056 Tx: 31121
ISBN prefix: 978–154
Chief exec: Michael O. Akinleye

Senegal

430 **Les Nouvelles Editions Africaines†**
10 rue Amadou A. Ndoye,
BP 260, Dakar
211381, 221580 ISBN prefix: 27236
Chief exec: O.P. N' Diaye

South Africa
Note: this listing of South African publishers is confined to the four leading progressive, anti-apartheid publishers who have been in the forefront of oppositional publishing in South Africa.

431 **Ad. Donker (Pty) Ltd**
111 Central Street, Houghton,
Johannesburg 2192
(728) 7121 Fax: (728) 6311
Found: 1975 ISBN prefix: 0–86852
Chief exec and contact: Adriaan Donker
AS titles: 4 ann
Spec: socio political-economic issues
Ms subm: literature, reference, socio-political
Ms L: 50,000w and more
Edit req: A4 typed or word processor-produced ms
UK distr: Premier Book Marketing, 1 Gower Street, London WC2; Tel: (01) 636 6005

432 **David Philip Publisher (Pty) Ltd**
208 Werdmuller Centre,
Newry Street, Claremont 7700
(021) 644136 Tx: 527566 CTCOC PHILIPUB
Fax: (021) 643358
Found: 1971 ISBN prefix: 0–86486
Chief exec: David H. Philip
AS contacts: David Philip, Marie Philip, Russell Martin, Mike Kantey
AS titles: 30 ann, 200 ip
Ser: 'The People of Southern Africa', 'Africasouth Paperbacks', 'South African Archaeological Society Series', 'Mantis Poets', 'Africasouth Playscripts', 'Africasouth Learners Series'
Spec: southern African history, politics, sociology, economics, anthropology, archaeology, theology and natural history; biography, fiction, drama and poetry; educational texts for pre-school, primary, secondary and adult learners; books for the children of Africa Ms subm: all of the above
Edit req: scripts typed or printed out from computer discs and d-s, or neatly hand-written and photocopied; preferably initially one or two page synopses of scripts with contents page and sample chapter
UK distr: Leishman & Taussig, 2B Westgate, Southwell NG25 0JH (*see* **463**)

433 **Ravan Press (Pty) Ltd**
POB 31134, Braamfontein,
Johannesburg 2017
(11) 403 3925/6/7/8/9 Fax: (11) 339 2439
Found: 1972 ISBN prefix: 0–86975
Chief exec and contact: Glenn Moss
AS titles: 10–15 ann, 120 ip
Spec: history, literature and poetry, children's books, theology, politics, sociology, labour studies, economics
Ms subm: as above, at levels ranging from the academic to the popular
UK distr: Third World Publications, 151 Stratford Road, Birmingham B11 1RD (*see* **470**)
NA distr: Ohio University Press, Scott Quadrangle, Athens, OH 45701 (*see* **405**)

434 **Skotaville Publishers†**
307 Hampstead House,
46 Biccard Street,
PO Box 32483,
2017 Braamfontein
3391871/4 Tx: 451149 SKOTAV
ISBN prefix: 0–947009
Chief exec: Mothobi Mutloatse
UK & NA distr: African Books Collective, The Jam Factory, 27 Park End Street, Oxford OX1 1HU, England (*see* **448**)

Zimbabwe

435 Baobab Books. An imprint of Academic Books (Pvt) Ltd
POB 567, Harare

706729/704910 Tx: 22514 ACADEM
Fax: 705121
Found: 1988 ISBN prefix: 0–908311
Chief exec: Hugh Lewin
AS contact: Irene Staunton
AS titles: 6 ann, 4 ip
Spec: tertiary, children's and new fiction from Zimbabwe and region
Ms subm: all areas above
Ms L: 50,000–75,000w
Edit req: d-s, typed, preferably with back-up disc

436 The College Press
POB 3041, Harare

66335 Tx: 3558 COLPRS
ISBN prefix: 086925
Chief exec: B.B. Mugabe
AS contact: M. Bedingfield
AS titles: 20 (excluding fiction) ann, 2–4 ip
Ser: 'New Directions in Education', 'Modern Writers' (mainly fiction but some historical),
Spec: teacher education, historical and popular reference, political/topical issues, African literature
Ms subm: all areas/levels although little tertiary/highly specialised materials i.e. theses
Ms L: maximum 250pp
Edit req: typed, 1½ spacing, author must retain copy, minimum of three months for full assessment
UK distr: Leishman & Taussig, 2B Westgate, Southwell NG25 0JH (*see* **463**)

437 Longman Zimbabwe Publishers (Pvt) Ltd
POB ST 125, Southerton, Harare

62711 Tx: 22566 LONZIM
Found: 1964 ISBN prefix: 0582
Chief exec: Sampson G. Mpofu
AS contacts: Nda Dlodlo, M. Poole
AS titles: 75 ann, 700 ip (total list figures)

Spec: primary and secondary level textbooks; novels, plays, poems, historical works; children's literature
Ms subm: primarily areas above by Zimbabwean authors
Edit req: typewritten ms preferred, accompanied by a synopsis and note on author
UK distr: Leishman & Taussig, 2B Westgate, Southwell NG25 0JH (*see* **463**)

438 Mambo Press
Senga Road, POB 779, Gweru

(154) 4016
Found: 1958 ISBN prefix: 0–86922
Chief exec: Albert B. Plangger
AS contact: Felix Matina
AS titles: 6 ann, 50 ip
Ser: 'Zambeziana', 'Shona Heritage Series', 'Exploring Zimbabwe'
Spec: history, anthropology, development studies, co-operatives, missiology
Ms subm: in areas above
Ms L: 25–30,000w
Edit req: only typed, d-s, ms accepted, typed on one side only, fn on separate pages, reading fee/assessment fee Z$2 per 20 pages of ms
UK & NA distr: African Books Collective, The Jam Factory, 27 Park End Street, Oxford OX1 1HU (*see* **448**)

439 Zimbabwe Publishing House (Pvt) Ltd
POB BW350, Harare

790148/9 Tx: 26035
Found: 1981 ISBN prefix: 0–949932
AS contact: Judy Norton
AS titles: 3 ann, 40 ip
Spec: political history of southern Africa; autobiographies of southern African political personalities
Ms subm: as above, secondary and tertiary levels
Ms L: 150,000w
Edit req: typed ms, d-s; full list of copyright material used with title and publisher of original work; if permission already granted, letter from copyright holders

VI. DEALERS AND DISTRIBUTORS OF AFRICAN STUDIES MATERIALS

This is a 'names & numbers' listing of the principal dealers, booksellers and distributors of African studies material in Europe and in North America. Many of those listed also stock records and cassettes, posters, arts and crafts, prints, etc. The list includes a number of general booksellers and retailers holding sizeable stocks of Africana, either new or antiquarian.

For a fuller annotated listing of dealers – with details of personnel, nature and range of stocks held, services offered, etc. – see 'A Directory of Dealers and Distributors of African Studies Material' in *The African Book World & Press: A Directory/Répertoire du Livre et de la Presse en Afrique*, 4th ed., pp. 289–295 (*see* 1).

EUROPE AND NORTH AMERICA

Canada

440 **Liberation Books Inc.**
2015 Drummond Street,
Montréal, Quebec H3G 1W7
(514) 287 9739

France

441 **L'Harmattan Edition-Diffusion**
16 rue des Ecoles, 75005 Paris
(also at 7 rue de l'Ecole
Polytechnique, 75005 Paris)
(1) 43 26 04 52
The leading bookshop in France with the most extensive stocks of African material, both in French and in English.

442 **Librairie Présence Africaine**
25bis rue des Ecoles,
75005 Paris
(1) 354 15 88 Tx: 200891 AFRISAC
Old-established specialist bookshop in the heart of Paris's Quartier Latin district.

Germany (Federal Republic)

443 **Books on African Studies**
Jerry Bedu-Addo,
Postfach 1224,
6905 Schriesheim
(06203) 62976
The main specialist dealer in Germany, with stocks of some 2,000 items in English and in German.

444 **Neue Horizonte. Fachbuchhandlung für Kulturaustausch**
Brückenstrasse 54,
6000 Frankfurt am Main 70
(069) 62 52 43 Tx: 4170425

Portugal

445 **Livraria Historica e Ultramarina Lda.**
Travessa da Queimada 28–1°,
1200 Lisbon
(1) 36 85 89

United Kingdom

446 Ad Orientem Ltd
2 Cumberland Gardens,
St. Leonards-on-Sea,
East Sussex TN28 0QR
(0424) 427186

447 Africa Book Centre
38 King Street,
Covent Garden,
London WC2E 8JT
(1) 240 6649 Tx: 264828 TWIN (for TWP)
Specialist bookshop on the premises of London's Africa Centre, operated by Third World Publications (*see* **470**)

448 African Books Collective
27 Park End Street,
Oxford, OX1 1HU
(0865) 726686 Tx: 94012872 ZELL G
Fax (0865) 793298
Major new self-help initiative by 19 African publishers, from West, East and Southern Africa, to collectively promote and distribute their books in Europe and North America. *Not* a retail bookshop, but Showroom maintained at ABC's offices in Oxford (visits by appointment only). Extensive range of catalogues and lists issued.

449 The Black Art Gallery & Bookshop
225 Seven Sisters Road,
Finsbury Park,
London N4 2DA
(01) 263 1918
Community organization with a gallery, bookshop, and poetry theatre; specialists in visual Black arts and crafts.

450 B.H. Blackwell's Ltd
50 Broad Street,
Oxford OX1 3EL
(0865) 792792 Tx: 83118
Oxford's famous bookshop. Has a good Africana section stocking some 1,500 titles.

451 The Book Company-Wiltshire
10 East Street, Warminster,
Wiltshire BA12 9BL
(0985) 213565 Tx: 49148

452 Bookmarks
265 Seven Sisters Road,
Finsbury Park,
London N4 2DE
(01) 802 6145
Socialist bookshop in North London; also mail order service.

453 The Book Place
13 Peckham High Street,
London SE15 5EB
(01) 701 1757

454 Books for a Change
52 Charing Cross Road,
London WC2N 0BB
(01) 836 2315
Stocks mostly on politics and development studies.

455 Centreprise Bookshop
136 Kingsland High Street,
London E8 2NS
(01) 254 9632
Community bookshop with a large stock of black fiction and non-fiction.

456 Dillons Bookstore
1 Malet Street,
London WC1E 6EQ
(01) 636 1577 Tx: 27950 (ref.2671)
Approximately 1,800 Africana titles held in stock; also some African news magazines.

457 Grass Roots Books
1 Newton Street, Piccadilly,
Manchester M1 1HW
(061) 236 3112
Manchester's alternative bookshop; specialists in feminist, socialist, black, and Third World books.

458 **Grassroots Storefront**
   71 Golborne Road,
   London W10 5NP
(01) 969 0687
Substantial stocks; also large
children's and women's section.

459 **Harriet Tubman Bookshop**
   27–29 Grove Lane,
   Handsworth,
   Birmingham B21 9ES
(021) 554 8479/5323
About 3,000 titles on black and
African/Caribbean studies and Black
Britain.

460 **Heffers Booksellers**
   20 Trinity Street,
   Cambridge CB2 3NG
(0223) 358351 Tx: 81298
Major bookshop, carrying about 1,200
Africana titles.

461 **Hogarth Representation**
   1 Birchington Court,
   Birchington Road,
   London N8 8HS
(01) 341 6570 Tx: 8951182 GECOMS
Largely library supplier; search service
and Standing-Order/Blanket order
services offered; extensive range of
catalogues and lists issued.

462 **Independent Bookshop**
   69 Surrey Street,
   Sheffield S1 21H
(0742) 758288
Stocks mostly on literature and
politics.

463 **Leishman & Taussig**
   2B Westgate,
   Southwell NG25 0JH
(0636) 813774
Carries some 1,200 titles, much of it
African-published, including material
in African languages; Standing-Order
plans and on-approval service offered.

464 **New Beacon Books**
   76 Stroud Green Road,
   London N4 3EN
(01) 272 4889
Very extensive stocks of ca. 10,000
titles covering fiction and non-fiction
from/about Africa, the Caribbean,
Afro-America and Black Britain. New
Beacon Books are the joint organizers
of the International Book Fair of
Radical Black and Third World Books,
held annually in London, usually in
March each year.

465 **Meridien Books Ltd**
   58 Railton Road, Brixton,
   London SE24 0LF
(01) 737 5473

466 **Arthur Probsthain Oriental**
   Bookseller
   41 Great Russell Street,
   London WC1B 3PH
(01) 636 1096
This firm also maintains a retail shop
on the premises of the School of
Oriental and African Studies,
University of London (*see* **318**)

467 **Raddle Bookshop**
   70 Berners Street,
   Leicester LE2 0AF
(0533) 24875
Some 2,000 titles stocked, with on-
approval service for libraries,
multicultural centres and community
organizations.

468 **Soma Books Ltd**
   Independent Publishing
   Company,
   38 Kennington Lane,
   London SE11 4LS
(01) 735 2101
Stocks especially strong on creative
writing and children's books.

469 **Walter Rodney Bookshop**
   5 Chignell Place, Ealing,
   London W13 0TJ
(01) 579 4920

470 **Third World Publications**
151 Stratford Road,
Birmingham B11 1RD
(021) 773 6572 Tx: 264828 TWIN (for
TWP)
A co-operative distributing books from
and about the Third World; distributor
of some African publishers; also
maintains the Africa Centre Bookshop
in central London (*see* **447**).

United States

471 **African American Book
Center**
7524 South Cottage Grove
Avenue, POB 730,
Chicago IL 60619
(312) 651 0070
Part of the Institute of Positive
Education.

472 **African Imprint Library
Services**
POB 350, West Falmouth,
MA 02574
Primarily library suppliers and blanket
order service, for virtually all printed
materials published anywhere in
Africa.

472a **Afro in Books 'n Things**
5575 NW 7th Avenue,
Miami, FL 33127
(304) 756 6107

473 **Common Concerns**
1347 Connecticut Avenue
NW, Washington DC 20036
(202) 463 6500
Leading bookstore in Washington
with very substantial stocks on Africa/
Third World, and Afro-Americana.
Also carries magazines, arts and
crafts, posters, etc.

474 **Deecee Books**
POB 506, Nyack, NY 10960
(914) 358 3989
Antiquarian only.

475 **Ethnographic Arts
Publications**
1040 Erica Road, Mill Valley,
CA 94941
(415) 383 2998
Mostly books on African art, artifacts,
material culture.

476 **The Family Album, A.B.A.A.**
Road 1, Box 42, Glen Rock,
PA 17327
(717) 235 2134

477 **Howard University
Bookstore**
2801 Georgia Avenue NW
Washington DC 20059
(202) 636 6656

478 **McBlain Books**
POB 5062, Hamden, CT 06518
(203) 281 0400
Scarce and rare books on Sub-Saharan
Africa.

479 **T'Olodumare Bookstore**
2440 Durant Avenue,
Berkeley, CA 94704
(POB 32386, Oakland, CA
94604)
(415) 843 3088
Specialists in African literature; also
albums, videos, prints, etc.

480 **Simon Ottenberg, Bookseller**
POB 15509,
Wedgwood Station,
Seattle, WA 98195
(206) 322 5398
Antiquarian only, especially African
art, history, ethnography, travel.

481 **Red Sea Press Inc**
556 Bellevue Avenue, Trenton
NJ 08618
(609) 695 3402 Tx: 3794257 AFRIC
Wide range of stocks; affiliate
company Africa World Press Inc. (*see*
393)

482 **Revolution Books**
  13 East 16th Street, New York
  NY 10003
(212) 691 3345
Strong on books on Marxism-
Leninism and Black liberation/
Women's oppression and liberation;
also international periodicals.

483 **Smithsonian Institution
  Museum Shops**
  Suite no. 295,
  600 Maryland Avenue,
  Washington DC 20560
(202) 287 3563 Tx: 229735 MUS
Stocks mainly on African art and
culture, including books for young
readers; also records and cassettes of
African music, and jewellery and craft
items.

484 **Terramedia**
  19 Homestead Road,
  Wellesley, MA 02181
(617) 237 6485
Fine and rare books, with emphasis on
early voyages, exploration and natural
history.

485 **University Place Book Shop**
  821 Broadway,
  New York, NY 10003
(212) 254 5998
Old established/specialist bookshop
founded by the late Walter Goldwater.

*Some UK & US distributors and
dealers of non-print materials:*

United Kingdom:

486 **African Video Centre**
  70 St. Mary's Road,
  London E13 9AD
(01) 471 9644
Mail order only.

487 **Concord Video and Film
  Council**
  201 Felixstowe Road, Ipswich,
  Suffolk IP3 9BJ
(0473) 715 754/760 12
The major distributor in the UK of
films and videos about Africa.

488 **Scottish Central Film Library**
  Dowanhill,
  74 Victoria Crescent Road,
  Glasgow G12 9JN
(041) 334 9314

489 **Stern's**
  116 Whitfield Street,
  London W1P 5RW
(01) 387 5550
London's major specialist and stockist
of African music; also Latin American
Salsa, Latin, Antilles and World
traditional music.

United States

490 **Africa Family Films**
  POB 1109, Venice, CA 90291
(213) 392 1020
Media production company
distributing films and videotapes
about Africa.

491 **African Record Centre
  Distributors**
  1194 Nostrand Avenue,
  Brooklyn, NY 11225
(212) 493 4500
Extensive selection of African records,
both traditional and contemporary.
Also manufactures its own records.

492 **Folkways Scholastic Records**
  906 Sylvan Avenue,
  Englewood Cliffs, NJ 07632

493 **Icarus Films Inc**
  200 Park Avenue South,
  Room 1319, New York NY
  1003
(212) 6743375

Media distribution company; exclusive distributor of the 'Africa Film Library'.

494 **Southern Africa Media Center**
California Newsreel
630 Natoma Street,
San Francisco, CA 94110
(415) 621 6196
Non-profit educational organization producing and distributing films on Southern Africa.

495 **University of Illinois Film Center**
University of Illinois at Urbana-Champaign,
1325 South Oak Street,
Urbana, IL 61802
(217) 333 1360
One of the largest rental libraries in the United States, distributing many films and video resources about Africa.

AFRICA

Listed below are a select number of major booksellers and distributors *in* Africa who may be willing to handle mail orders from overseas for locally published material. (In most cases this will require pre-payment).

For a comprehensive and fully annotated listing of some 400 booksellers throughout Africa, consult the appropriate sections in *The African Book World & Press: A Directory/Répertoire du Livre et de la Presse en Afrique* (*see* **1**)

Algeria

496 **Enterprise Nationale du Livre**
3 bd Zirout Youcef, BP 49,
Alger Strasbourg
63 96 43/63 92 67 Tx: 53845

Angola

497 **Instituto Nacional do Livro e do Disco**
Rua Cirilo de Conceição Silva no. 7–3°
CP 1248, Luanda
31544 Tx: 3056

Botswana

498 **Botswana Book Centre**
The Mall, POB 91, Gaborone
352931/2 Tx: 2327

Cameroun

499 **Centre de Diffusion du Livre Camerounais**, BP 611, Douala
42 20 44

500 **Librairie Editions CLE**
BP 1501, Yaoundé
22 35 54/23 27 09 Tx: 8438

Côte d'Ivoire

501 **Librairie de France**
av Chardy, BP 228, Abidjan 01
33 15 18/26 Tx: 2323

502 **Librairie Pociello**
01 BP 1757, Abidjan 01
33 15 65/33 26 93 Tx: 3896

Egypt

503 **Al-Arab Bookshop**
28 Faggalah Street, Cairo
908025

504 **Anglo Egyptian Bookshop**
165 Sharia Mohamed Bey Farid, Cairo
914337

505 **Lehnert and Landrock**
44 Sharif Street, POB 1013, Cairo
755324/747606

Ethiopia

506 **ECA Bookshop and Co-Op Society**
POB 60100, Addis Ababa

Gabon

507 **Librairie le Phenix**
BP 4102, Libreville
74 07 46 Tx: 5324

Ghana

508 **Omari Bookshop**
POB 4221, Accra
776212

509 **University Bookshop**
University of Ghana,
University Square,
POB 1, Legon
75381, ext. 8827

Kenya

510 **Africa Book Services (EA) Ltd**
Quran House,
Mfangano Street,
POB 45245, Nairobi
23641

511 **Text Book Centre Ltd**
Kijabe Street,
POB 47540, Nairobi
330430 Tx: 32027

Liberia

512 **National Book Store**
Carey and Mechlin Street,
POB 590/238,
Monrovia
222096, 223451 Tx: 4552

Madagascar

513 **Librairie Mixte**
37bis, av du 26 Juin 1960,
BP 3204,
Antananarivo 101
251 30

Malawi

514 **Central Bookshop Ltd**
POB 264, Blantyre
635447

Mauritius

515 **Librairie Allot Limitée**
Les Arcades Currimjee,
Curepipe
61253 Tx: 4277

Morocco

516 **SMER Diffusion**
3 rue Ghazza, Rabat
237 25 Tx: 32746

Mozambique

517 **Instituto Nacional do Livro e do Disco**
Avenida 24 de Julho 1921,
CP 4030, Maputo
28257/20839 Tx: 6288

Nigeria

518 **Bendel Library Bookshop**
17 James Watt Road,
PMB 1127,
Benin City, Bendel State
200810

519 **Jos University Bookshop Ltd**
37 Murtala Mohammed Way,
PMB 2084, Jos,
Plateau State
52118/9

520 **Odusote Bookstores Ltd**
     68 Lagos Bye-Pass, POB 244,
     Ibadan, Oyo State
316451 Tx: 31215

521 **University Bookshop
     (Nigeria) Ltd**
     University of Ibadan, Ibadan,
     Oyo State
400550, ext. 1208 Tx: 31433

522 **University of Lagos
     Bookshop**
     University of Lagos, Akoka,
     Yaba, Lagos State
820279

Senegal

523 **Librairie Africa SA**
     58 av Georges Pompidou,
     BP 1240, Dakar
214223

524 **Librairie Sankoré**
     25 av William Ponty,
     BP 7040, Dakar
217814

Sierra Leone

525 **Sierra Leone Diocesan
     Bookshops Ltd**
     Cathedral House,
     1 Gloucester Street,
     POB 104, Freetown
22302

South Africa

526 **Exclusive Books Ltd**
     48 Pretoria Street, POB 7724,
     Johannesburg 2001
4035050 Tx: 425011

527 **Logan's University Bookshop
     Literary Services (Pty) Ltd**
     POB 171199, Congella,
     Durban 4013
253221 Tx: 624583

Swaziland

528 **Africa South Books in
     Swaziland**
     Swazi Plaza, POB A456,
     Mbabane
45561

Tanzania

529 **University of Dar es Salaam
     Bookshop**
     POB 35090, Dar es Salaam
48300/49192, ext. 2388 Tx: 41327

Togo

530 **Nouvelles Editions
     Africaines Librairie**
     239 bd du 13 Janvier,
     BP 4862, Lomé
21 67 61 Tx: 5393

Tunisia

531 **Librairie Al-Manar**
     60 bd Bab Djedid, BP 121,
     Tunis 1015
260 641/243 224 Tx: 14894

Uganda

532 **Uganda Bookshop**
     Colville Street,
     POB 7145, Kampala
43756/8

Zaire Republic

533 **Librairie Universitaire**
     BP 1682, Kinshasa
24786/30652 Tx: 21394

534 **Librairie du Zaire**
     12 av des Aviateurs,
     BP 2100, Kinshasa
26748/69297

Zambia

535 **University Bookshop**
University of Zambia,
POB 32379, Lusaka
252576/213221, ext. 1242 Tx: 44370

Zimbabwe

536 **Alpha Books (Pvt) Ltd**
Paget House,
87 Union Avenue,
POB 1056, Harare
722553/790160

537 **Grassroots Books (Pvt) Ltd**
POB A267, Avondale, Harare
792551

538 **Kingstons Ltd**
POB 374, Harare
702051 Tx: 4431

539 **Mambo Press Bookshop**
Old Mutual House,
Speke Avenue,
POB 66002, Harare
705899

VII. ORGANIZATIONS

The listing that follows is a 'names & numbers' directory of the main African regional and international organizations together with the names of their current executive officers. Full information about their activities, organizational structure, history, officers, finance, membership, publications, etc. can be found in several sources, notably in the annual *Africa South of the Sahara* (*see* **45**), the *New African Yearbook* (*see* **46**), in *African International Organization Directory* (*see* **4**) or Richard Fredland's forthcoming *A Guide to African International Organizations* (*see* **14**).

1. The major regional African organizations

540 **African Development Bank** (ADB)
BP 1387, Abidjan 01,
Côte d'Ivoire
32 07 11 Tx: 23717
Exec Pres: Babacar N'Diaye (Senegal)
Exec Sec: Kofi Dei-Anang (Ghana)

541 **Arab Bank for Economic Development in Africa/ Banque Arabe pour le Développement Économique en Afrique** (BADEA)
Sayed Abdel Rahman
El-Mahdi Avenue,
POB 2640, Khartoum, Sudan
73646/73709/70498 Tx: 22248/22739
Chairman: Ahmad Abdallah Al-Akeil (Saudi Arabia)
Dir-Gen: Ahmad Al-Harti Al-Ouardi (Morocco)

542 **Communauté Économique de l'Afrique de l'Ouest/West African Economic Community** (CEAO)
rue Agostino Neto, BP 643,
Ouagadougou, Burkina Faso
33 22 32 Tx: 5212
Sec-Gen: Mamadou Haidara (Mali)

543 **Conseil de l'Entente/Entente Council**
Fonds d'Entraide et de Garantie des Emprunts,
BP 3734, Abidjan 01,
Côte d'Ivoire
33 28 35 Tx: 23558
Chairman Management Committee: Raphael Posset (Benin)
Admin Sec: Paul Kaya

544 **Economic Community of West African States** (ECOWAS)
6 King George V Road,
PMB 12745,
Lagos, Nigeria
636841 Tx: 22633
Pres of Council: Yao Grunitsky (Togo)
Sec-Gen: Momodu Munu (Sierra Leone)

545 **Economic Commission for Africa** (ECA)
Africa Hall, POB 3001,
Addis Ababa, Ethiopia
447200 Tx: 21029
Exec Sec: Adebayo Adedeji (Nigeria)

546 **Organization of African Unity** (OAU)
POB 3243, Addis Ababa,
Ethiopia
157700 Tx: 21046
Chairman: Pres Muhammad Hosni Mubarak (Egypt)
Sec Gen: Salim Ahmed Salim (Tanzania)

547 Southern African Development Co-Ordination Conference (SADCC)
Private Bag 0095, Gaborone, Botswana
51863 Tx: 2555
Exec Sec: Simbarashe Makoni (Zimbabwe)

2. Some other important regional and international organizations and institutes

Note: for guides to *teaching* institutions, or centres or institutes of African Studies, *see* entries **47** to **54**, and, in particular the *International Guide to African Studies Research/Etudes Africaines. Guide International de Recherches (see 51)*

548 The Africa Centre
38 King Street, London WC2E 8JT
(01) 836 1973
Dir: Nigel Watt

549 African Association for Literacy and Adult Education (AALAE)
Finance House, Tom Mboya Street, POB 50768, Nairobi, Kenya
22391/331512 Tx: 23240
Sec-Gen: Paul Wangoola

550 African Centre for Applied Research and Training in Development (ACARTSOD)
Africa Centre, Wahda Quarter, Zawia Road, POB 80606, Tripoli, Libya
833640 Tx: 20803
Exec Dir: Duri Mohamed

551 African Medical and Research Foundation (AMREF)
Wilson Airport, POB 30125, Nairobi, Kenya
501301 Tx: 23254
Dir Gen: C.H. Wood
(also at 833 United Nations Plaza, New York NY 10017;
(212) 949 6421; and at 11–12 Dover Street, London W1X 3PA)

552 African Regional Centre for Technology
Ave Cheikh Anta Diop, BP 2435, Dakar, Senegal
22 77 11 Tx: 3282
Dir: Babatunde Thomas (Nigeria)

553 African Training and Research Centre for Women (ATRCW)
United Nations Economic Commission for Africa, POB 3001, Addis Ababa, Ethiopia
447200, ext. 301 Tx: 21029
Dir: Mary Tadesse

554 African Wildlife Foundation
1717 Massachussetts Avenue NW, Washington, DC 20026, USA
(202) 265 8394
Exec Pres: Robinson MacIlvaine
(also at POB 48117, Nairobi, Kenya)

555 Afro-Asian Peoples Solidarity Organization/ Organisation de la Solidarité des Peuples Afro-Asiatiques (AAPSO)
89 Abdel Aziz Al Saoud Manial, Cairo, Egypt
845495/845014 Tx: 92627
Sec-Gen: Nouri Abdul Razzak

556 All Africa Conference on Churches/ Conference des Eglises de Toute l'Afrique (AACC)
Waiyaki Way, Westlands, POB 14205, Nairobi, Kenya
62601/4 Tx: 22175

Sec-Gen: Rev Jose Belo Chipenda
(also at BP 2268, Lomé, Togo)

557 **Association of African
Universities/ Association des
Universités Africaines** (AAU)
POB 5744, Accra North,
Ghana
65461, ext. 605–615 Tx: 2284
Pres: Donald E.U. Ekong (Nigeria)
Sec-Gen: L. Makany (Congo)

558 **Association of African
Women for Research and
Development** (AAWORD)
BP 3304, Dakar, Senegal
23 02 11 Tx: 3339
Dir: Patricia McFadden

559 **Centre Africain de Formation
et de Recherches
Administratives pour le
Développement/African
Training and Research Centre
in Administration for
Development** (CAFRAD)
avenue Mohamed V, BP 310,
Tanger, Morocco
36430 Tx: 33664
Pres: Abderrahim Benabdeljalal
Dir Gen: Tshianda Kasadi Basuebabu

560 **Centre for Black and African
Arts and Civilization**
PMB 12794, National Theatre,
Lagos, Nigeria
831734/802060
Dir: Zaccheus Simday Ali

561 **Centre International des
Civilisations Bantu** (CICIBA)
BP 770, Libreville, Gabon
72 33 14/72 32 22 Tx: 5680
Dir: Theophile Obenga
(*see* also **221**)

562 **Centre Régional de
Promotion du Livre en
Afrique/Regional Book
Promotion Centre for Africa**
(CREPLA)
BP 1646, Yaoundé, Cameroun
22 47 82/22 29 36
Dir: William Moutchia

563 **Conseil pour le
Développement de la
Recherche Économique et
Sociale en Afrique/Council
for the Development of
Economic and Social
Research in Africa**
(CODESRIA)
rue Leon G. Damas angle F
Fann Résidence,
BP 3304, Dakar, Senegal
23 02 11 Tx: 3339
Chairman: Claude Ake
Exec Sec: Thankika Mkandawire
(*see* also **227**)

564 **Encyclopaedia Africana
Secretariat**
PO Box 2797, Accra North,
Ghana
777651, ext. 30, 776939
Ag Dir: E.T. Ashong

European Council on African Studies
see **594**

565 **Institut Africain pour le
Développement Économique
et Social/African Institute for
Economic and Social
Development** (INADES)
08 BP 8, Abidjan 08,
Côte d'Ivoire
44 15 94
Dir: Alain Renard

566 **Institut Culturel Africain/
African Cultural Institute**
(ICA)
13 ave du Président Bourgiba,
BP 01, Dakar, Senegal
21 78 82/21 72 74 Tx: 3334
Dir-Gen: Basile T. Kossou

567 **Institute Fondamental
d'Afrique Noire – Cheikh
Anta Diop** (IFAN)
Campus Universitaire,
Corniche Ouest,
BP 206, Dakar, Senegal
22 00 90/21 16 52 Tx: 262 UNIDAK
Dir: Abdoulaye Bara Diop

568 **International African
Institute/ Institut Africain
International** (IAI)
Lionel Robbins Building,
10 Portugal Street,
London WC2A 2HD, England
(01) 831 3068 Tx: 24655 BLEPES
Chairman: William Shack
Hon Dir: Peter Lloyd
Sec: Jacqueline Hunt
(*see* also **148**)

569 **International Centre for
Insect Physiology and
Ecology** (ICIPE)
POB 30772, Nairobi, Kenya
43235 Tx: 22053
Dir: Thomas R. Odhiambo

570 **International Congress of
African Studies** (ICAS)
c/o Prof. Yusuf Fadhil Hassan,
Vice-Chancellor, University of
Khartoum, POB 321,
Khartoum, Sudan
75100
Sec-Gen: Sayyid H. Hurreiz

571 **International Council for
Research in Agroforestry**
(ICRAF)
Gigiru, Limiru Road,
POB 30677, Nairobi, Kenya

521450 Tx: 22048
Dir: B. Lundgren

572 **International Institute of
Tropical Agriculture** (IITA)
Oyo Road, PMB 5320, Ibadan,
Oyo State, Nigeria
400300 Tx: 31417
Dir Gen: Laurence D. Stifel

573 **International Laboratory for
Research on Animal Diseases**
(ILRAD)
POB 30709, Nairobi, Kenya
592311 Tx: 22040 ILRAD
Dir: A.R. Gray

574 **International Livestock
Centre for Africa** (ILCA)
POB 5689, Addis Ababa,
Ethiopia
183215 Tx: 21207
Dir Gen: John Walsh

575 **Nigerian Institute of
International Affairs** (NIIA)
11 Kofo Abayomi Road,
Victoria Island,
POB 1727, Lagos, Nigeria
615606/10 Tx: 22638
Dir: G.O. Olusanya

576 **Pan-African Institute for
Development/
Institut Panafricain pour le
Développement** (PAID)
BP 4078, Douala, Cameroun
42 37 70/42 30 68 Tx: 6048
Sec-Gen: A.C. Mondjanagni

577 **Pan African News Agency/
Agence de Presse
Panafricaine** (PANA)
BP 4056, Dakar, Senegal
23 08 98/22 61 20 Tx: 3261/3307

578 **Pan-African Women's Organization/ Organisation Panafricaine des Femmes** (PAWO)
23 bd Colonel Amirouche, Alger, Algeria

579 **Society of African Culture/ Société Africaine de Culture**
18 rue des Ecoles, 75005 Paris, France
43 54 57 69 Tx: 200891 Sec-Gen: Yandé Christiane Diop
(also at 19 rue Vincens, Dakar, Senegal)
(*see* also **129**)

580 **Unesco Regional Office for Education in Africa/ Bureau Régional de l'Unesco pour l'Education en Afrique** (BREDA)
BP 3311, Ave Roume, 12, Dakar, Senegal
22 50 82/22 46 14 Tx: 410
Dir: Baba Akhib Haidara

581 **Unesco Regional Office for Science and Technology in Africa/ Bureau Régional de l'Unesco pour la Science et la Technologie en Afrique** (ROSTA)
POB 30592, Nairobi, Kenya
333930/520767 Tx: 22275
Dir: M.S. Ntamila

582 **United Nations African Institute for Economic Development and Planning/ Institut Africain de Développement Économique et Planification**
rue 18 Juin, BP 3186, Dakar, Senegal
22 49 26/22 10/20 Tx: 579
Dir: Essam Montasser

583 **United Nations Institute for Namibia**
POB 33811, Lusaka, Zambia
216468/216649 Tx: 41960
Dir: Hage G. Geingob

VIII. AFRICAN STUDIES ASSOCIATIONS AND SOCIETIES

Information for this section was collected by means of a circular mailing. A † dagger symbol indicates an association which did not respond to our request for details of their activities, membership benefits, etc., and no further information is available.

Abbreviations used:

Exec sec – Executive Secretary/Director
Found – Year founded
Obj – Objectives
Pres – President
Publs – Publications issued

584 **African Literature Association** (ALA)
c/o George Joseph, Department of Modern Languages, Hobart and William Smith Colleges, Geneva, NY 14456, USA
(315) 789 5500
Obj: an independent non-profit professional society open to scholars, teachers and writers from every country. It exists primarily to facilitate the attempts of a world-wide audience to appreciate the efforts of African writers and artists.
Pres: Anne Adams
Sec: Georg Joseph
Membership dues: Institutional – $40, Sponsor – $50, Regular – $30, Student/Retired/Unemployed – $10
Membership privileges: n/a [Members receive *ALA Bulletin*; members may vote to elect officers of the Association]
Publs: *ALA Bulletin* (*see* **113**)

585 **African Studies Association** (ASA)
Emory University, Credit Union Building, Atlanta, Georgia 30322, USA
(404) 329 6410 Found: 1957
Obj: Welcomes to membership all persons with scholarly and professional interests in Africa. Founded in 1957 as a non-profit membership corporation, the African Studies Association provides useful services to the Africanist community, hosts a national convention of African studies annually, and publishes and distributes scholarly Africanist materials.
Pres: Simon Ottenberg (1989)
Exec sec: Edna G. Bay (1988–1992)
Membership dues: Individual – $35–$45 depending on annual income; $15 students, retired or unemployed; Institutional – $75 in US and overseas, $55 for African institutions
Membership privileges: members receive *ASA News*, the *African Studies Review*, and *Issue: A Journal of Opinion*; members may vote to elect officers of the Association, serve on ASA committees, organize panels at annual meetings, and receive special discounts on Crossroads Press publications.
Meetings: meeting held annually in the autumn, held in different regions of the US each year, and providing an occasion for panels, plenary sessions and discussion groups, exhibits and films.
Awards: Herskovits Award (*see* **664**), Distinguished Africanist Award (*see* **660**), Conover-Porter Award (*see* **659**), and The Robinson Award (*see* **667**)
Publs: *ASA News* (*see* **206**), *African Studies Review* (*see* **203**), *Issue: A Journal of Opinion* (*see* **211**); also occasional

publications, monographs, reference works, etc. published under the imprint Crossroads Press (*see* **396**).

586 African Studies Association of Australia and the Pacifict
c/o School of Social Sciences,
Deaking University,
Geelong, Victoria 3217,
Australia

587 African Studies Association of the UK (ASAUK)
18 Northumberland Avenue,
London WC2N 5BJ
(01) 930 1662 Found: n/a
Obj: n/a
Pres: A.H.M. Kirk-Greene
Hon Sec: Nici Nelson
Membership dues: £18 (Ordinary), £9 (Student), £50 (Corporate)
Membership privileges: members receive the journal *African Affairs*, and may participate (at privileged rates) in conferences, seminars, and symposia. Combined membership with the Royal African Society (*see* **596**) is possible at supplementary charge of £3.
Meetings: the ASAUK organises regular conferences and symposia which explore the frontiers of teaching and research in Africa; annual general meeting held Publs: *African Affairs* (jointly with Royal African Society, *see* **156**); *Directory of African Studies* (forthcoming)

588 Arbeitskreis der deutschen Afrika-Forschungs-und Dokumentationsstellen (ADAF)
c/o Institute für Afrika-Kunde, Neuer Jungfernstieg 21,
2000 Hamburg 36,
Federal Republic of Germany
(040) 3562523 Found: 1967
Obj: loose network of 33 member institutions in the Federal Republic of Germany with Africa-related research

and/or documentation activities and interests. Its main objective is to facilitate the exchange of information about on-going activities in the field of African studies and Africanist documentation.
Exec offs: Axel Halbach (Munich), Rolf Hofmeier (Hamburg), Herbert Weiland (Freiburg)
Membership dues: no dues
Publs: *ADAF-Rundbrief* (Newsletter), issued twice yearly by IFO-Institut‹für Wirtschaftsforschung, Abteilung Entwicklungsländer, Poschingerstrasse 5, 8000 München 86, Fed. Rep. of Germany

589 Archives and Libraries Committee of the African Studies Association
c/o John Bruce Howell,
International Studies Bibliographer,
University of Iowa Libraries,
Iowa City, IA 52242, USA
(319) 335 5885 Found: 1957
Obj: this is not an association, but a Standing Committee of the African Studies Association (*see* **585**). It has a broadly based membership including those whose full-time profession is Africana librarianship, as well as librarians in other areas but with interests in African studies collection development. There are two subcommittees: the Subcommittee on Bibliography provides a clearinghouse for information and support of bibliographic projects; the Subcommittee on Cataloging and Classification plays an important role in articulating the concerns of Africana librarians regarding the manner in which Africana materials are catalogued and classified.
Chairperson: John Bruce Howell (Iowa); Bibliography Subcommittee chairperson: Gregory A. Finnegan (Dartmouth College); Cataloging Subcommittee chairperson: Roy Ortopan (University of California-Berkeley)

Meetings: open semi-annual meetings are held in Spring and in Fall, the latter always coinciding with the annual meeting of the African Studies Association
Awards: Conover-Porter Award (*see* **659**)
Publs: *Africana Libraries Newsletter* (*see* **205**)

590 **Asociación Española de Africanistas†**
c/o Colegio Mayor Universitario N.S. de Africa,
c/Obispo Trejo 1,
Ciudad Universitaria,
28040, Madrid, Spain

591 **Association Belge des Africanistes†**
Musée Royal de l'Afrique Centrale
Steenweg op Leuven 13,
1980 Tervuren, Belgium

592 **Association of African Studies in the Netherlands**
c/o Afrika-Studiecentrum,
Stationsplein 12,
PO Box 9507,
2312 AK Leiden, Netherlands
(071) 273372/273373 Found: 1979
Obj: aims to promote African studies in the Netherlands; one of its main responsibilities is to play an intermediary role between its members and the government, particularly in respect of annual allocation of government research grants to Africanists in the Netherlands.
Pres: Rogier Bedaux
Sec: Piet Konings
Membership dues: no dues
Publs: *Newsletter on African Studies in the Netherlands* (irregular, published jointly with the African Studies Centre, Leiden (*see* also **283**)

593 **Canadian Association of African Studies†**
c/o Donald Savage, CAAS Treasurer, 308–294 Albert Street,
Ottawa, Ontario K1 P 6E6, Canada
(613) 237 6885

594 **Conseil Européen des Etudes Africaines** (CEEA)/
European Council on African Studies (ECAS)
c/o M.J.-P. Blanck, Centre de Géographie Appliquée-CEREG,
3 rue de l'Argonne,
F-67083 Strasbourg Cedex, France
(88) 35 82 47 Tx: 870 260 ULP
Found: 1985
Pres: A. Coupez
Exec sec: J.-P. Blanck
Membership dues: 1,5 ECU per national committee member
Obj: international non-governmental organization formed by the community of Africanists in Europe, and intended to serve all those who, in one way or another, are engaged in the study of African civilizations, cultures and societies. Membership is largely constituted of national committees of African studies of each European country, but is also open to Africanist scholars residing in a European country with no national committee or association.
Meetings: General Assembly meets every four years; the Standing Committee/Executive meets once or twice a year; the CEEA also organizes and encourages conferences and symposia both in Europe and in Africa.
Publs: *Bulletin du CEEA/ECAS Newsletter* (*see* **144**), *La Documentation Africaniste en Europe* (Actes du colloque: Paris 22–23 mars 1986) (*see* **87**)

595 **Danike Afrika Selskab†**
Ellehaven 25, 2950 Vedboek,
Denmark

596 **The Royal African Society**
18 Northumberland Avenue,
London WC2N 5BJ
(01) 930 1662 Found: 1901
Obj: to spread information about the
peoples and countries of Africa; to
strengthen and encourage an interest
in African affairs; to foster the development of relationships between
the UK and the countries of Africa and
to contribute to the creation of an
informed public opinion regarding
Africa; to further the study of Africa in
British universities, polytechnics, colleges, and schools.
Pres: J.P.G. Wathen
Sec: Mrs. M.L. Allan
Membership dues: £18 (Full), £9
(Student), £50 (Corporate)
Membership privileges: members
receive the journal *African Affairs* and
may attend speakers' meetings held
during the year; members are able to
use the library of the Commonwealth
Trust (formerly Royal Commonwealth
Society). The Society has close links
with the African Studies Association
of the UK (*see* **587**) and members may
participate in ASAUK conferences and
symposia.
Meetings: the Society holds discussion
meetings with distinguished politi-
cians, diplomats, aid officials,
academics and journalists; normally
about 25 meetings are held each year.
Publs: *African Affairs* (*see* **156**)

597 **La Société des Africanistes†**
c/o Musée de l'Homme,
Place du Trocadéro
75016 Paris, France

598 **Société Suisse d'Etudes
Africaines/
Schweizerische Afrika-
Gesellschaft**
3000 Bern, Switzerland

Found: 1974
Obj: promotion and coordination of
African studies research, particularly
in inter-disciplinary areas; organiz-
ation of meetings and seminars; col-
laboration with other academic institu-
tions in Switzerland and abroad;
collaboration with public and private
donor agencies; provision of docu-
mentation and information about
Africa.
Pres: Charlotte von Graffenried
Sec: Lukas Sosoe
Membership dues: Fr.50 (ordinary);
Fr.25 (Students) Fr.100 (Corporate)
Membership privileges: members
receive quarterly journal *Genève-
Afrique*, and also receive free copies of
occasional publications and the annual
Schweizer Afrika-Bibliographie
Meetings: regular meetings and study-
group get-togethers; annual general
meeting held
Publs: *Schweizer Afrika-Bibliographie;
Genève Afrique* (*see* **147**), plus occasional
publications

599 **Standing Conference on
Library Materials on Africa**
(SCOLMA)
c/o The Secretary, 27–28
Russell Square,
London WC1B 5DS
(01) 580 5876 Found: 1962
Obj: to provide a forum for librarians
and others concerned with the provision of materials for African studies
in libraries in the United Kingdom.
Membership is open to institutions
and libraries concerned with library
materials on Africa. Under the Area
Specialisation Scheme participating
libraries agree to specialise in the
acquisition of materials from particular
areas of Africa and to act as information centres.
Chairman: Peter B. Freshwater
Sec: Patricia Larby
Membership dues: £12
Membership privileges: members
receive a copy of *African Research and
Documentation*; institutional members

also receive discounts on publications
Meetings: regular meetings and
seminars held; three international
conferences have been held and the
proceedings published. (see **88, 90, 91**)
Publs: *African Research and Documentation* (*see* **166**); *SCOLMA Directory of
Libraries and Special Collections on Africa*
(*see* **83**), plus several other publications
and reference resources

600 **Vereinigung von
   Afrikanisten in Deutschland†**
   c/o Klaus von Freyhold,
   Uebersee Museum,
   Bahnhofsplatz 13,
   2800 Bremen 1,
   Federal Republic of Germany

IX. FOUNDATIONS, DONOR AGENCIES, NETWORK ORGANIZATIONS IN AFRICAN STUDIES (or active *in* Africa)

This section identifies the major foundations, donor agencies or network organizations either supporting research in African studies and/or active *in* Africa. Information was collected by means of a questionnaire mailing: 58 agencies were approached, and a total of 42 responded. The organizations which did not respond are included as a name and address/telephone listing only, and are marked with a † dagger symbol. In addition to those who did not respond a number of organizations approached declined to supply information or specifically asked us *not* to list them. These included major international donor agencies in Denmark (DANIDA) and in the Netherlands (NOVIB), as well as a number of development agencies elsewhere. They apparently feared that inclusion of their name and address, etc. would generate a large number of requests from scholars and students which they would have to reject, and which would lead to unnecessary administrative work for them.

For those who completed and returned questionnaires, the following information is provided: full name and address, telephone, telex, fax numbers, (and electronic mail address for some); year founded; a brief description of the organization's principal objectives and activities; source of finance/funding; name(s) of president of governing board or board of trustees; names of executive officer(s) and/or executive director; names of programme officer(s) in charge of Africa-related projects; details of activities, programmes, etc. in the African studies field, or activities *in* Africa; grants and awards made in the African studies field (including research grants, training support, workshop/conference support, publication support, etc.), *or* support of activities or relief operations, etc. *in* Africa; guidelines for applications for research support (where applicable) and/or procedures for submitting proposals; major publications issued.

Abbreviations used:

Act in AS	– Activities, programmes, etc. in the African studies field, or activities, project, or relief opertions support *in* Africa
Applic proc	– Application procedures [guidelines for submitting proposals]
ChGB	– Chairperson of Governing Board, or Board of Trustees
Exec Dir	– Executive Director
Exec off	– Executive officer(s) [with position where given]
Fin	– Finance/funded by
G/Aw	– grants and awards made

Gen Man   – General Manager
Gen Sec/Exec Sec – General/Executive Secretary
Obj   – principal objectives and activities
Pres   – President [of Governing Board or Board of Trustees]
Prog off   – Programme officer(s) in charge of Africa/African studies [or other areas]
Publs   – Publications
Reg dir   – Regional Director
Reg off   – Regional office(s) in Africa [with full addresses if provided]
VP   – Vice President

Australia

601 **Australian Council for Overseas Aid†**

POB 1562, Canberra ACT 2601
(062) 474 822 Tx: 61643

Austria

602 **Afro-Asiatisches Institut in Wien**

Türkenstrasse 3,
A-1090 Vienna
(0222) 344625 Found: 1959
Obj: support to Afro-Asian students; cultural and other exchange between Austria and African and Asian countries; economic and social research; lectures; seminars; art-exhibitions.
Fin: Austrian Ministry of Foreign Affairs, Austrian private Church organizations
Pres: Bishop Florian Kuntner
Exec off: Gerhard Bittner (Gen Sec)
Act in AS: investigations into and research on educational systems (mainly Universities) in Africa and Asia; development of training and educational programmes for overseas students in Austria.
G/Aw: grants to carry out field work at home for thesis (only for AAI scholars); lectures, seminars, art exhibitions and room-facilities in the building of AAI
Applic proc: application for scholarship only after arrival

Publs: *Treffpunkt-Studienförderung* (annually since 1988), *AAI Scholarships and Grants*

603 **Österreichische Forschungsstiftung für Entwicklungshilfe**

Türkenstrasse 3,
A-1090 Vienna
(0222) 340151 Found: 1967
Obj: documentation and information on development aid and developing countries with special emphasis on Austrian development aid and development policy.
Fin: Austrian Ministry of Foreign Affairs, Austrian Church organizations
Pres: Klaus Zapotoczky Exec off: Gerhard Bittner (Gen Sec), Gerda Kramer (head of documentation) Prog off: Mag Richard Langthaler
Act in AS: documentation and information on countries and regions, and special items on African development.
Publs: *Ausgewählte neue Literatur zur Entwicklungspolitik Bibliographie* (twice yearly), *Österreichische Entwicklungspolitik* (annually)

604 **Vienna Institute for Development and Cooperation**

Weyrgasse 5, A-1030 Vienna
(0222) 7133594 Tx: 613222343 VIDC

Obj: research, organization of international conferences
Fin: Federal Ministry for Foreign Affairs
Pres: Bruno Kreisky Exec off: Peter Jankowitsch MP Prog off: Erich Andrlik (Director of Vienna Institute)
Publs: *The World Ten Years after the 'Brandt Report', North-South Relations and UNCTAD, Decolonisation and After – The Future of the Third World*

Canada

605 **Canadian International Development Agency/Agence Canadienne de Développement International** (CIDA)
200 Promenade du Portage, Hull, Quebec K1A OG4
(819) 997 6100
Obj: the objective of CIDA's Non-Governmental Organizations Division is to support Canadian voluntary organizations in their development activities by (1) encouraging and facilitating the people-to-people participation of Canadians in international development through matching contributions to those projects and programmes of autonomous Canadian NGOs which are compatible with Canadian foreign and development policies; (2) supporting the efforts of people in developing countries, particularly the less advantaged, to meet their basic need and improve their quality of life through a development process which is sustainable and utilizes their own resources to the full in the context of their own values.
Fin: Canadian government
Exec: F.L.A. Ward (Dir General, Non-Governmental Organizations Division, Special Programs Branch)
G/Aw: The NGO division of CIDA does not provide grants or awards *per se* for African studies; rather it supports the development projects of Canadian NGOs in Africa and elsewhere.
Applic proc: 'Guide for preparing project submissions for NMGO Division' contained in *CIDA-NGO Division: Introduction and Guide* available from the Agency
Note: questionnaire not returned, information compiled from descriptive literature supplied.

606 **Canadian Organization for Development through Education** (CODE)
321 Chapel Street, Ottawa, Ontario K1N 7Z2
(613) 232 3569 Tx: 053 4880
Fax: (232) 7435
Found: 1959
Obj: to support and enhance formal and non-formal educational efforts in selected countries in Africa, the Caribbean and the Pacific.
Fin: Canadian public, Canadian International Development Agency, International donors
Pres: Madeline Hardy Exec off: Robert Dyck, Madeline Hardy, Tom Barnett, Alfred Best, *et al*
Prog off: Jamieson Campbell, David Foxall, Rosamaria Durand (Director, Book Program)
Act in AS: CODE has regional offices in West Africa, East Africa, and Southern Africa. CODE's assistance consists of shipments of books, educational equipment, paper and grants.
Applic proc: CODE provides assistance to eligible institutions in its program regions. Scholarships and grants to individuals are not provided.

607 **International Development Research Centre/ Centre de Recherches pour le Développement International** (IDRC)
CP 8500, Ottawa,
Ontario K1G 3H9
(613) 236 6163 Tx: 053 3753
Fax: (613) 7230
EM: IDRC-OTTA 2020: IDR001
Found: 1970
Obj: to promote scientific and technical research projects conceived and carried out by Third World researchers. The fields of investigation to which IDRC gives its financial and professional support include agriculture, health, social sciences, information sciences, earth and engineering sciences, training, and implementation of research results.
Fin: Parliament of Canada
ChGB: Janet M. Wardlaw Exec off: Ivan L. Head (Pres), Raymond J. Audet (VP Resources) James Mullin (VP Program)
Prog off: IDRC's internal structure is organized according to disciplines and not countries
Act in AS: very extensive, concentrating in five sectors: agriculture, food and nutrition sciences, health sciences, information sciences, social sciences, and communications
Applic proc: (1) pre-proposal letter should be prepared and forwarded to the closest Regional Office; (2) pre-proposal letter should include information of the following nature: community research priorities, objectives of the research, scientific methodology, resources available and required, expected results, rough budget, and timetable.
Reg off: IDRC Regional Office for Eastern and Southern Africa, POB 62084, Nairobi, Kenya (Reg dir: Daniel Adzei Bekoe); IDRC Regional Office for the Middle East and North Africa, POB 14, Orman, Giza, Cairo, Egypt (Reg dir: Kawzy Kishk); IDRC Regional Office for West and Central Africa, BP 11007, CD Annexe, Dakar, Senegal (Reg dir: Pierre Sané)
Publs: extensive, Publications catalogue available on request

Denmark

608 **Danish International Development Authority** (DANIDA)
Ministry of Foreign Affairs, Department of International Development Cooperation,
2 Asiatisk Plads,
DK-1448 Copenhagen K
(01) 92 00 00 Tx: 31292 ETR
Fax: (01) 54 05 33
[*Note:* DANIDA did not complete our questionnaire, but wrote to say that 'DANIDA is only financing science projects or networks through international research organizations or through our bilateral programmes with developing countries.']

France

609 **Agence de Coopération Culturelle et Technique** (ACCT) †
13 quai André Citroën,
75015 Paris
(1) 45 75 62 41 Tx: 2011916

610 **Alliance Française†**
101 boulevard Raspail,
7527 Paris Cedex 06

611 **United Nations Educational, Scientific, and Cultural Organization** (UNESCO)†
7 Place de Fontenoy, BP 3.07,
75700 Paris
(1) 568 10 00 Tx: 204461

Germany (Federal Republic)

612 Deutsche Welthungerhilfe
Adenauerallee 134, 53 Bonn 1
(0228) 22880
Obj: aims at protecting the interests of the rural population, in particular in the Third World; to improve the food situation and the rural living conditions in the Third World; support for self-aid programmes; emergency aid; compilation and distribution of information.
Fin: private donations, government subsidies, subsidies from the EEC
ChGB: Henselder-Barzel (Ch, Board of Directors)
Act in AS: none
G/Aw: none
Publs: publications catalogue available on request

613 Friedrich Ebert-Stiftung†
Godesberger Allee 149,
5300 Bonn 2
(0228) 8831

614 Evangelisches Missionswerk
Mittelweg 143,
D-2000 Haumburg 13
(040) 4158 1 Tx: 14504 EWEMI
Exec: Lothar Engel (Secretary for Africa)
[*Note*: this organization did not complete our questionnaire, but wrote to say that 'the mandate of our Association of Protestant Churches and Missions does not primarily refer to African studies; neither do we provide church research grants etc. in this field.' The organization is however active *in* Africa.]

615 Goethe Institut†
Zentralverwaltung,
Lenbackplatz 3,
D-8000 München 2
(089) 59 59 0

616 Friedrich Naumann Stiftung
Margaretenhof,
5330 Königswinter 41
(02223) 701 0 Tx: 8869997 FNST
Fax: (02223) 701 88
Found: 1958
Obj: the Friedrich Nauman Foundation seeks to promote political liberalism by developing citizens capable of informed and responsible decision-making in their social and political contexts. The Foundation's work in developing countries is in five areas: civic education, training for the media, legal services and human rights, self-help initiatives and small scale industries, and political dialogue on North-South and transatlantic issues.
Fin: Federal Government (95%), private donations (5%)
ChGB: Wolfgang Mischnick (Board of Directors), Walter Scheel (Board of Trustees)
Exec Dir: Fritz Fliszar
Prog offs: Mr. Fournier (West and Central African states), Mr. El-Ghannam (North African states), Ms. Köhler (Southern African states) Act in AS: activities in Africa include civic education projects in South Africa and Benin; regional self-help initiatives in Burkina Faso and Côte d'Ivoire; media projects in Egypt and the Congo; a self-help scheme for small businesses in Kenya; journalism training in Rwanda, the Sudan, Tunisia, Zambia and Zimbabwe; and legal aid services in South Africa and Zimbabwe.
G/Aw: most financial aid support for development projects are jointly carried out with like-minded liberal partners abroad.
Applic proc: (1) either through the Foundation's scholarship programme for study at a German university for which application .forms can be obtained from the Foundation's Berlin office (Im Dol 2–6, 1000 Berlin 33); (2) by submitting project proposals to the programme officers above for projects

to be carried out in Africa in local partnership.

Publs: extensive, complete list of publications available on request.

Italy

617 **Caritas Internationalis**
Piazza San Calisto 16,
00153, Rome

(06) 698 7197 Tx: 504 2014 CI VA

Fax: (06) 6987273

Found: 1950

Obj: provides emergency aid and activities in disaster stricken areas in all parts of the world. Caritas is an international confederation of 120 autonomous national member organizations directed by its statutes 'to spread charity and social justice in the world'.

Fin: member organizations

Pres: His Eminence Cardinal Alexandre do Nascimento

Exec off: Gerhard Meier (Sec Gen)

Prog off: Gaspard Gasana (Africa Liaison)

Act in AS: in line with four-year work plan decided by each CI General Assembly held every four years. Focus areas include: human rights and peace, social services, development, refugees and displaced persons, collaboration within and outside the Church. Regional work programmes in Africa, including workshops and seminars in areas linked to Confederation activities, on-site training in leadership and management, etc.

Applic proc: CI will consider only projects or programmes which have first been studied or evaluated by local national organizations.

Publs: *Intercaritas Bulletin, International Presence Newsletter*; monthly information flyer; occasional dossiers, reports and CI emergency manuals.

Netherlands

618 **Sichting Technische Ontwikkeling Ontwikkelings Landen** (TOOL)
Entrepotdok 68A/69A,
1018 AD Amsterdam

(020) 264409 Tx: 15080 KIT Attn: TOOL

Found: 1974

Obj: TOOL aims at improving the social and economic position of the poor in developing countries. Its role is in the transfer of knowledge and technology which, by being appropriate to local conditions, the poor can adopt and adapt in their efforts to alleviate poverty. Consists of Consultancy Sector and a Reference centre.

Fin: Directorate General of International Cooperation of the Dutch Ministry of Foreign Affairs as well as by the Dutch Cofinancing Organizations and own income from projects and selling books.

Pres: Y. de Wit Exec off: Jan Evers

Prog off: W. Parmentier

Act in AS: several, TOOL receives approximately 700 enquiries a year, the major part coming from organizations and individuals working in Africa.

G/Aw: none, TOOL is not a funding agency

Publs: 4-volume course on *Rural Building, More with Less/Mas con Menos* – aids for daily living for disabled people, *Rural Mechanics* (forthcoming)

619 **Netherlands Organisation for International Cooperation in Higher Education** (NUFFIC)
PO Box 90734,
2509 LS The Hague

(70) 510510/513 Tx: 33565 NUFIC

Fax: (70) 510513

Found: 1952

Obj: lays a central role in international cooperation in higher education; coordinates the Dutch participation in international student exchange pro-

grammes; coordinates cooperative links between Dutch institutions and their counterpart academic institutions in Africa, Asia and Latin America.
Fin: Dutch Government
ChGB: J.A. van Kemenade Exec off: T.G. Veenkamp
Prog off: O. Bruinsum, L.J. Boon
Act in AS: administers the 'Programme for Institutional Links of the Sector Programme for Education, Training and Research', comprising 120 projects in 26 countries, including 11 African countries.

Norway

620 **Norwegian Agency for International Development†**
(NORAD)
Ministry of Development Cooperation
PO Box 8142 DEP, 0033 Oslo 1
(2) 31 40 55 Tx: 16548 NORAD

Sweden

621 **Dag Hammarskjöld Foundation**
Ovre Slottsgatan 2,
S-752 20 Uppsala
(018) 128872 Tx: 76234 CHCENT
Found: 1962
Obj: The purpose of the Foundation is to organize seminars, conferences and courses on the political, social, economic, legal and cultural issues facing the Third World. Activities have developed from training courses in the strict sense into more comprehensive seminar projects with in-built research components. The Foundation now concentrates heavily on the sectoral aspects of the alternative development strategies proposed in the 1975 *Dag Hammarskjöld Report*, extensively elaborated in seminars on rural development, health, education, science and technology (especially plant genetic resources and biotechnology),

international monetary policy, information and communication, and participation. Works closely with SIDA (*see* **622**) the UN agencies, intergovernmental organizations and an increasing number of so-called 'third system' or popular organizations.
Fin: SIDA
ChGB: Ambassador Ernst Michanek (Ch, Board of Trustees)
Exec off: Sven Hamrell (Exec Dir), Olle Nordberg (Assoc Dir)
Act in AS: Seminar on The Development of Autonomous Capacity in Publishing in Africa, 1984; Seminar on The State and the Crisis in Africa: In Search of a Second Liberation, 1986. Further seminars, conferences and course details information available in booklet form.
G/Aw: the Foundation is an operating and not a grant-making foundation
Publs: *Development Dialogue. A Journal of International Development Cooperation* (*see* **146**). Book publications leaflet available on request.

622 **Swedish International Development Authority**
(SIDA)
Birger Jarlsgatan 61,
S-105 25 Stockholm
(08) 7285100 Tx: 11450 SIDA
Fax: 32214 Found: 1965
Obj: SIDA/ASDI – Autoridad Sueca Para El Desarrollo Internacional – administers programmes of bilateral development cooperation. Assistance is also provided via a number of other channels. 17 countries are in the main recipients of Swedish assistance. Countries in southern Africa received 50% of the bilateral assistance. Tanzania, Mozambique and Zambia are among those which receive most. The goals are to promote economic growth, economic and social equality, economic and political independence, democratic development and consideration of the environment.
Fin: the Swedish Parliament has decided to appropriate 1% of

Sweden's Gross National Income for development cooperation. SIDA's budget is channelled directly from the Ministry of Foreign Affairs
Exec off: Carl Tham (Dir Gen)
Prog off: Jan Cedergren (South Africa), Johan Holmberg (Eastern and Western Africa)
Act in AS: Two-thirds of the main recipient countries are in Africa, mainly in the southern and eastern parts.
Publs: publications catalogue available on request

623 Swedish Agency for Research Co-operation with Developing Countries
(SAREC)
S-105 25 Stockholm
(08) 7285100 Found: 1975
Obj: SAREC is an independent Government agency responsible for research cooperation with developing countries. It promotes research which can support the developing countries in their efforts to achieve self-reliance and economic and social justice. SAREC-funded research aims at strengthening an endogenous research capacity in the developing countries; addressing the conditions of underdevelopment; and changing the disadvantageous position of Third World countries in research cooperation. SAREC does not carry out research itself, but allocates funds for research cooperation with developing countries and between developing countries; international research programmes; and developing research in Sweden.
Fin: Swedish Government
G/Aw: requests should contain an identification of the research component and a governmental priority; funds are normally not intended for local costs, equipment or consultancy services; funds are not tied to the Swedish market; money can be used for specific projects, as a budget sup-

port to a research institution and for promotion of cooperation between research institutions in the recipient country and another country. A minor portion of SAREC's budget is earmarked for Swedish development research. One of the conditions on which grants are awarded for research in Sweden is that it must be relevant to the developing countries; and these grants are distributed annually.
Publs: *SAREC Report* series (research and survey reports), obtainable free of charge from SAREC

Switzerland

624 Aga Khan Foundation
POB 435, 1211 Geneva 6
(22) 36 03 44 Tx: 27545 AKF
Fax: (22) 36 09 48
Found: 1967
Obj: to promote social development in certain low-income countries of Asia and Africa, by funding programmes in health, education, and rural development.
Fin: donations and endowment income
ChGB: His Highness the Aga Khan, Prince Amyn Aga Khan, Maître André Ardoin
Exec off: Guillaume de Spoelberch (Gen Man)
Act in AS: supports action-oriented health and development programmes in Kenya and Tanzania.
G/Aw: a limited number of scholarships are awarded annually to Third World nationals for degree courses at internationally recognized institutions of higher education
Applic proc: does not support academic research; scholarship application forms may be requested from the AKF International Scholarship Programme Reg off: Aga Khan Foundation, POB 40898, Nairobi, Kenya (Reg exec off: Alnashir Visram)

625 Helvetas. Swiss Cooperation for Development/ Coopération Suisse au Développement
St. Moritzstrasse 15,
CH-8042 Zurich
(01) 363 50 60 Tx: 58946 HELAS
Found: 1955
Obj: politically independent and non-denominational private association of 30,000 members from all parts of Switzerland. Assists with development cooperation by providing technical advice and assistance and financial and material support of projects.
Fin: subsidies by Swiss Government, donations and fund-raising
Pres: Ambassador J.F. Sigismond Marcuard
Exec off: E. Werner Külling (Sec Gen)
Prog off: R. Helbling, A. Bürgi
Act in AS: no programmes in AS, but supports original local development efforts and self-help schemes, particularly appropriate rural instructure schemes and appropriate technical improvements at the village level, where Helvetas contributes technical help and personnel, or financial or material support.
Publs: *Partnerschaft*

626 Swisscontact. Swiss Foundation for Technical Cooperation
Doltschiweg 39,
CH-8055 Zurich
(01) 463 94 11 Tx: 814308
Fax: (01) 4623365 Found: 1959
Obj: vocational and technician training, promotion of miroenterprises and agricultural mechanization in Asia, Africa and Latin America.
Fin: Swiss private enterprises, Swiss Government, Communities and Cantons
Pres: Thomas E. Bechtler
Exec off: Robert Jenny (Sec Gen)
Prog off: Margrit Tappolet
Act in AS: vocational training in

Tanzania and promotion of micro-enterprises in Mali and Togo
G/Aw: none
Publs: annual report

627 World Council of Churches†
150 route de Ferney,
BP 66, 1211 Geneva 20
(022) 91 61 11 Tx: 23423 OIK
Fax: (022) 98 13 46

United Kingdom

628 Africa Educational Trust
38 King Street,
London WC2E 8JS
(01) 836 5075 Found: 1958
Obj: the general education in Africa for all persons and outside Africa for persons who in the opinion of the Trustees are wholly or partly of African descent.
Fin: SIDA (*see* **622**), Danish International Development Authority, Norwegian Foreign Ministry
Pres: Kenneth Kirkwood
Exec off: Kees Maxey
G/Aw: the Trust has a full and part-time scholarship programme for refugees and those whose education has been disrupted from South Africa and Namibia, and refugees from the Horn of Africa and other parts of Africa. It also administers small emergency assistance for non-refugee students in difficulties. All studies are in the UK.
Applic proc: all applicants have to be available for interview in the UK and only studies in the British Isles (including Eire) are accepted. For the refugee scholarship programme, applications must be received by the end of April for the following academic year. Applications for emergency help can be sent at all times. Unfortunately only a small proportion of applicants are successful.

629 **British Council**
10 Spring Gardens,
London SW1A 2BN
(01) 930 8466 Tx: 8952201 BRI COU
Fax: (01) 839 6347 Found: 1934
Obj: the British Council promotes
Britain abroad. It provides access to
British ideas, talents and experience in
education and training, books and
periodicals, the English language, the
arts, the sciences and technology.
Fin: three-quarters by the UK Govern-
ment, the rest from other earnings
ChGB: Sir David Orr
Exec off: Richard Francis (Dir Gen)
Act in AS: awards, chiefly short-term
for Africans to study in Britain. Contributions to training for development
of arts in Africa.
G/Aw: as above
Applic proc: Africans who want to use
British resources for advancement of
African studies and African arts
should write a brief statement of need
to the British Council Repesentative in
their country, and ask for an interview
Reg Off: all anglophone countries,
plus Senegal, Maghreb, Egypt, Sudan
and Ethiopia.

630 **Commonwealth Foundation**
Marlborough House,
Pall Mall, London SW1Y 5HY
(01) 930 3783 Tx: 27678 COMSEC
Fax: (01) 930 0827
Found: 1966
Obj: founded by Commonwealth
Heads of Government to promote
closer professional cooperation within
the Commonwealth; promotes better
understanding of the work carried out
by non-governmental organizations
and encourages the strengthening of
information links through facilitating
the establishment of Commonwealth
NGO liaison units (CLUs) in Commonwealth countries.
Fin: by Commonwealth Member
Governments. Target income is
£1.61m, of which some £1.2m was
available for grant-making in 1988
ChGB: The Hon. Robert L. Stanfield

Exec off: 'Inoke F. Faletau (Dir)
Act in AS: as outlined above; areas of
interest (Commonwealth-wide) include agriculture, education, health,
rural and community development,
planning, management, the media
and culture.
G/Aw: travel grants for participation in
small conferences and workshops and
for study visits and training attach-
ments within the Commonwealth;
provides financial support to Commonwealth professional associations
and professional centres; funds short-
term fellowship schemes in cooperation with other organizations; and
makes grants to facilitate the flow of
professional and development information through the distribution of
publications; does not fund students,
research or activities limited to one
country.
Applic proc: applications for grants
and bursaries may be submitted to the
Foundation directly. Application
forms are not required. Any Commonwealth citizen with the relevant
qualifications, or skill acquired
through practical experience, may
apply for any *ad hoc* award. A leaflet
outlining guidance for applications,
and guidance for conference organizers seeking support, is available
from the Foundation.

631 **Commonwealth Secretariat**
Marlborough House,
Pall Mall, London SW1Y 5HX
(01) 839 3411 Tx: 27678
Fax: (01) 930 0827
Found: 1965
Obj: The Commonwealth Secretariat
was set up to organize consultations
between member governments of the
Commonwealth and to run pro-
grammes of cooperation.
Fin: member governments
Exec off: HE Mr. Shridath S. Ramphal
(Sec-Gen)
Act in AS: save for special responses to
specific situations, the Secretariat does
not run separate African projects or

programmes; it responds to requests for assistance or expertise from all its member countries in five continents.

G/Aw: *Nassau Fellowships*: Commonwealth programme for South Africans, education for apartheid's victims. Bilteral awards, many at postgraduate level, are open to candidates living inside or outside South Africa, at the discretion of donor countries. Multilateral awards are principally for South African exiles, mainly for technical, vocational and first-degree courses – preference is given to those who have not yet obtained a technical or professional qualification and want to develop skills which offer a good chance of employment in developing countries. The administrators make no contact with the South African Government. *The Fellowships and Training Programme*: aimed at increasing the Commonwealth developing countries pool of skilled manpower in areas important to national development. Most recipients are middle-level technologists, managers or officials, and there is a priority for schemes which have a multiplier effect (training of trainers) or concentrate on training for women. *The Commonwealth Industrial Training and Experience Programme (CITEP)*: provides practical training and experience in industry, usually for six months, in developing and industrialised countries. Academic exchange awards are also made. *Programme for Namibians*: support for Namibian exiles on full-time courses to gain skills of benefit to Namibia after liberation.

Applic proc: in Commonwealth countries, advice and application forms from Ministry of Education or Commonwealth High Commission; in non-Commonwealth countries, advice may be sought from the Embassies of Commonwealth countries; or full particulars from: The Director, Fellowship and Training Programme, at the above address

Publs: catalogue available on request. Titles cover reports, analysis and information about Commonwealth co-operation and Commonwealth and world problems, resource directories, statistical and economic bulletins, reports of Commonwealth meetings and programmes, periodicals, and general information.

632 The Leverhulme Trust
15–19 New Fetter Lane,
London EC4A 1NR

(01) 822 6938 Tx: 265451 MONREF
EM: TELECOM GOLD 87:5QQ 604
Found: 1925
Obj: the provision of scholarships for education and research.
Fin: investments
ChGB: Sir David Orr
Exec off: Sir Rex Richards (Dir)
Act in AS: grants
G/Aw: mainly to UK institutions for research on African topics, but some grants for research to universities in Africa Applic proc: policies and procedures booklet available on request
Publs: annual reports on grants made, *Quinquennial Report*

633 The Harold Macmillan Trust
107–109 Temple Chambers,
Temple Avenue,
London EC4Y 0DT

(01) 583 4214 Tx: 262024
Fax: (01) 379 4204 Found: 1986
Obj: the Trust seeks to improve the quality of access to education in the developing world. It does this through supporting indigenous educational initiatives and by encouraging increased regional and international cooperation in education.
Fin: covenants and donations, both general and project specific, from individuals, companies, foundations, national and international aid donors
ChGB: International Board of six Trustees. Rotating Chair
Exec off: Michael Wills (Exec Dir), Gillian Gallagher (Dir of Dev), Laurie Johnston (Prog Asst)
G/Aw: The Trust exists exclusively to support the development of more effective education, especially (cur-

rently) in East and Southern Africa. It therefore supports individual developing country educators, professional associations and (very selectively) networking exercises aimed at supporting such individual groups and the institutions for which they work.
Applic proc: An outline proposal is adequate for a first submission
Publs: sponsorship of *Malawian Oral Literature* by Steve Chimombo

634 **The Nuffield Foundation**
28 Bedford Square,
London WC1B 3EG

(01) 631 0566 Fax: (01) 323 4877
Found: 1943
Obj: the advancement of health and the prevention and relief of sickness, particularly by medical research and teaching; the advancement of social well being, particularly by scientific research; the advancement of education; the care and comfort of the aged poor.
Fin: an original endowment of £10m in the form of Morris Motors shares. Until the early 1970s the Foundation was largely dependent on income from this endowment; since then the range of investments has been steadily diversified and the last of the British Leyland (including Morris Motors) shares were sold in 1975. The endowment is now represented by a portfolio of UK and foreign stocks, shares and properties with a total market value at 31 December 1987 of £85m.
ChGB: The Rt. Hon. Lord Flowers
Exec off: James Cornford (Dir), Patricia Thomas (Dep Dir, Social Research and Experiment; Viscount Nuffield Auxiliary Fund)
Prog off: Hilary Bullock & Sara Lonsdale (Elizabeth Nuffield Educational Fund), Barbara Anderson (Nuffield Foundation Commonwealth Fellowships and Commonwealth Relations Trust), Melanie Quin (The Interactive Science & Technology Project)
Act in AS: no programme in AS as such, though for many of the schemes

those interested in AS may apply
G/Aw: £3.5m grants disbursed in 1987. Grants and awards fall into five main categories: science and medicine, social research and experiment, education, care of old people and research into ageing, fellowships and awards for the Commonwealth. Within the five categories, there are three main forms of support: *Small Grants and Fellowship Schemes*, for the support of academic research in the sciences and the social sciences; *Major Grants*, in response to ad hoc proposals, amounting to some 50% of annual grant expenditure. No formal limits, major grants support experimental or developmental projects which may act as a model or example for others, and which cannot be supported from public funds, new projects are preferred and grants are seldom made for work already under way, research projects should generally have a practical application; *Special Interests*, which as well as responding to unsolicited proposals, takes a more active role in promoting developments which are of particular interest to the Trustees. Current special interests include family law, community interpretation, integrated education in Northern Ireland and public understanding of science. There are a number of specific funds, including the Commonwealth Relations Trust to encourage close relations within the Commonwealth by exchange visits between the UK and Commonwealth countries. Applic proc: *A Guide for Applicants*, with very full information, is available on request

635 **Overseas Development Institute** (ODI)
Regent's College,
Inner Circle,
Regent's Park,
London NW1 4NS

(01) 487 7413
Tx: 297371 quote ODI H5673
Fax: (01) 487 7590

EM: 72: MG 100474 Found: 1960
Obj: an independent non-govern-mental centre for development research, promoting discussion, study and public awareness of economic and social development issues. Maintains Agricultural Administration Unit (AAU) to examine practical problems in tropical agriculture, irrigation, forestry and livestock. Holds seminars and conferences and advises All-Party Parliamentary Group on Overseas Development (APGOOD).
Fin: grants and donations from busi-ness foundations, voluntary agencies, individuals, international organiz-ations and the British government
ChGB: Peter Leslie
Exec off: John Howell (Dir), Adrian Hewitt (Dep Dir), Terence Quirke (Fin & Admin off), Michele Low (Pub Aff off) *et al*.
Act in AS: discussion meetings, con-ferences, research projects
G/Aw: *Fellowship Scheme* which recruits young economists to work for two years in the public sector in Africa, the Caribbean and the Pacific; and *William Clark Visiting Fellowship*; ODI is not a grant-giving body Applic proc: for general information contact Public Affairs Officer; for information on Fellowship Scheme contact Nidhi Tandon, Programme Officer (Fellow-ship Scheme)
Publs: *Development Policy Review* (quarterly), Briefing papers, Working papers, studies in Development Policy, books (periodic), *Annual Report; Reference Bulletin* (bi-monthly)

636 OXFAM
274 Banbury Road,
Oxford OX2 7DZ
(0865) 56777 Tx: 83610
Fax: 57612 Found: 1942
Obj: main priority is long-term development world-wide – helping small groups and organizations to create and sustain their own oppor-tunities for change and improvement in their living and working conditions.

Different traditions and cultures are taken into account. Primarily non-operational, Oxfam invests in local people. In emergencies, where local skills are inadequate to meet the immediate needs, specialists are recruited for short-term assignments.
Fin: fund-raising activities by volun-teers and 800 shops in UK; some funds are given for specific projects on a joint funding basis by the Overseas Development Administration, the EEC and other agencies including sister organizations overseas; contri-butions from ODA and others for disaster funds
ChGB: Chris Barber
Exec off: Frank Judd (Dir)
Act in AS: activities arising from objec-tives; the main work is in the provision of funds and advice for small-scale community-based development pro-jects in agriculture, health, social development and income-generation; also helps in disasters although its work is essentially preventive.
G/Aw: grants are used as catalysts to generate other local initiatives when-ever possible, always aiming to advance the cause of the poor and to work for greater justice and the fulfil-ment of all humankind. £30.6m allo-cated in 1987/88 to 2,400 projects in 74 countries. *Brief details of grants allocated by Oxfam during the year 1987/88* avail-able.
Applic proc: Project Application Summary Form is available from the Overseas Dept.
Publs: catalogue of Oxfam Books avail-able on request

637 Plunkett Foundation for Cooperative Studies
23 Hanborough Business Park, Long Hanborough, Oxford OX7 2LH
(0993) 883636 Tx: 83147
Fax: (0993) 883576 Found: 1919
Obj: to promote and develop coopera-tive enterprises throughout the world by providing services to individuals,

cooperatives, national and international organizations; work comprises training, consultancy and research in the UK and overseas; library and information services; organization of study tours in the UK; publications and distribution of books; and provision of cooperative specialists and contacts worldwide.
Fin: independent charitable trust founded by Sir Horace Curzon Plunkett
ChGB: P. Dodds
Exec off: Edgar Parnell (Dir)
Prog off: Liz Cobbald (Man, Overseas Services)
Act in AS: work as described above, in Egypt and Botswana
G/Aw: no financial assistance available, only technical assistance
Applic proc: contact Liz Cobbald in first instance with details of specific enquiry
Publs: extensive, catalogue available on request; UK distributor for own titles and for titles on cooperatives from other imprints

638 **Third World Foundation for Social and Economic Studies**
1st floor, Rex House,
4–12 Lower Regent Street,
London SW1Y 4PE
(01) 930 8411 Tx: 8814201 TRIMED
Fax: (01) 930 0980 Found: 1977
Obj: to research and study North-South dialogue, Third World problems and prospects particularly South-South cooperation and publicise the results through a publications programme.
Fin: the Bank of Credit and Commerce International through a trust deed
ChGB: Agha Hasan Abedi
Exec off: Altaf Gauhar (Sec Gen)
Act in AS: South-South Dialogue, a seminar attended by Third World policymakers and negotiators held in Tanzania, 1978; Harare Conference 1985, to discuss past experiences, current context and future prospects for South-South cooperation.

Activities of the Foundation are governed through a trust deed between the funding Bank and the trustees; an Advisory Committee includes representatives from OAPEC, UNCTAD, Commonwealth Secretariat, Governments of Zimbabwe, Uruguay and Tanzania, and academics.
G/Aw: Third World Prize of $100,000 annually, not exclusively for Africa but for contribution to Third World development, particularly in the economic, social, political and scientific fields.
Applic proc: letter to Sec Gen
Publs: *Third World Quarterly* (*see* **192**) books and monographs list available on request

639 **War on Want†**
Three Castles House,
1 London Bridge Street,
London SE1 9SG
(01) 403 2266

640 **World Association for Christian Communication**
(WACC)
357 Kennington Lane,
London SE11 5QY
(01) 582 9139 Tx: 8812669
Fax: (01) 735 0340 Found: 1968
Obj: international non-profit-making organization registered as a UK charity, seeking to apply human values of equality and justice by means of communication. Priority given to less developed countries. Main activities include funding of Third World communications projects, training assistance, and co-publication of manuals and books on communication.
Fin: mainline churches and church agencies in Europe and North America
Pres: Rev. Dr. William F. Fore
Exec off: Rev. Carlos A. Valle (Gen Sec), Rev. Horace Etemesi
Act in AS: various communications programmes undertaken with partners in most countries of Africa, with

particular emphasis on community media. WACC is a partner of such organizations as the AACC Training Centre (Nairobi), All Africa Press Service (Nairobi), EDICEAS (Harare), ALC (Kitwe), Interchurch Media Programme (Johannesburg)

G/Aw: a *Training Assistance Programme* to which African students of communication may apply; support of various communications activities through a general programme of project support and through a Small Projects Fund; WACC is working with the African Council on Communication Education (Nairobi) to publish a series of books on communication in Africa, written by Africans

Applic proc: WACC screens projects annually for possible funding in the following year. In addition, applications to the Small Projects Fund may be made at any time for a decision within three months. Application forms and guidelines are available.

Publs: *Media Development* Newsletter (quarterly journal), *Action* (book series 'Communication and Human Values' published by Sage)

641 World University Services (UK)
20 Compton Terrace, London N1 2UN

(01) 226 6747 Tx: 9312102211
Fax: (01) 226 0482
Obj: an educational charity working to highlight the importance of education in development. It assists refugees and victims of repression through educational programmes and scholarships.
Fin: UK Government, E.E.C., Scandinavian governments, foundations and trusts
Pres: Jane Freeland
Exec off: David Bull
Prog off: Sarah Hayward and Sarah Lock
Act in AS: projects and research in field of education/training/employ-

ment in refugee-affected areas and areas of conflict and repression.
G/Aw: limited number of scholarships available, details available from WUS country committees
Applic proc: applications to be submitted via WUS relevant country committee
Publs: Refugee Education Research Papers, titles on Women, Education and Development, and on Education at Risk, Briefing papers, other resources; Refugee Education Advisers Information Packs, *WUS News* and *Annual Report*. Full details available on request

United States

642 The African-American Institute
833 United Nations Plaza, New York, NY 10017

(212) 949 5666 Tx: 666565
Fax: (212) 286 9493
Found: 1953
Obj: to improve the relationship between the US and African countries: to increase American understanding of Africa, to promote economic and human resource development in Africa, and to support equality and justice, particularly in southern Africa.
Fin: foundation grants, AID and USIA training and visitor contracts, individual and corporate gifts
Pres: Randolph Nugent Exec off: Frank E. Ferrari (Snr. VP & Act Pres), Jerry Drew (VP), Mary Wortman (Corp Sec), Michael Jennings (Trs) Prog off: Heather Monroe (Act Dir, Div of Ed), Charlotte McPherson (Prog Dir, Southern Africa Training Prog)
Act in AS: undergraduate, graduate and short-term training; visitor programs; conferences and seminars; placement of African students in educational institutions in US and Africa; policy studies US-African issues
G/Aw: achievement awards given at Annual Awards Dinner to outstanding

Americans and Africans for their contribution in improving relations between the US and African countries
Applic proc: n/a
Publs: Conference reports, *Africa Report* (*see* **198**)

643 Carnegie Corporation of New York
437 Madison Avenue,
New York, NY 10022
(212) 371 3200 Fax: (212) 754 4073
Found: 1911
Obj: a philanthropic foundation created by Andrew Carnegie to promote the advancement and diffusion of knowledge and understanding. It awards grants in four main program areas: Education, science, technology and the economy; Towards Healthy Child Development: the prevention of damage to children; Strengthening Human Resources in Developing Countries; and Avoiding Nuclear War.
Fin: the Corporation's capital fund, originally donated at a value of about $135 million, had a market worth of approximately $794.4m as of September 30, 1988
Pres: David A. Hamburg
ChGB: Helene L. Kaplan
Exec off: Adetokunbo O. Lucas (chair of the program, Strengthening Human Resources in Developing Countries)
Act in AS: the Corporation's African program is divided into the following sub-categories: Science & Technology for Development; Maternal & Child Health; US Public Understanding of Development; and South Africa.
G/Aw: numerous; interested parties should request a copy of the List of Grants and Appropriations from the Corporation
Applic proc: there is no formal procedure for submitting a proposal. Anyone seeking support for a project should submit a statement describing the project's aims, methods, personnel, and the amount of financial support required.
Publs: *Carnegie Quarterly*

644 Council for International Exchange of Scholars
3400 International Drive,
NW, Suite M-500,
Washington, DC 20008-3097
(202) 686 6230 Tx: 237401891
Fax: (202) 362 3442 Found: 1947
Obj: helps to administer the *Fulbright Exchange Program for Scholars*. The principal objectives of the program in sub-Saharan Africa are to increase mutual understanding between the people of various African countries and the people of the US, to increase scholarly knowledge in the US and Africa, and to meet needs of African universities.
Fin: The United States Information Agency, through an annual appropriation of the US Congress
ChGB: Jeswald W. Salacuse
Exec off: Cassandra A. Pyle (Exec Dir)
Prog off: Linda Rhoad (Area Chief), Ellen M. Kornegay (Prog Off)
Act in AS: grants for teaching and/or research at the university level
G/Aw: *for American scholars*: (i) 20–25 research awards open to most fields, including African studies, tenable 3–9 months in African countries with which the US has diplomatic relations; (ii) 60–65 lecturing awards in a variety of fields, for which scholars in African studies may apply. *For African scholars*: (i) 25 research grants for study in the US. Open to all fields, including African studies; (ii) 7 *Scholar-in-Residence Awards* for African lecturers who will enhance African studies programs in the US or assist US institutions in adding international content to programs
Applic proc: *for American scholars*: eligibility requirements include US citizenship, doctorate, and university teaching experience. Applications should be submitted by September 15 for awards a year hence. Applications re details etc. are available in early April each year. *For African scholars*: eligibility requirements include citizenship or permanent residence in home country, doctorate, and univer-

sity teaching experience. Applications must be obtained from US Embassy and submitted to Public or Cultural Affairs Officer in August or September of each year for awards that begin a year hence. For *Scholars-in-Residence;* US institutions, rather than African scholars, submit proposals by November 1 of each year for positions that begin during the following academic year. The institution names the person it wishes to host.

645 The Ford Foundation
320 East 43rd Street,
New York, NY 10017

(212) 573 5000 Tx: RCA: 224048
Fax: (212) 599 4584
EM: TCN 318
Found: 1936
Obj: The Ford Foundation is a private philanthropic institution chartered to serve the public welfare. Under the policy guidance of a Board of Trustees, the Foundation works mainly by granting and loaning funds for educational, developmental, research, and experimental efforts designed to produce significant advances on problems of worldwide importance.
Fin: when the Foundation became a national organization in 1950, its assets consisted almost entirely of 93 million shares of Ford Motor Company Stock bequeathed to it by the estates of Henry and Edsel Ford. In 1956 the Foundation began selling or otherwise disposing of its Ford Motor Company stock and investing the proceeds in other securities. By 1974 this process was complete, and the Foundation no longer holds shares in the company. The Foundation's assets are invested principally in a diversified portfolio that includes publicly traded equity and fixed-income securities.
ChGB: Edson W. Spencer
Exec off: Franklin A. Thomas (Pres), Susan V. Berresford (VP), William D. Carmichael (VP), John W. English (VP and Chief Investment Off), Barron M. Tenny (VP and Gen Counsel)

Prog off: John Gerhart & Richard Horovitz (Africa), William Duggan (West Africa), William Saint (Eastern & Southern Africa), David Nygaard (Middle East and North Africa), Alice Brown & Mark Quartermain (South Africa and Namibia)
Act in AS: grants are made primarily within six broad categories: urban poverty, rural poverty and resources, human rights and social justice, governance and public policy, education and culture, and international affairs. Program activities in individual countries are determined by local needs and priorities, within these subject areas.
G/Aw: the Foundation supports training, research and dissemination of findings through grants primarily to African institutions (and much more rarely individuals) working in the above-enumerated fields. The Foundation supports affirmative action goals in its grant-making and internal policies. The opportunities that prospective grantee organizations provide for minorities and women are considered in evaluating grant proposals. Activities must be charitable, educational or scientific, as defined under the appropriate provisions of the US Internal Revenue Code and Treasury Regulations. Support is directed to activities within the Foundation's current interests and likely to have wide effect. Thus, grants are not normally made for routine operating costs of institutions; programs for which substantial support from government or other sources is readily available; religious activities as such; or, except in rare cases, the construction or maintenance of buildings.
Applic proc: before any detailed formal application is made, a brief letter of inquiry is advisable in order to determinate whether the Foundation's present interests and funds permit consideration of a proposal. There is no application form. Proposals should set forth: objectives; the proposed

program for pursuing objectives; qualifications of persons engaged in the work; a detailed budget; present means of support and status of applications to other funding sources; legal and tax status. Applications are considered throughout the year. Grant requests in the US should be sent to the Secretary, Ford Foundation at the above address. Requests in foreign countries should be directed to the nearest Foundation office.

Reg off: *Office for West Africa*: The Ford Foundation, 29 Marina. POB 2368, Lagos, Nigeria (630141, Tx: 23311 FORWAN); The Ford Foundation, BP 1555, 60 rue Carnot, Dakar, Senegal (22 60 45, 21 88 98, 21 96 19, Tx: 3236 FONDAFO); *Office for Eastern and Southern Africa*: POB 41081, Silopark House, Nairobi, Kenya (338123/4, 21572, 22298, 25438)

Publs: annual report, *The Ford Foundation Letter*, etc.

646 The Hunger Project
One Madison Avenue, New York, NY 10010

(212) 532 4255 Tx: 4972126
Fax: (212) 532 9785
EM: Dialcom TCN 713
Found: 1977
Obj: an international non-profit organization committed to ending the persistence of world hunger. Through programs including education, communication and various initiatives, it works to make ending hunger a priority on the political and economic agenda.
Fin: private contributions
Pres: Ian Watson
Exec off: Joan Holmes (Exec Dir)
Prog off: Fitigu Tadesse
Act in AS: The Africa Prize for Leadership for the Sustainable End of Hunger. (*see* **655**)
G/Aw: none
Publs: *African Farmer* (*see* **202**) *A Shift in the Wind, World Development Forum*, The Hunger Project papers; *Ending Hunger: An Idea Whose Time Has Come*

647 Institute of International Education (IIE)
809 United Nations Plaza, New York, NY 10017

(212) 883 8200 Tx: TRT 175977
Fax: (212) 984 5452
EM: TCN 1509 (Daniel Heyduk)
Found: 1919
Obj: design and administration of international educational exchange and human resource development projects involving education and training in the United States and third countries and technical assistance, research publication, and information services.
Fin: programs are funded by US and foreign governments, international organizations, universities, foundations, and corporations
ChGB: Charles H. Percy
Exec off: Richard M. Krasno (Pres), Richard W. Dye (Exec VP), Sheila Avrin McLean (VP, Education & the Arts – overseas African projects)
Prog off: Dorothy Anderson (Dir, African Human Resources Development Projects), Daniel Heyduk (Dir, Development Assistance and Fellowship Programs, Bart Rousseve (Dir, South African Education Programs)
Act in AS: *Fulbright and Humphrey Programs, International Visitor Program, Energy Training Program, UNESCO Fellowships, Guinea Scholarship Program, South African Education Program, Zimbabwe Manpower Development Project, Malawi Human Resources Development Project*, etc. *IIE and Africa* paper, available on request, gives complete listing.
G/Aw: IIE administers scholarship and training programs for sponsoring agencies and organizations in Sub-Saharan Africa. The principal sponsor of these programs is the US Government through the US Information Agency (USIA) and the US Agency for International Development; also assists other organizations both public and private; not a grant-making institution

Applic proc: foreign nationals desiring to study in the US under IIE-administered programs usually apply through agencies in their home countries (Fulbright Commission or USIS posts). IIE will, however, respond to individual inquiries as helpfully as possible.

Publs: publications under the headings of IIE Study Abroad, IIE Foreign Nationals, IIE Research Reports, IIE Educational Associates, Seminar papers, Educational Associate Information and South Africa Information Exchange. Videotape on *The Fulbright Experience* also available

648 National Endowment for the Humanities†
Division of Research Programs/Interpretive Research Programs
Room 318 IR,
Washington DC 20506
(202) 786 0245

649 Robert S. McNamara Fellowship Program
The World Bank,
1818 H Street, NW,
Washington, DC 20433
(202) 334 8214 Found: 1982
Obj: research fellowships are awarded annually to approximately ten outstanding scholars who are nationals of World Bank member countries. Non-degree study or work is supported on innovative and imaginative topics in the general area of economic development.
Exec off: A. Robert Sadvoce (Coordinator)
Act in AS: as above. 60 fellowships have been awarded, the majority to nationals of developing countries – 19 to Asians, 16 to Africans and 10 to Latin American and Caribbean scholars
G/Aw: fellowships are normally for one year, non-renewable (July 1 – June 30); no restrictions on research topics

in the general field of economic development, although the Selection Panel determines topics of preference reflecting the central economic and social development concerns of the Bank. Individuals, or groups up to five persons, may apply; each applicant must (i) be a national of a World Bank member; (ii) hold a minimum of a Master's degree; (iii) normally not more than 35 years of age; (iv) have an outstanding academic background in the field of the proposed research work; (v) carry out the research work or activity in a World Bank member country other than the applicant's own country; and (vi) secure necessary government clearance or permission of the governments both of the applicant's home country and the host country and/or employment releases. Range of awards averages $20,000 for individuals to $35,000 for group projects.
Applic proc: write in the first instance to the Fellowships Office. Applications must be completed and returned no later than November 1 in each annual cycle. Write to The McNamara Fellowships Program, Economic Development Institute, The World Bank, at address above. Information sheet available on request

650 The Population Council
One Dag Hammarskjöld Plaza,
New York, NY 10017
(212) 644 1300
Tx: RCA 234722 POCO UR
Fax: (212) 755 6052
Found: 1952
Obj: an international, non-profit organization, which undertakes social science and biomedical research, advises and assists governments and international agencies, and disseminates information on population issues.
Fin: governments, international agencies, foundations, and private individuals
ChGB: Robert H. Ebert
Exec off: George Zeidenstein (Pres)

Prog off: George F. Brown
Act in AS: family planning and maternal-child health, management information systems, institution strengthening, operations research, acceptability studies in family planning, incomplete and septic abortion, contraceptive introduction, reproductive health.
G/Aw: research, postdoctoral fellows, computer training
Applic proc: proposals should be submitted to Dr. George F. Brown
Publs: Studies in Family Planning, *Population and Development Reviews*, Working papers

651 **The Rockefeller Foundation†**
1133 Avenue of the Americas, New York, NY 10036
(212) 869 8500

652 **Social Science Research Council** (SSRC)
505 3rd Avenue, New York, NY 10158
(212) 661 0280 Fax: (212) 370 7896
Found: 1923
Obj: seeks to achieve its purpose through the generation of new ideas and the training of scholars in research in the social sciences. It frequently convenes – at small meetings and large conferences – scholars from around the world to assess current knowledge, plan future research, and provide support to others for research and research training.
Fin: primarily private foundations. Africa Program is funded by the Ford Foundation (*see* **645**), the Rockefeller Foundation, the William and Flora Hewett Foundation, and the National Endowment for the Humanities
Pres: Francis X. Sutton Exec off: Frederick E. Wakeman, Jr.
Prog off: Tom Lodge
Act in AS: *Working Group on the African Humanities*: development of program to address problems in the area of resources, documentation and fragmentation of knowledge; *African*

Agricultural Fellowship for Researchers: fieldwork fellowships for doctoral students in African studies; sponsorship of workshops, conferences, panels, and research planning meetings.
G/Aw: African Agriculture: open to African and non-African researchers (post MA level but not research linked to doctoral study); International Doctoral Research Fellowships; grants for International Advanced Research (post-doctoral); fellowships for training (in the natural sciences) and doctoral research
Applic proc: with the exception of the African Agriculture awards, most fellowships are open to US citizens or non-US citizens affiliated to a US university. For further details see handbook available from the SSRC. Most awards are made annually but dates of submission for proposals differ.
Publs: occasional sponsored volumes; a sponsor of 'Overview' papers in *African Studies Review* (*see* **203**)

653 **Wenner-Gren Foundation for Anthropological Research, Inc**
1865 Broadway, New York, NY 10023
(212) 957 8750 Found: 1941
Obj: non-profit making private operating foundation. Its sphere of interest is the support of research in all branches of anthropology, including cultural/social anthropology, ethnology, biological/physical anthropology, archaeology, and anthropological linguistics, and in closely related disciplines concerned with human origins, development, and variation.
Fin: endowed in 1941 as The Biking Fund, Inc., by Axel Leonard Wenner-Gren
ChGB: Harold C. Martin
Exec off: Sydel Silverman (Pres)
G/Aw: *Small Grants*: up to $10,000 for basic research in all branches of anthropology; *Regular Grants* for

individual scholars holding the doctorate or equivalent in anthropology or a related discipline; *Richard Carley Hunt Memorial Postdoctoral Fellowships*, non-renewable regular grants up to $5,000 for scholars within five years of receipt of doctorate, to aid completion of specific studies or for preparation of field materials for publication; *Predoctoral Grants* for individuals to aid dissertation research, application to be made jointly with senior supervising scholar. *Conferences Program*: grants-in-aid to supplement other sources of support; also sponsors and directly administers conferences under the International Symposium Program. *Developing Countries Training Fellowships*: for scholars and advanced students from developing countries seeking additional training in anthropology; applicants must demonstrate unavailability of such training in their home country, their provisional acceptance by a host institution and their intention to return and work in their home country upon completion; awards up to $12,500 per year, for periods from six months to three years.

Applic proc: for Small Grants Program: application form on request, deadline for each calendar year May 1; for Conferences Program: initial letter describing the proposal conference, to be submitted at least twenty months prior to the conference date, and for Conference Grants-in-Aid, at least eight months prior to the date a decision is required; Developing Countries Training Fellowships: inquiries by means of a one-page Summary Statement of Purpose, briefly describing (i) scholarly goals; (ii) proposed training plan; (iii) institutional affiliation at home and at intended institution abroad; (iv) beginning date and estimated duration of training; (v) estimated budget for entire duration of training and itemized budget for the first year; (vi) other sources of aid; and (vii) prospects for employment and research upon return to home coun-

try. Applications should be initiated six months to a year.
Publs: Annual Reports, *Current Anthropology*

654 **World Education**
   210 Lincoln Street,
   Boston, MA 02111
(617) 482 9495 Tx: 200178
Fax: (617) 482 9485 Found: 1951
Obj: training and technical assistance in non-formal education for adults, with special emphasis on community development, small enterprise promotion, food production, literacy and health education. Works in partnership with indigenous organizations, both NGOs and government institutions.
Fin: foundation grants, private contributions, US Agency for International Development, Department of State
ChGB: Gerald Dun Levy
Exec off: Joel Lamstein (Pres)
Prog off: Jill Harmsworth (Senior Prog Off for Africa), Candace Nelson (Prog Off for Africa)
Act in AS: Rural Enterprise Program in Kenya; Training in Income Generation for Rural Women's Groups, in partnership with Tototo Home Industries of Mombasa, Kenya; support for non-governmental organizations in Mali and Senegal.
G/Aw: training in small enterprise promotion for women's groups with the Home Economics Officers of the Ministry of Agriculture and Cooperatives in Swaziland; training in the production of participatory learning materials with the Association for the Renaissance of Pulaar in Senegal; training for village health workers in rural Mali; training in organizational planning and project planning for NGO members of the CCA-ONG in Mali; training and institutional support for OMAES – a Malian NGO
Applic proc: World Education works in partnership with indigenous institutions that request a collaborative relationship, and seeks funding to do this from other sources.

Publs: *World Education Reports*, magazine for development workers; *Focus on Basics*, magazine for adult educators in the US; *Tested Participatory Activities for Trainers, A Study of the Structure of Opportunity on the Kenya Coast* (Women's Group Enterprises)

X. AWARDS & PRIZES

This section provides details of annual or biennial international awards, and book and literary prizes in the African studies field (and also including the major Commonwealth literary prizes). 'Closed' prizes, awarded only to nationals of a particular country, are not included. Information given includes full name and contact address, details about the founder/sponsors of the award and year founded/first awarded, the aims and objectives of each award, amount of prize/award money, conditions of entry and closing date for submitting entries/nominations, and details of past (or recent) winners of these awards.

Abbreviations used:

Cl date	– Closing date [for submissions]
Cond	– Conditions [of entry/competition]
Found	– Year founded
Obj	– Objectives [of prize/award]

655 **The Africa Prize for Leadership for the Sustainable End of Hunger**
The Hunger Project,
One Madison Avenue,
New York, NY 10010, USA
(212) 532 4255 Tx: 4972126 THPI
Fax: (212) 532 9785
Found: 1987 US$100,000
Obj: annually honours a distinguished African who has exhibited exceptional leadership in bringing about the sustainable end of the persistence of hunger at the national, regional or continent-wide level. The prize is awarded to individuals working in areas such as public policy, science, agriculture, education, and health, whose leadership and policies reflect courage, initiative, creativity, and, in some cases, personal sacrifice.
Cond: nominations for the prize, which can be submitted by individuals or by organizations, can be made by letter or by using a special nomination form available from the Hunger Project. Current biographical information about the nominee should be included, as well as a brief statement concerning the attributes of leadership that qualify him or her for the prize.

Cl date: 1 June each year
Past winners:
1987: Abdou Diouf (Senegal)
Thomas R. Odhiambo (Kenya)
1988: Robert Mugabe (Zimbabwe)

656 **All-Africa Okigbo Prize for Poetry**
c/o Association of Nigerian Authors,
Guardian Newspapers Ltd.,
PMB 1217, Oshodi, Lagos, Nigeria
524080/524111
Found: 1987 US$1,500
Obj: endowed by Wole Soyinka and in honour of Christopher Okigbo, the Nigerian poet who died fighting on the Biafran side during the Nigerian civil war. Aims to give recognition to the best African poetry, and to encourage a continent-wide poetic sensibility.
Cond: open to African authors for a book published in any language spoken in Africa. Published works only are eligible for entry, and may be submitted by individual poets or their publishers.
Cl date: 31 July each year

Past winners:
1987: J.B. Tati-Loutard (Congo Republic) *La tradition du songe* (Présence Africaine)

657 **Commonwealth Poetry Prize**
Commonwealth Institute,
Kensington High Street,
London W8 6NQ
(01) 603 4535 Tx: 8955822
Found: 1982 £6,000 (£2,000 for best first-time published poet; £1,000 for regional award winners)
Obj: sponsored by British Airways and awarded annually for the best book of poetry published in the Commonwealth. There is an annual overall winner, plus regional 'Area Awards' and a prize for the 'Best first-time published poet'. Cond: open to citizens of all Commonwealth countries who must submit five copies of published volumes. Entries must be in English or officially recognized Commonwealth languages. Entries must be works which have been published during the previous twelve months prior to the closing date.
Cl date: 30 June each year
Recent past winners:
1985: Overall winner
Lauris Edmond (New Zealand) *Selected poems* (OUP)
Best first-time published poet
Timothy Holmes (Zambia) *Double element* (Wordsmiths Zambia)
Africa Area Award
Kobeni Ayi Acquah (Ghana) *The man who died* (Asempa Publishers)
1986: Overall winner
Niyi Osundare (Nigeria) *The eye of the earth* (Heinemann Educational Books Nigeria Ltd);
joint winner with Vikram Seth (India) *The golden gate* (Faber)
1988: Africa Area Award
Kofi Awoonor (Ghana) *Until the morning after: collected poems 1963–1985* (Greenfield Review Press)

658 **Commonwealth Writers Prize**
The Book Trust, Book House,
45 East Hill,
London SW18 2QZ
(01) 870 9055
Found: 1987 £10,000 (£1,000 for runner-up and for each regional winner)
Obj: sponsored by the Commonwealth Foundation, in association with the Royal Overseas League and the Book Trust, this is an annual prize for the best novel, full-length play or collection of short stories or one-act plays by a Commonwealth citizen. In addition to the first prize there are runner-up prizes and four regional prizes for Africa; the Caribbean and Canada; South East Asia and the South Pacific; and Eurasia. Preliminary heats take place in these four regional centres.
Cond: works must be written in English and must have been published before each year's closing date.
Cl date: 31 December each year
Past winners:
1987: Overall winner
Olive Senior (Jamaica) *Summer lightning* (Longman)
Africa region winner
Ben Okri (Nigeria) *Incidents at the shrine* (Heinemann)
1988: Overall winner
Festus Iyayi (Nigeria) *Heroes* (Longman)
Africa region joint winners
Festus Iyayi, as above, and Charles Mungoshi (Zimbabwe) *The setting sun and the rolling world* (Heinemann)

659 **Conover-Porter Award**
c/o Phyllis B. Bischof, Chair,
ASA Subcommittee on Bibliography,
208 Main Library, University
of California,
Berkeley, CA 94720, USA
(415) 642 0956
Found: 1980 US$300
Obj: sponsored by the African Studies
Association (*see* **585**) and administered
by the ASA's Archives and Libraries
Committee, this prize is presented
biennially to the author of the most
outstanding achievement in Africana
bibliography and reference works,
published during the previous two
years. The Award is named after two
pioneers in the field of African studies
librarianship and bibliography, Helen
F. Conover and Dorothy B. Porter.
Cond: open to any Africa-related reference work, bibliography or bibliographic essay published separately or
as part of a larger work. Books may be
nominated by individuals or by
publishers.
Cl date: 31 December in alternate years
Past winners:
1980: Julian Witherell *The United States
and Africa; guide to US official documents
and government-sponsored publications on
Africa, 1785–1975* (Library of
Congress)
1982: Roger Hilbert and Christian
Oehlmann *Foreign direct investments
and multinational corporations in sub-
Saharan Africa: a bibliography* (Campus
Verlag)
1984: Hans M. Zell, Caroline Bundy,
and Virginia Coulon *A new reader's
guide to African literature* (Heinemann/
Africana Publishing Corp)
1986: Tore Linne Eriksen *The political
economy of Namibia: an annotated critical
bibliography* (Scandinavian Institute of
African Studies)
1988: Joint winners
Jean E. Meeh Gosebrink *African studies
information resources directory* (Hans
Zell Publishers)

Daniel P. Biebuyck *The arts of Central
Africa: an annotated bibliography* (G.K.
Hall)

660 **Distinguished Africanist
Award**
African Studies Association,
Emory University,
Credit Union Building,
Atlanta, Georgia 30322, USA
(404) 329 6410
Found: 1984 Not a cash award; award
consists of a Certificate of Lifetime
Membership in the African Studies
Association
Obj: offered in recognition of a lifetime's distinguished contributions to
African studies. Criteria for the Award
are the distinction of or contribution to
Africanist scholarship, as measured by
a lifetime of accomplishment and
service in the field of African studies.
Cond: any member of the African
Studies Association (*see* **585**) is eligible
to propose a candidate. The nomination must include a *vitae* of the
nominee, a detailed letter of
nomination justifying the candidature
in terms of the criteria for the Award,
and three similar letters from ASA
members seconding the nomination.
At least two of the latter must be
affiliated with institutions other than
that of the nominee. The complete
dossier of the candidate must be
submitted to the ASA secretariat.
Cl date: must be submitted by 31
December each year, for consideration
for the following year
Past winners:
1984: Gwendolyn M. Carter
1985: Elliot Skinner
1986: Jan Vansina
1987: Joseph Greenberg
1988: Elizabeth Colson

661 Edgar Graham Book Prize
c/o D. Matias,
School of Oriental and
African Studies,
University of London,
Malet Street,
London WC1E 7HP
(01) 637 2388 ext. 2336
Found: 1986 £1,000
Obj: Sponsored by the School of Oriental and African Studies, this prize is awarded every two years for a published work of original scholarship on agricultural and/or industrial development in Asia and/or Africa.
Cond: works must have been published during the preceding two years
Cl date: 31 December in alternate years
Past winner:
1988: Paul Collier, Samir Radwan, and Samuel Wangwe *Labour and poverty in rural Tanzania: Ujamaa and rural development in the United Republic of Tanzania* (Oxford University Press)

662 Grand Prix de la Fondation Léopold Sédar Senghor de Littérature
rue Seydou Nourou Tall angle
René Ndiaye, BP 2035,
Dakar, Senegal
21 53 55
Found: 1985 CFA1,000,000
Obj: to stimulate literary research and creative writing; to promote the dissemination of black African cultures; to promote reading in Africa. The prize is given biennially and is open to writers from any part of the world, regardless of race or nationality.
Cond: novels, short-stories, folk tales and works of poetry published within the preceding two years of each Award are eligible; they must either be written in the French language, or translated into French from an African language. Submissions must portray African cultural, political and social realities. Seven copies of each title entered must be sent to the Award's organizers.

Cl date: 31 December in alternate years
Past winners:
1985: Ibrahima Ly *Toiles d'araignée* (L'Harmattan)
1987: *La trilogie de Kouta* (Le Coiffeur, Le Boucher, et le Lieutenant de Kouta) (Hatier)

663 Grand Prix Littéraire de l'Afrique Noire
Association des Ecrivains de
Langue Française,
15 rue la Perouse,
75016 Paris, France
40 70 02 89
Found: 1961 FF2,000
Obj: awarded annually for a work making an original contribution in the French language. All literary forms are eligible: novels, short stories, tales, history, biography, poetry, etc.
Cond: works published in the year of the Award, and the preceding year, are eligible. Ten copies of each title submitted must be forwarded to the Award's administrators.
Cl date: 1 October each year
Recent past winners:
1980: Aminata Sow Fall (Sénégal, *La grève de Battu* (Nouvelles Editions Africaines)
1981: Jean-Marie Adiaffi (Côte d'Ivoire) *La carte d'identité* (CEDA)
1982: Joint winners
Yodi Karone (Cameroun) *Nègre de paille* (Editions Silex); Frédéric Pacere Titinca (Burkina Faso) *La poésie des griots* and *Poèmes pour l'Angola* (Editions Silex)
1983: Sony Labou Tansi (Congo Republic) *L'anté-peuple* (Editions du Seuil)
1984: Modibo Sounkalo Keita (Mali) *L'archer bassari* (Editions Karthala)
1985: Jean-Pierre Makouta-Mboukou (Congo Republic) *Introduction à l'étude du roman négro-africain de langue française* and *Les grands traits de la poésie négro-africaine* (Nouvelles Editions Africaines)

1986: Joint winners
Bola Baenga (Zaire Republic) *Cannibale* (Ed. P.M. Favre); Thierno Monemembo (Guinea) *Les écailles du ciel* (Editions du Seuil)

664 **Melville J. Herskovits Award**
    African Studies Association,
    Emory University,
    Credit Union Building,
    Atlanta, Georgia 30322, USA
(404) 329 6410
Found: 1965 US$500
Obj: offered annually to the author of the oustanding scholarly work published on Africa during the previous year. The Award is named in honour of Melville J. Herskovits, one of the original founders of the African Studies Association (*see* **585**), and the man who is considered to be the father of modern African studies.
Cond: nominations must be original non-fiction scholarly works published in English and distributed in the United States. The subject matter must deal with Africa and/or related areas. Edited collections and compilations, bibliographies and dictionaries are not eligible. Books may be nominated by publishers; four copies of each title nominated must be sent to members of the Award Committee.
Cl dte: usually 15 May each year
Past winners:
1965: Ruth Schachter Morganthau *Political parties in French-speaking West Africa* (Oxford University Press)
1966: Leo Kuper *An African bourgeoisie* (Yale University Press)
1967: Jan Vansina *Kingdoms of the Savanna* (University of Wisconsin Press)
1968: Herbert Weiss *Political protest in the Congo* (Princeton University Press)
1969: Paul and Laura Bohannan *Tiv economy* (Northwestern University Press)
1970: Stanlake Samkange *Origins of Rhodesia* (Praeger Publishers)
1971: Rene Lemarchand *Rwanda and Burundi* (Praeger Publishers)

1972: Francis Deng *Tradition and modernization* (Yale University Press)
1973: Allen F. Isaacman *Mozambique – the Africanization of a European institution: the Zambezi Prazos, 1750–1902* (University of Wisconsin Press)
1974: John N. Paden *Religion and political culture in Kano* (University of California Press)
1975: Lansine Kaba *Wahhabiyya: Islamic reform and politics in French West Africa* (Northwestern University Press)
1976: Ivor Wilks *Asante in the nineteenth century* (Cambridge University Press)
1977: M. Crawford Young *The politics of cultural pluralism* (University of Wisconsin Press)
1978: William Y. Adams *Nubia: corridor to Africa* (Princeton University Press)
1979: Hoyt Alverson *Mind in the heart of darkness: value and self-identity among the Tswana of Southern Africa* (Yale University Press)
1980: Richard B. Lee *The !Kung San* (Cambridge University Press)
1981: Gavin Kitching *Class and economic change in Kenya: the making of an African petite bourgeoisie, 1905–1970* (Yale University Press)
Gwyn Prins *The hidden hippopotamus: reappraisal in African history: the early colonial experience in western Zambia* (Cambridge University Press)
1982: Frederick Cooper *From slaves to squatters: plantation labor and agriculture in Zanzibar and coastal Kenya, 1890–1925* (Yale University Press)
Sylvia Scribner and Michael Cole *The psychology of literacy* (Harvard University Press)
1983: James W. Fernandez *Bwiti: an ethnography of the religious imagination in Africa* (Princeton University Press)
1984: Paulin Hontoundji *African philosophy* (Indiana University Press)
J.D.Y. Peel *Ijeshas and Nigerians: the incorporation of a Yoruba kingdom* (Cambridge University Press)
1985: Claire Robertson *Sharing the same bowl* (Indiana University Press)
1986: Sara Berry *Fathers work for their sons: accumulation, mobility, and class*

formation in an extended Yoruba community (University of California Press)
1987: Paul M. Lubeck *Islam and urban labor in northern Nigeria: the making of a muslim working class* (Cambridge University Press)
T.O. Beidelman *Moral imagination in Kaguru modes of thought*
1988: John Iliffe *The African poor: a history* (Cambridge University Press)

665 The Noma Award for Publishing in Africa
c/o Hans Zell Associates,
11 Richmond Road,
POB 56, Oxford OX1 3EL,
England
(0865) 511428/(0993) 775235
Tx: 94012827 ZELL G
Found: 1979 US$5,000
Obj: this annual book prize is available to African writers and scholars whose work is published in Africa. It is one of the aims of the Award to encourage the publication of works by African writers and scholars *in* Africa, instead of abroad as is too often the case at present. The Award is given for an outstanding new book – published during the preceding twelve months – in any of these three categories: (i) scholarly or academic, (ii) children's books, (iii) creative writing, including fiction, drama or poetry. The Award's founder is the late Shoichi Noma, formerly president of Kodansha Limited, the Japanese publishing giant. Mr. Noma died in 1984 after a lifetime's devotion to making books more readily available in developing countries, to actively promoting readership in these countries and to bridging the gap between north and south.
Cond: (1) the Award is open to any author who is indigenous to Africa, but entries must be submitted through publishers, (ii) In order to qualify for consideration, each work submitted must have been published (regardless of its place of manufacture) by a publisher domiciled on the African continent or its offshore islands. (iii) Published works only qualify for consideration and unpublished manuscripts will not be eligible. (iv) Any original work written in any of the indigenous or official languages of Africa is eligible for consideration. Translations, anthologies, edited collections, and similar compilations are not eligible. (v) Three copies must be submitted to the Award's administrators.
Cl date: 28 February each year
Past winners:
1980: Mariama Bâ (Sénégal), *Une si longue lettre* (Nouvelles Editions Africaines)
1981: Felix C. Adi (Nigeria), *Health education for the community* (Nwamife Publishers)
1982: Meshack Asare (Ghana), *The brassman's secret* (Educational Press & Manufacturers Ltd)
1983: A.N.E. Amissah (Ghana), *Criminal procedure in Ghana* (Sedco Publishing Ltd)
1984: Joint winners
Gakaara wa Wanjau (Kenya), *Mwandiki wa Mau Mau ithaamirio-ini* (Heinemann Educational Books East Africa Ltd)
Njabulo Ndebele (South Africa), *Fools and other stories* (Ravan Press)
1985: Bernard Nanga (Cameroun), *La trahison de Marianne* (Nouvelles Editions Africaines)
1986: António Jacinto (Angola), *Sobreviver em Tarrafal de Santiago* (Instituto Nacional do Livro e do Disco)
1987: Pierre Kipré (Côte d'Ivoire), *Villes de Côte d'Ivoire, 1893–1940* (Nouvelles Editions Africaines)
1988: Luli Callinicos (South Africa), *Working life. Factories, townships, and popular culture on the Rand, 1886–1940* (Ravan Press)
1989: Chenjerai Hove (Zimbabwe), *Bones. A novel* (Baobab Books)

666 **Trevor Reese Memorial Prize**
c/o The Director, Institute of
Commonwealth Studies,
University of London,
27–28 Russell Square,
London WC1B 5DS
(01) 580 5876
Found: 1987 £500
Obj: awarded every two years to what
is in the opinion of the adjudicators an
outstanding work of scholarship in the
field of imperial and Commonwealth
history in the preceding two years.
The prize is given in honour of the late
Trevor Reese, former Reader in Com-
monwealth Studies at the Institute of
Commonwealth Studies and scholar of
imperial history, who died in 1976.
Cond: works must have been pub-
lished during the preceding two years
Cl date: 31 December in alternative
years
Past winner: 1988: James Belich *The
New Zealand wards and the Victorian
interpretation of racial conflict* (Auckland
University Press)

667 **James H. Robinson Award**
c/o Professor Ralph Austen,
Committee on African
Studies, University of
Chicago,
5826 South University
Avenue, Chicago, IL 60637,
USA
(312) 969 8344
Found: 1989 US$250
Obj: sponsored by the African Studies
Association in cooperation with
Operation Crossroads Africa and
named in memory of the founder of
Operation Crossroads Africa, this is a
biennial award to the author of what is
judged to be the best essay or creative
work (tape, film, photo-essay or pic-
torial art) based on a first experience in
Africa not exceeding one year.
Cond: open to anyone who can document such experience whether undertaken individually or under the
auspices of an organized programme.

The experience should have occurred
within the preceding three years and it
alone, as opposed to any subsequent
visits to Africa, must be the subject of
the work submitted. Works by persons who visited Africa in a professional capacity are not eligible for
consideration.
Cl date: 1 April in alternate years
Past winner:
1989: Details of first (1989) winner not
available at press time

XI. ABBREVIATIONS & ACRONYMS IN AFRICAN STUDIES

The abbreviations and acronyms listed below include all the organizations listed in this book, plus those of a number of other bodies, as well as including some other acronyms commonly used in African studies

AACC	All Africa Conference on Churches
AALAE	African Association for Literacy and Adult Education
AAPSO	Afro-Asian Peoples Solidarity Organization
AAU	Association of African Universities
AAWORD	Association of African Women for Research and Development
ABC	African Books Collective
ABPR	*The African Book Publishing Record*
ACARTSOD	African Centre for Applied Research and Training in Development
ACCT	Agence de Coopération Culturelle et Technique
ADAF	Arbeitskreis der deutschen Afrika-Forschungs- und Dokumentationsstellen
ADB	African Development Bank
AFESD	Arab Fund for Economic and Social Development
AID	Agency for International Development
ALA	African Literature Association
AMREF	African Medical and Research Foundation
ARD	*African Research and Documentation*
ASA	African Studies Association (US)
ASAUK	African Studies Association of the United Kingdom
ATRCW	African Training and Research Centre for Women
BADEA	Banque Arabe pour le Développement Économique en Afrique
BCEAO	Banque Centrale des Etats de l'Afrique de l'Ouest
BREDA	Bureau Régional de l'UNESCO pour l'Education en Afrique
CAFRAD	Centre Africain de Formation et de Recherches Administratives pour le Développement
CAMP	Cooperative Africana Microform Project
CBAA	*Current Bibliography on African Affairs*
CEEA	Conseil Européen des Etudes Africaines
CEAO	Communauté Economique de l'Afrique de l'Ouest
CFA	Communauté Financière Africaine
CICIBA	Centre International des Civilisations Bantu
CIDA	Canadian International Development Agency
CMEA	Council for Mutual Economic Assistance

CODE	Canadian Organization for Development through Education
CODESRIA	Conseil pour le Développement de la Recherche Économique et Sociale en Afrique
CREPLA	Centre Régional de Promotion du Livre en Afrique
DANIDA	Danish International Development Authority
EAC	East African Community
ECA	Economic Commission for Africa
ECAS	European Council on African Studies
ECOWAS	Economic Community of West African States
EDF	European Development Fund
EEC	European Economic Community
EIU	Economist Intelligence Unit
FAO	Food and Agriculture Organization of the United Nations
FRELIMO	Frente de Libertação de Mocambique
GATT	General Agreement on Tariffs and Trade
GDP	Gross Domestic Product
GNP	Gross National Product
IAB	*International African Bibliography*
IAI	International African Institute
IBRD	International Bank for Reconstruction and Development
ICA	Institut Culturel Africain
ICAS	International Congress of African Studies
ICIP	International Centre of Insect Physiology and Ecology
ICRAF	International Council for Research in Agroforestry
IDA	International Development Agency
IDEP	Institut Africain pour le Développement Économique et de Planifaction
IDRC	International Development Research Centre
IFAN	Institute Fondamental d'Afrique Noire
IIE	Institute of International Education
IITA	International Institute of Tropical Agriculture
ILCA	International Livestock Centre for Africa
ILO	International Labour Organization
ILRAD	International Laboratory for Research on Animal Diseases
IMF	International Monetary Fund
INADES	Institut Africain pour le Développement Économique et Social
JASPA	Jobs and Skills Programme for Africa (ILO)

LC	Library of Congress
LDC	Less Developed Country
MPLA	Movimento Popular de Libertação de Angola
NIEO	New International Economic Order
NIIA	Nigerian Institute of International Affairs
NORAD	Norwegian Agency for International Development
NOVIP	Netherlands Organization for International Development Cooperation
NUFFIC	Netherlands Organization for International Cooperation in Higher Education
OAU	Organization of African Unity
OCAM	Organisation Commune Africaine et Mauricienne
ODI	Overseas Development Institute
OECD	Organisation Européen de Coopération et Développement
OPEC	Organisation of Petroleum Exporting Countries
ORSTOM	Office de la Recherche Scientifique et Technique d'Outre-mer
OXFAM	Oxford Committee for Famine Relief
PAID	Pan African Institute for Development
PANA	Pan African News Agency
PAWO	Pan African Women's Organization
PRO	Public Record Office (UK)
PTA	Preferential Trade Area for East and Southern Africa
ROSTA	Bureau Régional de l'UNESCO pour la Science et la Technologie en Afrique
SADCC	Southern African Development Coordination Conference
SAREC	Swedish Agency for Research Co-Operation with Developing Countries
SCOLMA	Standing Conference on Library Materials on Africa
SIDA	Swedish International Development Authority
SSRC	Social Science Research Council
TOOL	Sichting Technische Ontwikkeling Ontwikkelings Landen
UDEAC	Union Douanière et Économique de l'Afrique Centrale
UN	United Nations
UNCTAD	United Nations Conference on Trade and Development
UNDP	United Nations Development Programme
UNEP	United Nations Environment Programme

UNESCO	United Nations Educational, Scientific and Cultural Organization
UNHCR	United Nations High Commissioner for Refugees
UNICEF	United Nations Children's Fund
UNIDO	United Nations Industrial Development Organization
WACC	World Association for Christian Communication
WHO	World Health Organization

INDEX

This index comprises authors of books, titles of journals and continuing sources, names of journal editors (but not names of book review editors), and names of publishers, libraries/institutions, dealers and distributors, organizations, associations, foundations and donor agencies, and names of awards and prizes. Names of personnel (other than journal editors) are *not* indexed. Similarly not indexed are names of special collections in libraries, or references to publications issued by libraries or donor agencies, etc. unless they also appear as a main entry. All references are to entry numbers. Book titles and journals appear in *italics*.